Breaking Ice and Breaking Glass: Leading in Uncharted Waters

"In this engaging and invaluable book, Vice Admiral Stosz has delivered a prime resource for any leader's library. Principled, pragmatic, and personal, her passion for teamwork is succinctly delivered. Sharing her wisdom from decades of sea service, illuminated by enduring wisdom drawn from classic literature, she reveals how character shapes our success."

> —**James Mattis**, General, US Marines (ret.), and 26th Secretary of Defense

"Sandra Stosz is the uncommon combination of leader and trailblazer, reflected in her shining character and integrity. *Breaking Ice and Breaking Glass* is a must-read for those who seek to lead in both military and civilian life."

> —**Jeh C. Johnson**, Former Secretary of Homeland Security

"*Breaking Ice and Breaking Glass* teaches you how to adjust and adapt leadership styles to succeed at the next level. Through personal experience leading at every level in the US Coast Guard, Admiral Stosz provides a roadmap for those eager to lead their people and organizations to achieve excellence."

> —**Marshall Goldsmith**, New York Times #1 Bestselling Author of *Triggers, Mojo*, and *What Got You Here Won't Get You There*

"I've admired Admiral Sandy Stosz for over a decade and am thrilled she's sharing what she's learned over her extraordinary career. Who better to help us navigate the uncharted waters unleashed by the disruptions of 2020 than the first woman to lead a US Service Academy, commanding ships and leading all male teams? *Breaking Ice and Breaking Glass* is the kind of navigational tool we need now."

> —**Sally Helgesen**, Author of *How Women Rise, The Female Advantage, The Web of Inclusion*

"*Breaking Ice and Breaking Glass* is a barrier-breaking book by a barrier-breaking leader. Admiral Sandra Stosz writes with brilliant clarity, revealing transparency, and absolute integrity about her experiences in navigating uncharted waters. The lessons she shares are timeless, yet especially relevant at this moment in history. Admiral Stosz is a role model for all leaders and living proof of the power of grace, skill, character, and determination. From the opening story to the closing one, this is a book about adhering to core values and how that simple principle is what earns you respect, rank, and reputation. Her moving stories and experience-based tips make this book practical, but it's her honesty and transparency that make *Breaking Ice and Breaking Glass* a must-read. This book, and its author, will restore your trust and faith in the capacity of leaders to put others before self and the greater good before personal gain."

> —**Jim Kouzes**, Coauthor of the Bestselling *The Leadership Challenge*, and Fellow, Doerr Institute for New Leaders, Rice University

"Through engaging, insightful stories, Admiral Sandy Stosz illustrates how to lead with character, build trust, and earn respect in a diverse workplace. The proven principles in this indispensable guide are for leaders at every level. It is a must-read for anyone who wishes to inspire others to achieve their full potential."

> —**Donald T. Phillips**, Author of *Lincoln on Leadership* and *Character in Action*

"*Breaking Ice and Breaking Glass* creates a pathway for leaders from their first responsibility through the executive level—one of the few true 'cradle to grave' books on leadership. Vice Admiral Stosz pursues building leaders with character and ethical judgment as if it were the Holy Grail of leader development, and she now places the chalice in our hands with her new book. *Breaking Ice and Breaking Glass* is my top choice for this year's graduation book for new leaders; we desperately need Vice Admiral Stosz's character-based approach to take our youth, as well as our seasoned leaders, to a level of performance that is ethically and morally straight. Our country's future depends on it."

> —**Thomas A. Kolditz**, PhD, Director, Doerr Institute for New Leaders, and Author of *Leadership Reckoning: Can Higher Education Develop the Leaders We Need?*

"I have had the privilege of knowing Sandy Stosz for almost thirty years as Kellogg business school classmates. After a very successful trailblazing career, Sandy shares her leadership lessons and experiences in a book that will be extremely valuable not only for military leaders but also for those leading in the corporate, not-for-profit, and academic sectors. *Breaking Ice and Breaking Glass* is a necessary resource for current and aspiring leaders. What a fantastic gift from a terrific leader!"

> —**Ana Dutra**, Corporate Board Director, Former CEO, Korn Ferry Consulting, and Author of *Lessons in LeadershiT: Detoxing the Workplace*

"The capacity to lead in difficult times is a skill that is timeless in its value and is a necessity in today's world. This capacity has its essence in true character, which is both critical and essential in order to lead decisively, perform confidently, and to inspire successfully in even the most difficult circumstances. Sandy Stosz, in her forty-year career as a Coast Guard officer, embodied and regularly demonstrated leadership qualities and principles that will never become dated. In *Breaking Ice and Breaking Glass: Leading in Uncharted Waters* she brings these vital skills forward in a manner that every aspiring leader can learn from and use successfully every day. This book is a must-read for leaders in all walks of life!"

> —**Sandy Ogg**, Founder, CEO.works, and Author of *Grow: The CEO's Master Playbook for Coaching Value into Existence*, US Coast Guard Academy Class of 1976

"Admiral Sandy Stosz's captivating book, *Breaking Ice and Breaking Glass,* details her compelling rise as one of the first women to reach the executive ranks in the Coast Guard. Her proven principles provide a roadmap for others to follow, showing leaders how to develop and employ the character attributes and core values necessary to lead and succeed with an ever more diverse workforce."

> —**Carol Mutter**, Lieutenant General, US Marine Corps (ret.), and first woman in the US Armed Forces nominated to the grade of three-star

"Vice Admiral Stosz's expansive addition to leadership literature considers both the tactics and the deep heart of leadership based on her forty years of service in the US Coast Guard, including as the first woman to lead the Coast Guard Academy. Stosz offers exceptional generosity of heart and spirit in a missive of leadership for a changing world. *Breaking Ice and Breaking Glass* is universal in time and situation, and invaluable to every leader navigating uncharted waters."

> —**Shannon Huffman Polson**, Author of *The Grit Factor: Courage, Resilience and Leadership in the Most Male Dominated Organization in the World*

"Vice Admiral Stosz has combined her unique experience as a high-ranking officer in the Coast Guard with the character-building lessons she experienced coming up through the ranks at sea and in her exceptional leadership in presiding as superintendent of the Coast Guard Academy. Her insights about how character builds great leaders are true life lessons for anyone seeking a firsthand look through the lens of someone *Newsweek* named 'one of the women who shake the world.'"

> —**Joe Moglia**, Former Chairman of the Board, TD Ameritrade, Former Head Football Coach, Coastal Carolina University, and Author of *Coach Yourself to Success: Winning the Investment Game*

"Admiral Sandy Stosz reveals how to succeed as a leader of character by standing by one's core values in the face of adversity. Her proven principles show leaders how to emerge with their honor and integrity intact, having earned the trust to become respected, successful influencers. Those yearning to serve a greater purpose and make a positive impact on an organization and its people will find a roadmap to success in *Breaking Ice and Breaking Glass*."

> —**Guillermo Barrera**, Admiral, Columbian Navy (ret.), Former Commander of the Columbian Navy, and Distinguished International Fellow at the US Naval War College

"If you or your organization is adrift in a sea of change, Admiral Sandy Stosz's new book, *Breaking Ice and Breaking Glass: Leading in Uncharted Waters,* will be just the buoy you need. Admiral Stosz brings forty years of leadership experience to help leaders at all levels learn how to work with role models and mentors, how to improve teams, and how to embrace diversity. Highly recommended!"

—**Cathy Fyock**, Author of *Authority: Strategic Concepts from 15 International Thought Leaders to Create Influence, Credibility, and a Competitive Edge for You and Your Business*

"*Breaking Ice and Breaking Glass* delivers! If you're looking for inspiration on how to become the kind of leader people follow, Sandy Stosz's character-centered leadership lessons will show you how to lead from your core values to help everyone on your team reach their full potential."

—**Dr. Ginny A. Baro**, CEO, ExecutiveBound, International Motivational Speaker, Leadership Coach, Bestselling Author of *Healing Leadership* and *Fearless Women at Work*

"All leaders will face times of crisis that require navigating in uncharted waters. In *Breaking Ice and Breaking Glass*, Admiral Stosz draws upon lessons learned throughout her forty-year leadership journey to show leaders how to keep clear of shoal water and succeed by steering on their moral compass."

—**Robert Wray, Jr.**, Rear Admiral, US Navy (ret.), CEO, BlueStar SeniorTech, and Author of *Saltwater Leadership*

Breaking Ice and Breaking Glass:
Leading in Uncharted Waters

by Vice Admiral Sandra Stosz, USCG (ret.)

ISBN 978-1-64663-525-2
LCCN: 2021908120

Author cover photo by Artist Tony Falcone of Falcone Art Studio

A portion of the proceeds from this book will be donated to the US Coast Guard Academy James M. Loy Institute for Leadership

Published by

 köehlerbooks™

3705 Shore Drive
Virginia Beach, VA 23455
800-435-4811
www.koehlerbooks.com

Breaking Ice & Breaking Glass

LEADING IN UNCHARTED WATERS

Vice Admiral Sandra Stosz,
United States Coast Guard (ret.)

VIRGINIA BEACH
CAPE CHARLES

TABLE OF CONTENTS

★ ★ ★

DEDICATION

*Leading with character means treating everyone
on the team with equal regard and respect, from the duty
driver to the senior executives.*

—Samuel K. Skinner, former US Secretary of Transportation

THIS BOOK IS DEDICATED to the many women who went before me, on whose shoulders I stand—members of the US Coast Guard Women's Reserve, known as SPARS for the Service's motto, *Semper Paratus* (Always Ready). The SPARS were remarkable and vibrant women who served our nation during World War II, performing duties on the home front while men shipped off to war.

They were women like Captain Dorothy Stratton, who served as the first director of the Coast Guard Women's Reserve (she died in 2006 at the age of 107). They were women like Yeoman Second Class Olivia Hooker, the first female African-American Coast Guard member (she died in 2018 at the age of 103).

And this book is dedicated to Mr. Sam Skinner, who as Secretary of Transportation reached down to give a young, female Coast Guard lieutenant a leg up to stand on those strong shoulders and learn how to lead with character.

FOREWORD

I REMEMBER FONDLY THE hours Admiral Sandy Stosz spent alongside the team that worked determinedly to refine the leadership development program at the Coast Guard Academy. As the new superintendent at the Academy, she was the boss. She joined several more of us, all committed dreamers, who had recognized the character foundation provided during our years as cadets. It was our objective to define and crystalize that formative period of our collective young adulthood and to replicate our experience—improving it, honing it, and refining it to provide an even better program for the cadet corps of today.

The constant Admiral Stosz provided to our discussions was that *character* is the essential underpinning of a successful leader. This book describes the life journey she lived that brought her to that conclusion. As a lifelong student of the leadership genre, I have tried diligently to observe and to learn. Years ago, I came across a great little book (still in print) titled *Lincoln on Leadership* by Donald Phillips. Its lesson for me was that a simple but powerful set of ideas, studied diligently, can become the foundation of one's core values and then be used as a sounding board or testing device against which to assess behavior and performance throughout one's life. Don and I later teamed to write two books about *character* and *leadership*, and Stosz' *Breaking Ice and Breaking Glass* brings to life the structural framework that is the focus of those books.

Admiral Stosz tells personal stories from her journey, beginning with the self-proclaimed shy, young woman who entered the Coast Guard Academy lacking confidence and unsure of her direction. She writes about lessons learned in crisis moments at sea, early as a deck watch officer and later as a commanding officer. She helps us understand the possibility, even the assured likelihood, that we can learn every bit as much from subordinates as from bosses and, in equal part, how to lead . . . and how *not* to lead. Stosz' cumulative experience and life lessons returned her to the Coast Guard Academy as superintendent, coming full circle, no longer shy, certainly not lacking in confidence.

This book also reinforces the learning opportunity presented by studying the great leaders of history. Many well-known figures of the past are cited as positive examples of the traits and skills exhibited by great leaders. But equal attention is also given to the value of counsel from the tactical expert in the middle of a demanding operation . . . notwithstanding the fact that the tactical expert might be a junior subordinate or a newly arrived team member. The citation in her conclusion from President Teddy Roosevelt's famous "Man in the Arena" speech is the perfect reference to capture the point she is making. There is an old aphorism that says, "Talk's Cheap and Behavior Counts." Admiral Stosz adds the imperative that said behavior must be based on sound character, and it's that leader who is validated in Roosevelt's arena.

There are many books available to the reader in the Leadership/ Management section of the library or the bookstore. *Breaking Ice and Breaking Glass* is set apart by two things. First, it is grounded in a simple, understandable set of principles. A glimpse at the chapter titles reflects life circumstances we have all experienced. It's as if the reader can opt to read a chapter from his or her own life journey and be given a chance to compare those experiences to the stories told by the author. Second, it leaves the reader with a hint about an answer but ultimately leaves the challenge on the table for the reader to figure it out for themselves. This challenge is illuminated as infinitely doable if an adequate personal investment is made. Stosz validates that premise with her succession of intriguing stories that bring to life her journey from young cadet to the flag officer responsible for fully half the people and resources of the service she grew to love and respect.

Breaking Ice and Breaking Glass gives us a chance to pause in our busy lives and revisit our own stories. They remind us life provides us with endless opportunities to prepare ourselves as leaders of character. Admiral Stosz affirms that in order to produce the behavior that counts when serious outcomes are at stake, the successful leader invariably leads based on a set of core values that have been decisively and confidently developed over time. This book is a great read for anyone on the journey from novice to expert. Educators and trainers will be better at their work for having read it. Leaders who are in the arena as operators and leaders who are responsible for support will be reminded that value and character-based behavior will help them excel. I've been reading leadership books for over sixty years. Admiral Stosz has written a really good one.

Williamsburg 2020

—James M. Loy

Admiral, US Coast Guard (ret.)
Former Commandant, US Coast Guard
Former Chair, US Coast Guard Academy
James M. Loy Institute for Leadership

INTRODUCTION

Character is like an anchor to windward,
holding one steady and true in tumultuous seas.

—Sandra Stosz, Vice Admiral, US Coast Guard (ret.)

IT HAD BEEN A long, arduous day at sea in the Pacific Ocean. I was the boarding officer in charge of a small team of US Coast Guard members inspecting a fishing vessel. Our job was to ensure the vessel's compliance with laws and regulations. If it failed, I would have to issue a warning or costly citation. Fortunately, the vessel we were inspecting met all the appropriate safety and fishing gear requirements, leading to an agreeable conclusion.

As we prepared to disembark into our small boat and return to our ship, the vessel's master, who had been cooperative throughout the boarding, extended a nice catch of fish, asking us to take it as a gift. I could see some of my boarding team members' eyes light up at the prospect of finishing up a tough day with a fresh seafood dinner back aboard the ship. We had worked hard since dawn, struggling through choppy seas to pull ourselves up and over the slimy gunwales, or sides, of fishing vessels that first pitched then rolled like a bronco trying to buck us off. We slipped and slid in cold, wet, and stinky fish holds inspecting gear, struggling to keep our balance. We even missed lunch. Surely those fish would be a fitting reward for such effort!

Perhaps the vessel master understood the hardships and hazards of the job and offered the seafood as a sincere gesture of appreciation for the Coast Guard's service to mariners. After all, the Coast Guard not only inspected fishing vessels for compliance, it saved them when in distress at sea. Yet I respectfully declined the vessel master's generous offer. Regardless of his intentions, taking the fish wouldn't be appropriate. The Coast Guard exercises regulatory authority over fishing vessels and must maintain an unbiased, unimpeachably professional presence in its proceedings with those it regulates. Although initially disappointed, the boarding team members understood and respected my decision and the importance of adhering to our core values.

Today, our nation is like a ship being tossed in tumultuous seas. The winds and waves of change have divided and distanced our society, threatening to wash away the very principles upon which our nation was founded. Decency and civility have been thrown overboard in favor of outrage and intolerance. The forces of change are driving us into uncharted waters.

Leading in uncharted waters requires character-centered leadership. Now more than ever, our nation needs leaders of character—those anchored with the moral courage to stand strong and steady against the battering waves that, if unchecked, could erode our core values. Such leaders would unite people in support of a shared purpose by building the trust and respect necessary for organizations and their people to thrive.

Leading with character means being true to yourself, true to your coworkers, and true to the organization you serve. To succeed, organizations need exceptional leaders who motivate their people to do the right thing—always. That kind of bold leadership is vital to the organization I served, the US Coast Guard. A member of the US Armed Forces, the Coast Guard protects and defends United States interests at home and abroad. Poorly led organizations fail and, for the Coast Guard, failure is not an option.

The challenge for any organization is to identify, develop, and retain inspirational leaders whom others choose to follow and desire to emulate. Such individuals will lead their organizations to success, even when battered by tumultuous seas. The question is, "Who are these leaders, and what makes them exceptional?"

Although no textbook solution exists, most people recognize exceptional leadership when they experience it. Exceptional leaders are guided by character-centered core values, which are shaped over a lifetime of learning and experience. The Coast Guard Academy James M. Loy Institute for Leadership offers a compelling definition of a leader of character that has helped me steer a straight course: *A leader of character is one who embodies the Coast Guard Core Values and influences and inspires others to achieve a goal by seeking to discover the truth, deciding what is right, and demonstrating the courage to act accordingly, always.*

Exceptional organizations, like exceptional leaders, are defined by their core values. The Coast Guard subscribes to the core values of honor, respect, and devotion to duty. As each service member internalizes those core values, a virtuous cycle ensues. For 230 years, the Coast Guard has been developing leaders of character who live its core values. Those leaders, in turn, sustain and advance an organizational culture that builds trust by valuing and respecting all its members.

Leaders of character have core values that orient their moral compass, alert them to decisions warranting deliberate moral reflection, and govern their actions and behaviors. The difference between a *person* of character and a *leader* of character is action. Leaders of character navigate uncharted waters by steadying up and steering on the north star of character. They hold true to their course, demonstrating the moral courage to make tough decisions, intervene and engage to move an organization and its people toward excellence.

Those who lead with character are virtue-driven. When their actions and behaviors are in alignment with their values, they succeed, regardless of the possible adverse consequences of making difficult, value-based decisions. They are humble when on top and maintain their professional demeanor and dignity when knocked down. They work hard and persevere, never giving up on themselves or others. Leaders of character do not make excuses; they take responsibility for their actions and the actions of their subordinates.

Duty-bound by far more than achieving results and meeting organizational objectives, leaders of character are servants. They recognize their moral obligations to demonstrate ethical integrity and deliver selfless service to the people and organizations they lead. Those who lead with character inspire others to achieve their personal and professional goals, to seek the truth, and to always do what is right—that is, what fidelity to their core values demands—regardless of the consequences.

The age-old question is, are leaders of character born or made? I contemplated that question throughout my career and have concluded the answer is *both*. Some people might possess more natural talent than others, but all leaders can develop their skills and strengthen their character. Indeed, I contend that character is dynamic. Every time leaders face a situation involving difficult moral considerations, they can choose to either strengthen their character . . . or erode it.

With the right tools, a person who lacks natural leadership talent can develop over time into a strong leader of character. I will provide a structured and simple approach to character-centered leadership development that will help all who so desire, particularly those in entry-level and mid-level positions, to lead with character and succeed across a lifetime of learning.

Drawing upon the basic principles of the Coast Guard's proven leadership development framework,[1] my Framework for Leadership Development demonstrates a continuum centered on character and core values.

Framework for Leadership Development

- Leading Self and Leading Others
  - ◊ **Entry-level Trainee/First-line Supervisor**
- Leading Programs and Making Policy
  - ◊ **Mid- to Senior-level Leader**
- Leading the Organization
  - ◊ **Executive Leader**

Each part of this book stands independent and includes information pertinent to leaders at every level. Part One, "Leading Self and Leading Others," explores the journey of self-discovery that serves as the foundation for leadership development. It introduces models and tools valuable to those who supervise and lead teams. Issues explored include mentoring, power, control, and exhaustion. Part Two, "Leading Programs and Making Policy," addresses the obligations and opportunities that accompany leading with character at the middle to senior levels. In Part Three, the discussion advances to "Leading the Organization" and offers advice on leadership at the executive level.

Many of the leadership lessons shared here are based on my personal experiences leading in uncharted waters during a forty-year career in the Coast Guard, including twelve years at sea. Much has changed since I entered the Coast Guard. There are different challenges facing leaders today, particularly with advances in technology and the proliferation of social media. Everyone will have to navigate uncharted waters at some point in their career. It's how people meet those challenges that will determine whether they succeed or fail. Successful leaders of character possess attributes relevant across time: they work hard and persevere, they take responsibility for their actions, and they adapt and innovate to grow with change. I am excited to share my thoughts on leading with character and hope this book will serve as an inspiration to those who aspire to lead up to the executive level.

PART ONE

Leading Self and Leading Others

★ ★ ★

The key to discovering your true self is letting go of the limitations you perceive and imagining the possibilities of who you can become.

—Sandra Stosz, Vice Admiral, US Coast Guard (ret.)

EVERY LEADER'S CHARACTER AND core values are shaped early in life. Reflecting on formative developmental experiences helps leaders at all levels better understand themselves. In doing so, I discovered three elements of identity foundational to leadership development. They are personality (*who* you are), abilities (*what* you can do), and core values (*why* you choose to do something).

Core values are the most significant and nuanced of the three elements and are what define a leader's character. Unlike personality and abilities, which I consider to be part of a person's inherent make-up, core values must be instilled early and constantly reinforced. Young people need strong parents, teachers, mentors, coaches, and other influencers to teach them the core values they will need to navigate life in a complex and challenging world. Core values are a leader's North Star. They guide a leader in setting and pursuing goals, making good choices, and doing the right thing, always.

Part One begins with the story of my formative years of leadership development, from childhood through my time as a junior officer. In this part of the book, I will share the tools and models that helped me develop as a leader of character and prepared me to move up to the next level of leadership in the Coast Guard.

★ CHAPTER ONE ★

GETTING UNDERWAY IN UNCHARTED WATERS

A pathfinder's north star is character.

—Jonathan Treacy, Major General, US Air National Guard (ret.)

THE WIND-DRIVEN SLEET stung my face and hurt my eyes. I closed them tightly, wiped, then opened them again to scour the tumultuous seas for icebergs and other hazards to navigation. Drawing a deep breath of frigid, sea-sprayed air, I savored the taste of the stinging saltiness on my lips. I was a new ensign standing watch on board the Coast Guard icebreaker, *Glacier*, sailing to Antarctica. As a break-in underway officer of the deck, I was learning under the tutelage of a qualified watchstander and was responsible to the commanding officer[i] for directing the movements of the ship. Never had I experienced such responsibility or such excitement. I was living my dream!

Antarctica is my favorite place in the entire world. It is the most amazing, remarkable, and ruggedly beautiful place on Earth. The fifth-largest of the seven continents, it hosts the world's southernmost active volcano, the 12,500-foot Mount Erebus. Despite being covered

---

i   The commanding officer of a Coast Guard cutter is the top person in authority. The commanding officer is fully responsible for everything that happens on the ship.

with ice up to four miles thick, Antarctica boasts one of the world's largest mountain ranges, and its renowned Dry Valleys are the driest place on Earth. It's no great surprise it also ranks as the windiest and coldest place on Earth.

Regardless of these seemingly inhospitable conditions, marine life abounds. Numerous species of seals, penguins, whales, birds, fish, and colorful invertebrates inhabit the Antarctic Ocean and surrounding ice. The Adelie penguins are my favorite. Incredibly cute and very curious, they would waddle right up to the ship to get a closer look at us.

On the voyage from *Glacier*'s homeport in Long Beach, California, down to Antarctica, we crossed the equator, with its oppressive heat and doldrums. The ship wasn't air-conditioned, and the temperature rose to well over one hundred degrees in some of the berthing areas. The heat forced people topside to sleep. At night, crew members of all ranks and rates covered the decks, wrapped in their bedding, to escape the suffocation of the berthing areas. From my spot looking down from my watch station high up on the bridge, or pilothouse, of the ship, the starlight played upon the motionless, mounded bodies. It looked for all the world like the deck of a ghost ship moving silently through the darkness.

Our trackline continued down through the South Pacific to the "roaring 40s," "furious 50s," and "screaming 60s" as we entered the southern latitudes. There, the weather could become notoriously rough and deadly. Even though our ship was 310 feet long, the incredibly strong winds and huge seas battered us mercilessly as we crossed those harsh latitudes. The ship, which had a rounded hull designed for breaking the ice, rolled wildly in the open sea.

Sure enough, our first casualty came when a huge wave hit the ship and threw the helmsman off the wheel. The helmsman suffered severe injuries from crashing into the leeward side of the 75-foot-wide bridge. Blood mixed with spilled coffee and seawater to create a treacherous surface on the dielectric deck covering. We medically evacuated the injured crew member by helicopter the next day when the seas subsided. I came away from that experience with a much deeper respect for Mother Nature.

The first iceberg we encountered was small but made for much conversation. For many of us in the crew, it was our first ice. The novelty wore off as we very quickly found ourselves navigating an entire sea of small icebergs, or bergy bits, like a minefield. They popped up, seemingly out of nowhere, through dense fog formed by the cold Antarctic current meeting the warmer surface air. We were engaged in a dangerous and scary exercise.

Although the bergy bits looked small, much of their mass lay below the waterline, and striking one could significantly damage the ship, big and heavy as it was at 310 feet and over 8,000 tons. I quickly came to understand and deeply appreciate the breadth of responsibility that would be entrusted to me once I earned my qualification as an officer of the deck. I resolved to be worthy of that trust and to earn my qualification as soon as possible.

Within a few days, the fog gave way to sparkling blue skies and scintillating icebergs, many of them emanating an ethereal, deep cobalt hue denoting their old age. Not long after, we heard the shout, "Land ho," and our gazes met the mountains of Antarctica on the horizon. To my astonishment, the mountains were still 150 miles away. The clean, clear polar atmosphere deceived us into believing they were much closer.

The sea and sky teemed with the marvels of Antarctic Ocean marine life. The omnipresent minke whales lolled past, feeding idly on plentiful krill. Looking skyward, I gazed with wonder as wandering albatross, the largest sea bird in the world with a wingspan of up to ten feet, curiously circled to check out the ship.

Finally, after weeks of transit, we arrived at our destination—the ice edge. The channel leading to the ice pier at the US Naval Station in McMurdo, Antarctica, was covered in sea ice for twenty to thirty miles. *Glacier*'s role was to break a path through the ice, open the channel, and escort the merchant ships that supplied the station and its residents.

I loved my job and could hardly believe I was getting paid to participate in a once-in-a-lifetime adventure that few other people would ever realize. Who else would have the opportunity to break open the shipping channel in the shadow of Mount Erebus? An active volcano, it simmered mysteriously, releasing gas into the atmosphere as if it were a living, breathing entity.

My euphoria was dampened daily. Despite standing two four-hour watches per day under instruction, I had not yet received my coveted deck watch officer qualification. Once qualified, I would be authorized to stand my own, independent watch without another officer supervising me. My eagerness to earn that qualification surpassed all else.

Unfortunately, no matter how hard I worked and how well I progressed, my supervisor didn't see what he wanted. Earning my qualification was proving to be harder than navigating through the seas of icebergs I encountered on watch. My frustration mounted when my supervisor admitted I'd demonstrated the technical proficiency and judgment to stand the watch. In his mind, I lacked something in my command presence, but he couldn't articulate the details to help me advance.

One of my shipmates, Ray, was an old salt and a qualified watchstander who was helping me break in. He had served in the Coast Guard for over twenty years, and he became my first mentor. Ray encouraged me, telling me I was doing a good job, to trust my instincts, and be patient. His support kept me focused and motivated when I became discouraged.

One day after watch, my boss called me in and told me he had figured it out. I was too quiet. He wouldn't qualify me until I stood at my post on the bridge of the ship "barking orders like John Wayne with a six-gun in each hand." John Wayne was a macho movie star and the consummate male role model for my generation. Perhaps it was only natural for my boss to think a leader had to establish a demanding and bold command presence to earn respect.

My personality is different. I'd always struggled as a shy introvert in an extrovert's world. I wasn't loud and outspoken; I was quietly competent. No one would ever mistake me for John Wayne.

Standing watch, I spoke in a voice loud enough to be heard and to deliver the necessary commands but did not shout unless I needed to. I enjoyed getting to know my fellow watchstanders and built professional relationships with them. I usually didn't need to raise my voice to compel compliance; the crew members knew their jobs and wanted to perform well. In my view, the officer of the deck's duty required leading the team and coordinating the efforts while trusting the competent watchstanders to perform their duties. It worked for me to lead by building trust and earning respect, not by demonstrating my authority as the one in charge.

When my boss told me, "You've got to change your leadership style to get qualified," I felt distressed and confused. After giving it much thought, and listening to my mentor, Ray, I realized succeeding meant accepting myself for who I was. I had to be true to myself and stop trying to be someone else. I let go of the image of John Wayne and immediately felt as free as one of the albatrosses soaring over our ship. With that newfound courage came confidence.

My boss noticed. I think he came to realize and accept that my style of leadership got the job done, even if it differed from his. I learned it wasn't my leadership style or personality that held me back—it was my lack of self-confidence. Other people wouldn't have confidence in me until I demonstrated confidence in myself.

Finally, my boss recommended me to the commanding officer, who gave me my deck watch officer qualification. At last, I was fully qualified! The excitement and enthusiasm elevated my spirits as high as Mount Erebus. On my first solo watch, I climbed a long ladder inside the ship's hollow mast high above the deck to the control station known as *aloft conn*. To cut the channel, I needed a good view to see where the ice cracked so I could find a path. I followed the cracks, or leads, to ease our progress through the thick ice. The bridge is normally where the watchstanders control the ship, but for icebreaking, it is too low. Aloft conn provides a better line of sight and includes a full control station for engines and steering.

Operating the ship in aloft conn, far above the decks and removed from the rest of the ship and crew, was an otherworldly experience. I stood many watches alone up there, feeling like an eagle on its eyrie, keenly searching for the leads to follow as I broke a path down the channel. I was astounded at the diversity of wildlife that appeared to be enjoying the endless Antarctic summer days as much as I was. As the ship surged forward through the ice, I blew the whistle to urge lounging seals or penguins to hasten out of our track. They waddled or wriggled away at their best speed, looking so ridiculously funny I would laugh. As we opened a pathway behind us, whales followed to take advantage of new waters and food sources.

During the Antarctic summer, the sun never sets, creating a sensation of timeless energy. Mount Erebus, rising high above the rugged landscape, watched over me whenever I stood watch, never failing to elicit within me awe at the grandeur of what is truly the world's Last Frontier. Standing aloft on the bridge of the mighty *Glacier*, gazing forward upon the vast expanse of the Antarctic, I felt confident and excited about the future despite the icebergs I could foresee in my path.

Reflecting on my humble start in life, I realized every barrier I'd faced and overcome had shaped my character, my north star that had guided me to where I stood on the bridge of *Glacier* the day I earned my coveted watchstander qualification. I knew then I was ready to lead in uncharted waters.

CHAPTER TWO

DEVELOPING CHARACTER AND CORE VALUES

Out of suffering have emerged the strongest souls;
the most massive characters are seared with scars.

—Kahlil Gibran

I GREW UP AS a tomboy in the 1960s, the eldest of four siblings raised in the small town of Ellicott City, Maryland. My brothers—Mark, Tom, and Jay—and I were less than four years apart, so as children, we did everything together. My parents, both from Massachusetts, met at college, married, and then moved to Maryland where my father worked as an explosives research scientist for the US Navy.

My parents raised us all the same. I even wore boys' clothes, and my mom, a homemaker and substitute teacher, economized by passing them down to the next child. Mom taught us discipline at a young age by assigning and holding us accountable for completing household chores. The allowance we earned bought us treasured penny candy at the local five and dime.

I participated equally with my brothers in competitive swimming, backyard sports, and other athletic activities. I got used to holding my own with the boys and willingly adapted to fit in with the majority. When it came time for our daily thirty minutes of television, the vote from the boys was always to watch a western or war show. That may explain why I became such an avid reader. It was no surprise that I grew up enjoying outdoor activities like hiking and shooting.

My parents, both very athletic, were competent marksmen and archers. On weekends, they led us on long hikes through the woods. We would often leave the safety of the established trail and navigate over hill and dale with just my dad's compass and a topographical map to guide us. My mom and dad were always prepared. They made sure each child had a hunting knife and knew how to use it. Even more fun was target practice with our shared .22 rifle and 20-gauge shotgun. Although I wasn't always the best shot, learning how to properly use a weapon empowered me.

Despite those confidence-building experiences, I was definitely not a born leader. To the contrary, I was painfully shy and lacked self-esteem. From my earliest years, I compared myself to the loud, bold kids who were always the first to be selected to a team or to be called upon by the teacher. I wished I could be more like them.

What I didn't understand at the time was the power of the firm foundation of values my parents had instilled in me through their high expectations. Honesty was foremost. We were taught from the beginning to never lie, cheat, or steal. That value was deeply ingrained and immutable. It needed no explanation. Perseverance, hard work, and humility were mainstays I learned through experience and internalized during my youth. Looking back, my parents helped shape me as a leader of character and prepared me for future success by instilling the following personal core values:

Core Values to Live By
- Honesty
- Perseverance
- Hard work
- Humility

Perseverance

When I turned twelve years old, my father took my three brothers and me on a two-week hiking trip in the White Mountains of New Hampshire. Mark was eleven, Tom ten, and Jay almost nine; we weren't seasoned hikers! A big, strong man, my dad loved a challenge. It came as no surprise that he charted a course across one of the most grueling sections of the Appalachian trail, a popular hiking trail extending from Maine to Georgia. Our route took us over the Presidential Range featuring Mount Washington, the highest peak in the northeast.

It was August and stifling hot. We got out of the car at the parking lot and loaded up with our backpacks and two-quart metal canteens, preparing for our big trek. Reality hit, and we knew there would be no turning back once we started; we would have to persevere to the end. I weighed in at about ninety pounds, and my backpack was a hefty twenty-three pounds, not including the pesky canteen that cut into my shoulder and bounced irritatingly against my side. Add to these discomforts the fact that my father had dutifully bought each of us brand-new leather hiking boots that hadn't yet been broken in.

Our journey started with a jolt of reality. This was no walk in the park. The first day we labored for hours up a steep incline to the top of Mount Liberty. Our small bodies and short legs toiled under the weight of the packs, and our feet became painfully sore and blistered adapting to the new hiking boots. The climb exhausted us. We were all in tears. When we finally reached the top, my brother Tom knelt to drink out of a stream. The weight of the heavy backpack upended him, pinning him face down in the cold water. My siblings and I were too tired and stunned to act. We stood there staring, because we knew if we leaned down to help Tom up, we would tip over too. My dad, bringing up the rear, had to rescue the hapless boy. At that point, all the kids wanted to quit.

Life on the trail didn't get any easier. Despite our small size, we were burdened with big appetites and couldn't carry enough food to satisfy our hunger. Since provisioning along the trail wasn't an option back then and our wilderness trek didn't take us near any towns, hunger was a constant companion. A typical breakfast consisted of Carnation instant powdered milk mixed with water. Lunch might be a Slim Jim and a handful of trail mix. In the early 1970s, freeze-dried food developed for space travel trended for hikers, so a typical supper consisted of freeze-dried beef stew and mashed potatoes.

We never had enough. Hiking in the heat on a dry, dusty trail, always hungry and thirsty, I mechanically placed one foot in front of the other, mile after grueling mile. Mentally zoned out, I stayed motivated by fantasizing about the sweet taste and tingling sensation of an ice-cold Coca-Cola gushing down and revitalizing my parched throat.

The day of judgment arrived two-thirds of the way through the trip when it came time to scale the venerable Mount Washington. The highest peak in the Northeast is infamous for its erratic weather with extremely strong winds, cold, and snow—even in the summer. Mount Washington holds the record for the highest wind speed outside of a tornado or tropical cyclone. The menacing sign at the trailhead warning travelers to beware, listing ominously how many people had died trying to make it to the top, is etched in my mind. We started up the mountain on a cloudy day that turned cold and stormy as we pushed on toward the summit.

Above the timberline, the clouds burst, and we could scarcely follow the faint white blazes marking the trail across the barren rocks. They blended in with the heavy fog and clouds. There was no turning back. My dad decided to stop and set up our rain tarp, since wandering off the trail was how most of the people who failed to make it had died. It seemed like we spent forever trying to set up that makeshift shelter, but it couldn't stand the onslaught of the howling winds and sideways rain. Dad decided we were better off on the move, so we packed up and soldiered on. Finally, through the rain and fog, we spied our destination—the Lake of the Clouds Hut. What a welcome sight!

Never had I felt such relief. Soaked to the skin, we shivered with cold. Inside the cozy lodge, a crackling fire soothed our wet, frigid hands. After warming up, my dad and three brothers headed to the men's bunk room, while I reported to the women's. Upon entering, my welcome turned sour. Some of the women, noticing my pixie haircut and boy's hiking garb, questioned my presence, thinking I was a boy.

Along the trail, other hikers had mistaken my brothers and me for a Boy Scout troop, but this was different—I had to get into the women's bunk room for the night. Shy and startled, not knowing what to make of the situation, I stood agape and staring. Finally, one of my interrogators looked at me closely and exclaimed, "I can tell she's a girl by her eyes."

With that pronouncement, they decided I could stay. Climbing gratefully into a top bunk, I curled up like a squirrel in its warm, leafy nest and fell fast asleep. Fortunately for us, the weather system cleared during the night. The next day dawned beautifully for our journey to the summit and subsequent descent.

Many days later and some pounds lighter, our perseverance paid off, and we finally reached civilization. The last leg of our two-week journey led us along a road teeming with stores and places to eat. Eagerly anticipating the end of our ordeal, we were exuberant and overstimulated like work horses headed back to the barn after a long day plowing. My dad indulged us with hamburgers and even ice cream on the long walk back to the parking lot. When we got back to the car, we were thrilled to find a big bag of M&M's dad had stashed for the trip home.

Never had food tasted so good! But the thrill was short-lived. Overnight, every kid became wretchedly sick from having been starved for so long then stuffed. My mom had wisely not made the trip, choosing instead to spend a relaxing interlude with her parents at their beach home on Cape Cod, Massachusetts. Her serenity was shattered when we showed up in need of immediate attention. It took us a week to recover from the intestinal upset. I don't think my mom ever forgave my dad for his lack of judgment!

Despite the trials and tribulations on the trail, I'm thankful to my father for providing me such a growth opportunity as a pre-teen. Getting to know real deprivation, in the form of hunger, thirst, and fear, built character and shaped me as a leader. I learned to appreciate persevering through adversity could yield a wellspring of opportunity. As a result, throughout my career, I never quit when the going got tough. I embraced bad bosses and hardship as sources of deeper learning and opportunities for leadership development.

Hard Work

A year after hiking the White Mountains, at the age of thirteen, I made the tough decision to quit the summer league swim team I'd been part of for most of my young life. I was a good swimmer and held the pool record for the butterfly stroke but felt compelled to work during the summer to earn money for college. The economic times were tough, and with four kids to raise, my parents didn't have much money left over to save.

I thought about my paternal grandparents who owned a farm in Amherst, Massachusetts. My brothers and I had spent an adventure-packed week or so visiting them each summer. Perhaps I could stay with them and find employment on a farm.

Grandma and Grandpa were hard workers whose families had come to America from the old country in Eastern Europe. Grandpa immigrated directly from Romania and worked in a shop in New York City. Grandma's family had come from Lithuania and bought the farm in Amherst. They met in New York City, moved to the farm, and raised seven children.

Grandma and Grandpa had old-fashioned values and placed a big emphasis on family. Their house was always filled with children, grandchildren, and other relatives. The chaotic environment was exciting and stimulating. Though I had an aunt a few years older than me, my playmates at the farm consisted of fifteen boys between my cousins and my brothers. We ran barefoot in the pastures and through the barns, slipping in cow flaps and bleeding from barbed wire scrapes acquired from rolling under the fence to escape the enraged bull. My early family experiences in a mostly male environment helped prepare me for a career of leadership in a predominantly male organization.

The fertile Connecticut River Valley offered abundant farm work. I landed a job working for my great uncle on his nearby farm, picking cucumbers grown for the pickling industry. Commercial cucumber picking was accomplished utilizing old, modified trucks with wings constructed on each side of the flatbed. Used mattresses lined the wings, so young workers could lie on their stomachs and pick cucumbers as the truck slowly moved up and down the rows.

Each wing accommodated four or five pickers. We sorted in unison through the prickly vines to find the cucumbers and place them in baskets hanging in front of us. Another worker emptied the baskets into big, burlap bags. If a picker missed too many cucumbers, the supervisor walking behind the truck checking the work noticed, and the picker was reprimanded or fired. We were all expected to pull our fair share as part of the team, and we accepted that responsibility. No one made excuses.

At the end of each day, we stacked the bags of cucumbers into the bed of an old pickup truck then drove them to the pickle factory. It was exciting riding down the road bouncing around on top of all those shifting bags—no one thought anything of the dangers back in the 1970s. That summer, I learned the value of hard work and perseverance when I took home my first paycheck. Although my paltry paycheck amounted to a little over one dollar per hour, the money seemed like a lot to me, and I was proud to have earned it on my own.

For two more summers, I lived with my grandparents in Amherst. By then, I'd moved up to a better-paying job working on a commercial tobacco farm. Consolidated Cigar Corporation farmed a crop called shade tobacco, which is grown under cheese cloth tents to filter the light and increase humidity levels for optimal growing conditions. The huge leaves, over two feet long, were used as the outer wrapping for premium cigars.

Taking that job was ironic. Never in my life had I tried a cigarette, and I always detested being anywhere near a smoker. During the mid-1970s, America suffered from the disastrous effects of the infamous oil shock of 1973. There were precious few jobs to be had for a teenager, and I gladly took the available work.

The tobacco farm hosted a mélange of laborers. The Puerto Rican migrant workers, both men and women, came to America for summer employment. They worked in the barns where the tobacco was sewed and hung in the rafters to dry. Anibal was one of them. A young man, he was working to earn money to support his family back home. Although he spoke no English and I spoke no Spanish, I learned how to bridge the gap and communicate in other ways. Despite the grueling work, Anibal always had a ready smile to brighten my day.

Juvenile delinquents joined the ranks of workers, bussed up from detention facilities to the south. They stayed in the University of Massachusetts college dorms after the students vacated for summer break. Many of the girls had a hard edge. They weren't people with whom I would normally choose to associate, but most of them stayed in line and did their jobs.

Then there were the few local kids, like me, who found themselves in the distinct minority. One of the girls, Colleen, came from an Irish family with sisters Maureen and Doreen. Colleen was fit and fast, and we competed to see who could sew the most tobacco each day. Despite my best efforts, she usually beat me. Another local girl, Cindy, was known for her decadent chocolate chip cookies. Nothing tasted as good during the lunch break after laboring all morning in the fields or barn.

Best of all was my supervisor, Sue. Sue was my first real boss and from a local family like I was. Although a few years older, she looked out for me and taught me, by her example, the importance of being an engaged leader. She helped to steer me straight and avoid trouble. To this day, I'm thankful for her mentorship. Best of all, she married my uncle John and remains one of my most treasured friends to this day.

Regardless of our diverse origins and, in some cases, dubious backgrounds, we all worked well together and respected each other's roles. I came to know and appreciate many decent, competent people among the migrants, juvenile delinquents, and locals. Despite our considerable differences, we were united by the common goal of producing a tobacco harvest. I learned to judge individuals based on their character and work ethic, not on preconceived notions about their race, ethnicity, culture, or socioeconomic conditions.

Tobacco farming was tough, backbreaking work entailing a rigorous disciplinary ethic. Out in the fields, girls and boys worked separately under tents. The girls tied up the young plants so they would grow straight and tall. Hundreds of times a day, I bent down, tied a string around a small plant, then reached up and tied the same string to a wire running high above the row. We had to wrap adhesive tape around our hands so the string wouldn't cut our skin when we broke it off the roll. The boys came behind us, scooching along the rows of dirt and mud on their rear-ends to remove all the small suckers at the bottom so the big leaves would thrive.

It was scorching hot in the fields. Temperatures rose to well over one hundred degrees under the tents, which trapped the hot, humid air. I finished each day drenched in sweat and covered with nicotine. My arms became coated in brown from constant contact with the sticky substance secreted from the tobacco plants. I couldn't wait to get back to the farm and jump in the cool, clear brook to wash off.

When the tobacco plants reached maturity at about six feet tall with leaves over two feet long, the girls moved from the fields to the barns. There, my job entailed sewing the big tobacco leaves onto wooden lats, three-foot-long sticks that held the leaves so they could dry. I stood in front of a huge machine with a belt rotating around at a set speed. Grabbing a lat from a bundle of fifty, I fastened a string to it and placed it on a rack above the belt. Another girl piled leaves in front of me on a table in neat stacks with stems facing inward, so I could easily grasp them.

All day long, my hands went down, without my looking, to pick up two leaves by their stems and insert them into slots on the rotating belt. The pair of leaves would attach to the lat as a large, industrial needle pierced the stems, sewing them onto the string. The next slot came right behind the first and so on, for a total of approximately twenty-five slots per lat. Sewers couldn't afford to miss a slot; if they missed too often, termination soon followed. Those of us who sewed lived in constant fear of having a finger impaled by the needle in our haste to shove leaves into the slots.

When a lat was filled with leaves, I passed it to a Puerto Rican woman. She took the lats and handed them up to the rafters of the barn through a human ladder of Puerto Rican men. The men hung the lats of tobacco leaves on special rafters throughout the barn. There, the leaves dried, turning from green to the familiar brown color of a cigar. On an average day, I sewed hundreds of lats.

Every day, we had to make our quota, a required level of productivity. Those who failed to achieve the minimum requirement faced dismissal. On the other side of that coin, piecework incentivized us. Productivity beyond the quota was rewarded with extra money. Sweating in the tobacco fields and barns is how I came to appreciate the merit-based system that rewarded hard work and top performance. I toiled to the limit of my ability to earn more money through the piecework. Not only did I take home more pay for college, but I also felt pride in my accomplishments and recognition as one of the fastest and most productive workers.

Humility

In between working summers on the farm, I attended Mount Hebron High School in Ellicott City, Maryland. The year was 1974, two years following the enactment of the education law commonly known as Title IX. That seminal legislation mandated equal opportunity in education, including sports for girls and women.

In my freshman year, I tried out for the girls' track team. Young people at that formative age need strong role models, and Coach Ed Holshue set the standard. A serious, no-nonsense man, he nonetheless possessed a dry sense of humor. Sometimes I couldn't tell if he felt disappointed in me or secretly pleased—each of us had to earn his praise. Coach Holshue was an athlete, fit and wiry. From his intensity, he must have been a fierce competitor in his day.

Coach Holshue was dedicated to his duties and devoted to his students. Although he never mentioned it, the girls all suspected he wanted to coach football instead. Nonetheless, he embraced his role as the girls' track coach with passion and commitment. I suspect Title IX required girls' teams to have standing and coaches like the boys' teams. As a result, we had the good fortune to be assigned a talented coach and consummate leader of character.

A taciturn individual who always demanded the most of us, Coach also looked out for us. One day early in the season, he showed up and unceremoniously presented us each with a pair of white athletic socks, which he had procured and paid for himself. In those days, women's teams weren't well-equipped for sports, and many of us wore our thin dress socks from the school day to track practice. Athletic shoes and other gear targeted to specific sports weren't available. We all wore basic sneakers, shorts, and T-shirts except when we wore school uniforms to team meets. As a result, we often nursed blisters and shin splints. At the time, I didn't fully appreciate Coach Holshue's thoughtful, compassionate gesture. His humility stayed with me over the years as a shining example of what we would nowadays refer to as true servant leadership.

On the track team, I struggled to find my fit. Despite my athleticism, I lacked the speed to sprint and the endurance to run distance. I wasn't built to run, and no amount of hard work and perseverance was going to turn me into a runner. At five feet nine inches, I was tall, so I turned to the high jump and tried to master the technique. Once again, I didn't have what it took; I lacked the explosive power needed for vertical lift. I couldn't figure out why I failed at every aspect of track and field. *What was wrong with me?*

The constant failure taught me a lesson in humility, reinforcing my core values.

Coach Holshue didn't give up and continued to encourage me as I participated with the team and tried to find my place.

One day, as I walked past the area where the shot put and discus throwers practiced, a senior named Ann called me over.

"Hey, Sandy, you look like you could throw. Come over here and try this." She unceremoniously handed me an eight-pound metal shot put. Ann was graduating that spring and was looking for someone to replace her in the throwing events.

Throwing the shot put requires a certain technique. It involves a hop and turn, but I didn't know the move at the time. I stood awkwardly in the throwing circle and chucked that ball of iron as best I could. To everyone's amazement, especially mine, it arced gracefully through the air and landed with a thud a long way off. The others stared with their mouths open. From thence onward, I became a thrower. The discus throw came even more naturally, and I went on to win the state championship in my junior year.

I never gave the track and field throwing events a thought because I couldn't throw a softball in a straight line, but the two activities require far different abilities. With the help of Coach Holshue and Ann, who saw something in me, I found my true ability and purpose on the track team. There, in the throwing circle, I developed the confidence, tempered by the humility of prior failure, I would later need to succeed at the Coast Guard Academy.

★ CHAPTER THREE ★

FINDING PASSION AND PURPOSE

Twenty years from now you will be more disappointed by the things that you didn't do than by the ones you did do. So, throw off the bowlines. Sail away from the safe harbor. Catch the trade winds in your sails. Explore. Dream. Discover.

—Mark Twain

EARLY IN LIFE AND throughout your career, it's necessary to continually evaluate the direction to take and the choices to make. It's important to pursue options that truly excite your interest and to pair that passion with an intended purpose that will lead to a desired outcome. Finding that passion and purpose is hard for most people. For me, it involved the following components:

Finding Passion and Purpose
- Analyze alternatives
- Make a commitment
- Seek experiences
- Defy the odds
- Recognize and seize opportunities
- Enjoy the job
- Show fortitude
- Make a difference

Analyze Alternatives

While my youthful experiences shaped my character and core values, my summers on Cape Cod helped me discover my passion and purpose to pursue a life at sea. My maternal grandparents retired from the hubbub of the South Shore of Boston to spend their later years on the peaceful shore of Great Bay in Falmouth, Massachusetts. My grandfather had been raised on the Saint Lawrence Seaway in the early 1900s. His father had been captain of Senator George Fulford's 126-foot private yacht, the *Magedoma*, in Brockville, Ontario. My grandfather always dreamed of having a boat and living near the water.

I spent a couple of weeks each summer at my grandparents' home on Cape Cod, communing with nature and learning to love the sea as did my grandfather. He took me out in his old wooden rowboat and taught me how to maneuver the heavy, clunky oars. We rowed across the bay, enjoyed a lunch packed by grandma, then meandered back to shore. We didn't concern ourselves with the passing hours during those carefree, idyllic days.

My grandfather didn't say much, but he taught me through his actions and deeds. He was a man of character, whom I looked up to and greatly respected. He taught me responsibility and values. I always remember Grandpa's advising me when I was a little girl, "Don't get married until you've finished college and have ten thousand dollars in the bank." He and Grandma had learned the value of thrift and hard work following their marriage during the Great Depression. I respected Grandpa and was inspired when he told me I could be anything I wanted to be in life.

Unfortunately, Grandpa was wrong. When I was a young person, many barriers to access and advancement for women still existed in education and the workplace. Thankfully, that changed in 1976 during my junior year in high school when an awesome opportunity came along that would alter my life.

It all started with legislation passed in 1975 requiring the US

Armed Forces Service Academies[ii] to open their doors to women. One day a neighbor, who knew I was applying to colleges, passed me an article in the *Baltimore Sun* announcing the US Naval Academy in Annapolis, Maryland, would be admitting women.

The article went on to describe the educational and career opportunities available for young men, and now for young women, who could persevere through the incredibly demanding nomination and admissions process. Straightaway I started the application process and obtained a coveted nomination from Senator Paul Sarbanes. Then my application entered the next step, competition for an appointment.

Fortunately, an observant high school guidance counselor looked out for me. PJ Kesmodel had also been my youth league swimming coach. He had dedicated himself to helping young people perform at their very best and had been instrumental in discovering and leveraging my talent as a swimmer. Now, he helped me find the right fit in a college.

PJ informed me of another armed forces service academy to consider, the US Coast Guard Academy, located on the Thames River in New London, Connecticut. He advised me of the importance of having more than one option to evaluate. Examining the brochure together, we decided the Coast Guard looked like a small navy and I should give it a try.

The Coast Guard Academy offered educational opportunities similar to those at the Naval Academy but operated on the direct admission process. I applied there as a backup and was soon offered an appointment as a cadet, or student. Pleased and proud to have been admitted to a top college that valued me entirely on my merit, I decided to accept.

---

ii   The US Armed Forces Service Academies include the Coast Guard Academy in New London, CT, the Naval Academy in Annapolis, MD, the Air Force Academy in Colorado Springs, CO, and the Military Academy in West Point, NY. The Merchant Marine Academy in Kings Point, NY, commissions some graduates directly into the Armed Forces, but most go into the Merchant Marine or into service in the maritime industry.

In walking away from the Naval Academy, I rejected the more politicized congressional nomination system required of the other armed forces service academies. It meant a lot to me that I earned my appointment to the Coast Guard Academy based on my achievements, through hard work and perseverance, not because of political connections. I came to rely on those core values—hard work and perseverance—as my key to success throughout the rest of my career.

Make a Commitment

I arrived at the Coast Guard Academy as a member of the third class to include women. The Class of 1982 started with approximately 280 men and 30 women. At the end of our four years, we graduated with just 156 people, including 10 of the 30 women who started. The attrition rate was incredibly high, averaging approximately one-half for each class. For women, it was higher—closer to two-thirds. I didn't want to become a statistic, so early on, I committed to persevere.

In those early days, women only made up five percent of the cadet population, and they had few choices for varsity sports. The newly established women's teams had to scrimmage against local high school teams as they worked toward establishing varsity teams. Women who had never played sports were recruited to help fill out teams. As a swimmer, I was invited to practice with the men's swim team. Although I could never have competed with the men at meets, I was included and accepted as a member of the team.

In pursuit of my dream to serve at sea, I joined the cadet sailing team—both the intercollegiate dinghy and offshore ocean racing squadrons. Fortunately for me, the Coast Guard's leadership development program is built around leadership experiences on the water.

Although I knew I'd made a wise choice in selecting the Coast Guard over the Navy, I can't say I did so with deliberate purpose to pursue a known passion. Sometimes in life, we must evaluate choices and select the best one with the information we have at hand, believing it will lead to a positive outcome.

The penultimate sailing opportunity and leadership development experience is a voyage on America's tall ship, the 300-foot square-rigged barque *Eagle*. At the end of the first summer of training at the Coast Guard Academy, cadets are shipped out to the *Eagle* for a one-week, experiential, real-life leadership opportunity. My class was lucky. We got to travel across the country, flying from New London, Connecticut, to Seattle, Washington, to meet the tall ship during her summer cruise.

We embarked on the ship and commenced our voyage to San Francisco, California, the next day. Manning our special sea detail watch stations, we witnessed crowds of people cheering on the pier to see us off. How electrifying! Underway, the ethereal experience of sailing an old-fashioned, square-rigged tall ship enthralled me. Instead of sleeping, I spent my time at night on deck taking in the majesty of the heavens and the stars in all their glory. Experiencing the deep darkness of the clear night sky, free from the tarnishing intrusion of ambient light, made me feel closer to heaven.

Hauling on a line in unison with other cadets, I raised canvas to the wind, controlling the movement of the huge sailing ship. All the while, I thrilled to the feeling of disciplined power that surged through my body. The sense of belonging to the crew and being part of an honorable service like the Coast Guard was deeply satisfying. Yes, I was hooked on the Coast Guard! I'd found my passion and purpose during that first summer at the Academy on board the *Eagle*.

The next summer, training took me on a very different and action-packed adventure on board the *Eagle*. This time we got underway from the Academy in New London, Connecticut, bound for Cork, Ireland. A couple of nights into the voyage, a big squall suddenly slammed the ship. It was late at night, and the alarm sounded for all hands to man their emergency sail stations.[iii] The ship listed dangerously far toward the water, and sails had to be taken down fast to bring the ship back upright.

Startled by the alarm, we cadets all jumped out of our racks, or beds, and scrambled up on deck as fast as we could. The night was pitch black. The wind howled so strongly and loudly we could hardly hear the commands shouted by those on duty. I struggled to move on deck as the wind funneled fiercely through the rigging, forcing me backward. The blinding sea spray stung my eyes, and the heel of the ship caused me to slip and slide precariously on the wet decks.

A square-rigged sailing vessel like the 300-foot *Eagle* has two masts 150 feet high—the foremast and the mainmast—along with a mizzen mast on the stern. There are five sails on the fore and main masts, with the highest one hanging way up near the 150-foot mark. As inexperienced trainees, we followed orders issued by the permanent crew in charge of our training. A few of us were ordered aloft to furl, or take in, the uppermost sail called the "royal." I was both terrified and thrilled to have been chosen.

Three of us cadets cautiously climbed aloft and positioned ourselves on one side of the yardarm. Battered by the howling gale, we desperately tried to get our arms around and bring in the huge sail. We stood on wiggling foot ropes holding onto a metal bar running along the yardarm, while the billowing sail threatened to knock us off. *Eagle* seamanship requires "one hand for the ship; one hand for yourself," and we took that "one hand for yourself" part very seriously that dark and stormy night! It was very, very scary, and my adrenaline rushed as fast as water through a fire pump.

Once we finished furling the sail and securing it to the yardarm with attached lines, we were supposed to work our way along the

---

iii   Sail stations is an emergency alarm sounded on the Coast Guard's only tall ship, *Eagle*, to alert the crew to proceed to their assigned positions, called stations, to adjust the sails and rigging. Sail stations are often required when the ship is under sail and unexpectedly hit by high winds that could cause damage to the ship and/or that could hurt people.

yardarm back to the mast and climb down to the deck. One cadet had frozen in place on the yardarm in a complete state of panic and wasn't responding to commands. Both of his hands clutched the metal bar in a death grip, and he could not move. We had to unpeel his fingers one at a time and talk him back to the mast and down to the deck.

Later that night, once the intense excitement ended and I was back in my cozy little rack, a wave of emotion surged through me. I felt as if I'd passed a personal test on the yardarm. I had not been the one to freeze. Despite my shortcomings in the classroom or on the athletic field, I discovered an untapped strength. Under incredible pressure, I found the courage to perform a difficult duty and to help others.

It dawned on me how this seminal experience validated my purpose in choosing a path in the Coast Guard. Serving at sea with shipmates I could trust, to accomplish a purposeful mission, ignited a passion within me. I didn't fully realize it at the time, but that fateful night was one in a series of inflection points that helped chart the course of my career.

Despite my passion for the Coast Guard and desire to serve my country, I often doubted my chances of making it through the Academy. Passion is one thing, but it's nothing without purpose and commitment to that purpose.

I took consolation that the Academy offered a five-year graduation plan for some cadets who couldn't make the necessary grades. I was glad to have learned humility early in life, because I wasn't the fastest, smartest, sharpest, or best at anything. I was a very average cadet, even below average in academics. I struggled with the science and math classes, graduating lower in my class as a result. I owe a debt of gratitude to one of my smarter classmates, John Welch, who tutored me through the mysteries of calculus. Kind and patient as Job, John helped me get through that arduous class.

Despite the hardships, having a passion and purpose and committing myself through my core values of hard work and perseverance helped level an uneven playing field. In the end, I not only made it through the four-year degree program at the Academy but continued to complete forty remarkable years of service in the Coast Guard. I found deep satisfaction in the Service's awesome missions, along with an enduring admiration of its amazing people.

Seek Experiences

Upon graduating from the Coast Guard Academy in 1982, I jumped at the chance to see the world by sailing the four winds and the seven seas. While many of my classmates opted for ships as close to home as possible, I set my course across the country for Long Beach, California, where I reported aboard the polar icebreaker *Glacier* as a brand-new ensign.[iv]

Designed to break ice in support of scientific and national security missions, *Glacier* was heavy and wide, shaped like a football. The ship was painted bright red to make it visible in the ice so deployed helicopters and small boats could safely return. The ship's crew numbered over two hundred, and I was one of two female officers on board. Within weeks, we got underway on a five-month patrol, Operation Deep Freeze '83, bound for Antarctica to support the United States science mission.

Although the US National Science Foundation is the lead agency for the US Antarctic Program, it has been supported over the years by the US Armed Forces, including the Coast Guard. The Coast Guard conducts icebreaking operations each year during the Antarctic summer through an operation called "Deep Freeze." Operation Deep Freeze supports science research and involves a heavy icebreaker clearing the channel leading into the nation's primary logistics facility, McMurdo Station.

---

iv   In the military, officer ranks start at the entry-level with O-1, which is an ensign in the Coast Guard and Navy and a second lieutenant in the Marine Corps, Army and Air Force. Likewise, O-2 is a lieutenant junior grade or first lieutenant; O-3 is a lieutenant or captain; O-4 is a lieutenant commander or major; O-5 is a commander or lieutenant colonel; O-6 is a captain or colonel and O-7 through O-10 are admirals or generals (flag or general officers).

That's where *Glacier* fits in, and it explains why the US Coast Guard took me halfway around the world to Antarctica, the most remote place on Earth.

Most people mistakenly think of the Coast Guard as a shallow-water service, but it's so much more. The Coast Guard has a network of coastal facilities, including small boat rescue stations and air stations scattered along America's waterways, yet its missions span the world. From the polar regions to the Caribbean, to the South China Sea and the Persian Gulf, the Coast Guard must meet the threats where they originate and provide services where they're most needed to protect the homeland and serve the American people. That mission space includes Antarctica.

After deploying for five months, *Glacier* completed the Deep Freeze '83 science mission and returned to homeport. In extreme disrepair from decades of hard running, the ship entered an extended maintenance availability. Most of the crew transferred, including me. Having completed only one year of what should have been a two-year, first tour afloat, I was reassigned to another polar icebreaker, *Polar Star*, homeported in Seattle, Washington, to finish my training. That new ship had been built to replace *Glacier* and other old icebreakers. *Polar Star* was even bigger than its predecessors at 400 feet and 14,000 tons. The prospects of a new start with a new ship and crew elated me.

My first deployment on board *Polar Star* took me in the opposite direction from Antarctica. We headed north to conduct a two-and-one-half-month science mission in the waters of the Arctic Ocean. The Arctic Winter West mission was far different from Operation Deep Freeze in Antarctica. Since the Arctic is an ice cap, not a landmass, there was no science station to support. We transported the scientists to conduct research drilling ice cores, sampling water, and studying marine mammals and birds.

Winter in the Arctic is frigid cold, dark, and desolate. The wind howls low across the ice, driving it to pile up on itself into deep pressure ridges that are far thicker than the surrounding sea ice. Those pressure ridges were fun to break. I would back the ship up then push the throttle full ahead to ram the pressure ridge at top speed. The ship would ride up on the ridge, and the ice would groan as it fell apart under the crushing weight of the ship. I felt a satisfying sense of conquest over nature when demolishing pressure ridges.

As in the Antarctic, the Arctic is replete with wildlife. I thrilled to see my first polar bear rise menacingly from behind a pressure ridge. We observed walrus, seals, and stunning celestial phenomena. I loved the Arctic!

By the time I made lieutenant junior grade, I had experienced both the Arctic and the Antarctic and enjoyed exotic, educational ports of call everywhere in between. One of my most memorable travel experiences came along by chance while serving aboard *Polar Star*. One day while in homeport, I was working in my spaces, preparing for the Operation Deep Freeze '85 mission to Antarctica. Andy, an enlisted member in my workgroup, approached to ask if I planned to participate in the ship's morale trip during our port call in Lima, Peru.

Andy explained the morale committee wanted to get enough people signed up to sponsor a trip to visit Machu Picchu. I couldn't believe what I'd just heard. The educational travel opportunity of a lifetime was there for the taking. The cost seemed like a lot at the time, but I jumped at the chance.

We arrived in Lima, and I couldn't wait to start our great adventure to visit the ancient Incan citadel. The evening before the trip, the wardroom, comprised of all the ship's officers, was invited to a reception hosted by the Peruvian Navy. At the time, two women served on board *Polar Star*. No women served in the Peruvian Navy. During the reception, *Polar Star* leadership made much of how progressive the Coast Guard was in sending women to sea, boasting that women performed the same jobs as the men. The Peruvian officers slyly exchanged knowing looks with each other upon hearing this. They were convinced we served a much different purpose on the ship!

I was glad to leave the Peruvian Navy behind and head for the airport the next day. We boarded a plane and took off on the first leg of our voyage to the ancient Incan city of Cusco in the Andes Mountains. Although Cusco is located at a relatively high altitude of over 11,000 feet, the Andes Mountains rise far higher. Instead of flying over the mountains, our flight took us on terrifying twists and turns through the mountains! During that frightful transit, I must admit to questioning my judgment in signing up for the trip.

Thankfully, we arrived safely at a small, unimproved airstrip outside of Cusco. After settling into our rustic quarters, we sallied forth to partake of the local culture. As we wandered, we explored markets where Incan women sold exotic wares such as colorful, handmade woven blankets and warm clothing spun from alpaca fiber. The people were very friendly, and one of them coaxed us into a small eatery where we enjoyed hearty Andean cuisine. Exhausted from the travel and altitude, and satiated from the good food, our small group retired to rest up for the next day's activities.

We awoke early and boarded a train for the second leg of our journey to Machu Pichu. The train ride was almost as amazing as the ruins themselves. We spent several hours chugging along through the grand Andes Mountains, taking in some of the most spectacular scenery in the world. Upon arriving in the iconic foothold of Aguas Calientes, we disembarked the comfort of the train. The final leg to our destination was the toughest, as we began the steep hike up Machu Picchu.

The view at the top was breathtaking, and a sensation of otherworldliness coursed through me. I could almost feel the spiritual presence of members of the ancient civilization that had lived and worshipped on the same ground upon which we stood. It struck me how civilizations the world over have their unique versions of hallowed sites. Those few cherished days spent in the Andes among the Incan people significantly enriched and expanded my worldview. I learned to see through the many differences between civilizations to the common traits and ideals that unite us as fellow members of the human race.

People often ask me what job I liked best in the Coast Guard. I know they expect me to name one of the important, high-visibility jobs I held later in my career as a senior officer. But I don't. The best job I ever had was my very first assignment, serving as an ensign on board the polar icebreakers *Glacier* and *Polar Star*. I owe my success to that initial tour of duty. It offered me the educational and developmental experience of a lifetime. It taught me how to navigate around obstacles and break through barriers, and it prepared me well to lead at the next level in the Coast Guard.

Defy the Odds

At age twenty-five, I was finishing up my tour of duty aboard *Polar Star*. I'd received orders to report aboard the Coast Guard Cutter *Clover* in Eureka, California, as operations officer and senior boarding officer. Again, I'd be the first and only woman on a ship with an all-male crew of fifty.

A *Polar Star* shipmate Kevin had been previously assigned in Eureka. When I shared my orders with him, instead of congratulating me, he expressed sympathy. He informed me Eureka, located in the far northern reaches of California, was a small town of lumberjacks and fishermen. He cautioned me it would be very hard and lonely there for a young woman. I loved the outdoors and, despite his warning, kept my spirits high. I would defy the odds.

Stepping into such a responsible role without knowing anyone was hard, but I felt comfortable with the officers and crew. The ship conducted law enforcement patrols from Canada to Mexico, an exciting and rewarding mission. My responsibilities included training, outfitting, and leading all-male boarding teams to enforce fisheries laws and other laws on the high seas.

To conduct a boarding, we lowered a small boat[v] from the *Clover* and motored over to a fishing boat. The vessels ranged from small salmon trollers and mid-water trawlers to big foreign fishing vessels. Once alongside, I informed the vessel master we intended to come aboard to conduct an inspection.

The Coast Guard has unique authorities under Title 14 of the US Code allowing the Service to board vessels on the high seas— something the Navy cannot do. Authorities notwithstanding, we were seldom received with open arms. The busy fishermen had to accommodate the boarding party while simultaneously working fishing gear and navigating the ship.

I always tried to put myself in the fishermen's position and treat the master and crew with respect, even if they occasionally seemed rude and resistant. After many encounters with fishermen, I found being firm in my resolve to come aboard while showing professional courtesy was what worked best. It was also an advantage, in some ways, to be a woman. On occasion, a boarding party out on a mission would call back to the ship on the radio to say, "Ma'am, we need you to come out here; this guy won't let us aboard."

Conducting boardings was a dangerous activity, and the situation always turned tense when a vessel master refused the boarding team. Most of the fishermen carried guns, which they needed to kill huge, flopping fish, like halibut. It wasn't an option to allow a master to refuse being boarded, but neither was it prudent to storm aboard the boat against the master's will. The objective was to get the boarding done properly with the lowest possible risk.

One time when I'd remained on board *Clover* to run law enforcement operations, the boarding party I dispatched called me out to deal with a sailboat owner/operator who wouldn't let them board. Far out to sea in the Pacific Ocean, the independent, single-

---

v   In the Coast Guard, most ships carry small boats in cradles. The small boats are launched to conduct ship's missions, such as search and rescue or law enforcement. They're run by a small boat coxswain, an enlisted member who assumes full responsibility for the small boat when it is away from the ship.

handed sailor was transiting south. When asked as part of the standard pre-boarding questions, he informed my boarding team he had a gun, which heightened the boarding party's concern. Upon arriving on the scene, I directed our small boat to approach the sailboat and engaged the man in conversation.

The tension seemed to deescalate when the boat operator noticed I was a woman. He was a bit eccentric, and I tried to earn his trust. I very politely and patiently explained our role and why we had to board his boat. Since I was a sailor, I understood sailboat operators' concerns about heavy black boots marking up their white decks. I assured him we would be very careful not to mar his sailboat with our shoes.

At last, the operator agreed to let us aboard, and we conducted an uneventful boarding. I attribute my success to using personal and professional power to persuade the vessel operator to allow me on board instead of issuing demands based on my authority. If the persuasive approach hadn't worked, I would have escalated to using position power which was seldom, if ever, necessary.

On the personal side, Eureka turned out to be a wonderful place to live. My shipmate Kevin was wrong. I moved into a quaint little fourplex outside of town where I met a young woman my age. Julie, a lifelong Eureka resident, worked for the telephone company. Like me, she enjoyed exploring the outdoors. Through Julie, I made quite a few female friends. My new friends taught me how to dive for abalone, where to bike ride among the magnificent coastal redwood trees, and where to meet for a delicious brunch.

Being so satisfied with both my personal and professional lives, I asked my assignment officer to extend my tour of duty in Eureka from two years to three. He readily agreed, given the dearth of people clamoring for assignment to that remote outpost. My experiences on board the *Clover* and in Eureka taught me to develop the confidence to defy the odds. Instead of feeling isolated, I made friends and found interests outside of work. My girlfriends in Eureka provided a comfortable counterbalance to the male crew I served with every day on the ship. I also discovered you can live a fulfilling life in a small town equally as well as in a big city. Perhaps most importantly, I learned there are advantages to being different.

Recognize and Seize Opportunities

The conclusion of my three-year assignment on board *Clover* marked the completion of six straight years of sea duty upon graduating from the Coast Guard Academy. Since sea duty was all I'd known, I would have served another tour afloat if given the chance. Instead, my assignment officer told me the time had come to transfer ashore. He had even picked out a job for me on the icebreaker acquisition staff at Coast Guard Headquarters in Washington, DC.

My first reaction was chagrin, as no junior officer wants to hear she has orders to headquarters. Having experienced significant growth as a leader through my years of seagoing operations, I thought a staff job as a lieutenant would surely end my career. I could never have envisioned how the staff job would launch my career instead.

I loved working on the icebreaker acquisition staff and felt valued as the only operator amongst a team of engineers and logisticians. I advised the team on practical matters and attention to human factors to ensure the design was functional. For instance, watchstanders had to be able to reach all the equipment on the bridge and to see out the windows. Although I'd resisted an assignment to Coast Guard Headquarters, it provided a remarkable opportunity for me to grow and learn.

One morning, I decided to visit my assignment officer, whom I'd never met, and thank him for sending me to headquarters. He was understandably surprised to see me, as officer assignments can be a thankless job. I introduced myself, paid my respects, and told him how much I loved my job.

The next day, I received a phone call from my assignment officer. He asked me if I would like to interview for a position as military aide to the newly installed secretary of transportation, Mr. Samuel Skinner.[vi] Secretary Skinner made it known early on how much he valued having a component of the armed forces as a member of the department. He was very proud to be the secretary of the Coast Guard and took great interest in raising the Coast Guard's profile during his tenure. In pursuing that goal, he asked the Coast Guard to provide him a military aide.

I was taken aback by my assignment officer's offer for me to interview for the position. I politely explained, "I'm truly honored, sir, but yesterday I told you how much I love my job on the icebreaker acquisition staff. They need me on the team, and I'm not going to abandon them for a better offer."

I took a deep breath and got back to work, thinking that was the end of it and vaguely wondering what I'd passed up.

My assignment officer called again the next day. This time, he said to me in no uncertain terms, "Let me rephrase my question. When are you available to interview with the secretary of transportation?"

I had no choice but to comply. In any case, my assignment officer had already proven he knew best regarding my career. I trusted him.

The interview with Secretary Skinner was completely unstructured with no specific questions. The secretary and I were the only participants in his cavernous office at L'Enfant Plaza in Washington, DC. It greatly relieved me to discover Secretary Skinner did not live up to my image of an imposing figure sitting sternly behind his desk waiting to size me up. Rather, he met me at the door, greeted me kindly, and tried to put me at ease.

Leading me over to a computer screen, he showed me a new Federal Aviation Administration air traffic control system under development. Secretary Skinner embraced technology and expressed great enthusiasm about the new capability. I knew nothing about the

---

vi   At the time, the US Coast Guard fell under the Department of Transportation. It wasn't until March 1st, 2003, that the Department of Homeland Security was established, with the US Coast Guard as a component.

new technology and came away from the interview thinking, "Well, that was fascinating, but there's no way I'll be selected."

Shortly after the interview, the word came down informing me I'd been selected for the job. Perhaps it was because I came to the Secretary's door and presented as my authentic self. What an amazing job it turned out to be! That assignment provided me the incredible opportunity to broaden my perspective and understand where the Coast Guard fit in the much bigger scheme of the entire department. A high visibility position, it allowed me access and interactions at the top levels of government and industry. The initially dreaded staff job ended up being the turning point in my career.

Enjoy the Job

While serving Secretary Skinner, I was selected for my first command at sea. I would report aboard the 140-foot icebreaker *Katmai Bay*, homeported on Lake Superior in Sault Ste. Marie, Michigan. I happened to be the first woman ever chosen for such an assignment. It pleased me to learn from a mentor who had served on the selection panel that the decision was based on my operational expertise and not my gender.

At the time, the Coast Guard was going to great lengths to assign women to high visibility and command positions to increase representation across the Service. Heading for my first command, I wanted to stand on merit and not have anyone judge me based on misperceptions. I didn't want my crew, who would entrust me with their safety, to think I might not be best qualified for such an important position.

People in the maritime community had already told me I wouldn't be accepted as the first and only female commanding a vessel on the Great Lakes. They said the old, experienced shipmasters would never put their trust in following an icebreaker commanded by a female. I decided to prove them wrong.

Upon reporting aboard *Katmai Bay*, I contacted one of the big shipping companies to ask if I could ride along on one of their ore carriers for familiarization. The gigantic vessels, many of them 1,000 feet long, barely fit into the locks and through the St. Mary's river. They carried approximately 75,000 tons of iron ore mined in Wisconsin and transported down through the lakes and rivers to the steel mills in Indiana.

My familiarization ride was approved. A very experienced master welcomed me into the pilothouse of a 1,000-foot iron ore carrier. Although reserved, he treated me with courtesy. I asked him many questions about what I needed to know to best serve the shipping fleet. Since *Katmai Bay* was only 140 feet long and the ore carriers were 1,000 feet long and far wider, I wanted his advice on the kind of path I needed to cut through the ice.

The master seemed a little surprised by my questions and warmed up to our engagement. He gladly called my attention to the most dangerous passages in the narrow river and showed me the points of greatest concern, where a very wide turn was needed in the ice. At the end of our transit, the master let me know he was used to the Coast Guard simply informing him of their icebreaking intentions, which often did not meet the mariner's needs. He expressed both surprise and pleasure to see me consulting the customers.

The Coast Guard had taught me from a young age that asking questions is empowering. People want to help others grow and learn, and the relationships that form help break down any existing barriers. Reaching out to meet the mariners where they were and trying to understand how I could best serve them helped me build trust. In the long run, it helped me succeed in best serving my new customers.

Nothing can compare with that first command assignment. The Coast Guard is a small service with a strong culture of responsiveness, as evidenced by the motto *Semper Paratus* (Always Ready). Responsibility is pushed down to the lowest reasonable level. As a result, junior officers are eligible for significant leadership responsibilities, like commanding the *Katmai Bay*. After serving for three years on board polar icebreakers conducting missions in both the Arctic and the Antarctic, the chance to leverage my experience on the Great Lakes excited me.

Icebreaking is a neat mission. The *Katmai Bay* was big, heavy, and round, ideal for clearing a wide track through the ice. To break the ice, the ship would back up and then come ahead, often at full speed, riding up on top of the ice and crushing it down. Meanwhile, a compressed air "bubbler system" pushed air out of ports in the hull below the waterline. The stream of bubbles would rise alongside the steel hull, introducing water as a lubricant between the ice and the ship's hull. Imagine a snow shovel in the winter; a coat of wax helps keep the snow from sticking. As the ship moved forward, ice broken upfront would flow back to the stern where the ship's over-sized propeller milled it into small chunks, like a coffee grinder. Below decks, the icebreaking noise was deafening, stifling conversation. It sounded like an army of workers pounding on the hull with hammers.

We performed icebreaking operations at close quarters alongside giant merchant vessels beset in the ice. To free the merchant vessel, the icebreaker had to make high-speed passes close aboard down its sides. Such maneuvers loosened up the ice, releasing tension so the merchant vessel could get moving again. The icebreaker had to approach unnervingly close to achieve the desired result and risked scraping alongside the beset vessel. I can recall times on *Katmai Bay* when we came too close for comfort.

Such is the nature of icebreaking; it comes with much responsibility and considerable risk. The job was among the most exciting and empowering I ever had. I loved it! Where else in the maritime industry, Navy, or Coast Guard can you intentionally ram a ship into a solid substance as a legitimate part of the mission? I came away from my first command assignment feeling like the Coast Guard had prepared me well for a job I loved, with both the technical and leadership skills I needed to succeed.

Show Fortitude

My next assignment, back at Coast Guard Headquarters, required me to summon everything I'd learned in my short Coast Guard career. This time, I worked for the chief of staff in the highly visible office of program review. The staff was already lean, with about a dozen reviewers assigned to Coast Guard programs. As a result of new budget pressures, the Coast Guard had recently started a streamlining effort to drastically downsize. The Service had committed to cutting 4,000 people and $400 million during the four-year term of the commandant,[vii] from 1994-1998.

The office of program review suffered a one-position cut as its share of the streamlining effort. Consequently, as the newly reporting officer, I was saddled with relieving two officers, each of whom was working at least twelve-hour days. One of the officers programmed funds for the Coast Guard's capital budget, while the other reviewed the major systems acquisition account. As is typical in the Coast Guard, staffing was one person deep for each position, with no backup.

I was overwhelmed with information. At any given time, four budget years were in some stage of development, and I had to understand dozens of major acquisitions inside and out. The duties of a program reviewer included briefing congressional staff on the status of the budget and programs, and I had to be ready for that task. After an all-too-short relief week, I felt unprepared to assume all the new duties and responsibilities.

I sat at the head of a big, long table in the executive conference room on that fateful Friday afternoon, the last day of my relief process. The two officers I would relieve had done their best to prepare me in the time they had. The table was filled with people looking at me anxiously and expectantly, hoping the information they had leveled at me through fire hoses all week had sunk in. I struggled to hold back

---

vii   The Coast Guard commandant is the service chief, equivalent to the administrator in another government agency, or the chief executive officer in a private organization.

involuntary tears of exasperation. Were these people serious? I wasn't fully prepared to take on the combined duties performed by two highly competent professionals. I would have to sink or swim.

Thankfully, I swam. Three years went by in that pressure-cooker office where I worked incredibly long and hard to get the job done. I was single at the time and vividly recall the stress of the unpaid bills stacked on my desk at home and uniforms left unclaimed at the dry cleaners. Some nights, I slept at the office, as did other program reviewers. The organization was stressed, and people were exhausted. But no one recognized the signs of exhaustion and the impact it had on an overtaxed workforce.

One morning I arrived at the office to learn a colleague had checked into the hospital for what ended up being an extended period. He joined others who had developed stress-related medical issues, ongoing illnesses, and marital problems. Yet no one—neither leadership nor those in the peer group—took a step back to examine the situation and take remedial action. Enduring the hardship was like a badge of courage, and nobody wanted to be the one to show weakness.

One day a new supervisor reported in. He had a big personality and seemed pleasant. We allowed ourselves to be a little bit excited, hoping he would bring a new perspective along with some relief from the stress. Unfortunately, that wasn't the case. He saw the new job as a major career advancement opportunity and wanted to make a dramatic first impression. He called us into the conference room to warn us he had very high expectations and "we could sleep when we were dead." We all made our best effort to keep our mouths from dropping, and morale plummeted right then and there. It would take fortitude to keep going, but it didn't need to be that way.

Leading with character means putting people first. Exceptional leaders understand succeeding in a tough mission means being fully aware of the stressors in the workplace and knowing their people's limits. Their duty requires providing people the resources and support required to manage stress, avoid exhaustion, and maintain wellness.

Make a Difference

In the Coast Guard, we have a saying. "A bad day at sea is better than a good day ashore." Finally, after three years streamlining the Coast Guard as a program reviewer, my trackline led me back to sea, where there would be good days and some bad days. In the summer of 1997, I reported in as executive officer[viii] aboard the Coast Guard cutter *Confidence*, a 210-foot ship homeported in sunny Cape Canaveral, Florida. Cape Canaveral is nestled in the heart of the Space Coast. To the north lies the Kennedy Space Center, where shuttles and rockets are launched. The port was booming as cruise ships took advantage of the location to accommodate surging demand. It was a very exciting place to be stationed.

Underway, we enforced laws and conducted search and rescue in the Caribbean Sea. In those days, we lacked the intelligence information needed to effectively drive operations. Therefore, our missions ranged from mundane, routine patrols to crisis response.

On the morning of September 9th, 1997, we were patrolling back and forth in the Windward Pass between Cuba and Haiti. The seas were calm and the wind light; it was another idyllic morning in the Caribbean. Below decks, crew members not on watch were eating breakfast, preparing for the day's work. Suddenly, we received orders to divert to Haiti. The ferry *La Fierte Gonavienne*, transiting from the island of La Gonave to the mainland, had capsized and sank early that morning with hundreds of people on board.

Unfortunately, Haitian ferries were often grossly overloaded, and such was the case of *La Fierte Gonavienne*. As the ferry approached the mainland, which had no pier, it turned to put its stern to shore so passengers could disembark by rowboat or by stepping onto the shoulders of people who waded out to carry them in. As the ferry

---

viii   The executive officer of a Coast Guard cutter is second in authority to the Commanding Officer. The executive officer is responsible for safety and security, training, medical, personnel and running the day-to-day business. In the Coast Guard, the executive officer function is akin to the chief operating officer of a private sector company or the deputy position in another government agency.

maneuvered, the passengers moved to one side, causing the unstable vessel to instantly overturn. The bottom dropped off steeply, and although close to shore, the vessel sank immediately in over one hundred feet of water. Some passengers managed to escape, but hundreds had been trapped below decks or knocked overboard and drowned.

At the time, Haiti was going through a period of instability. The president, Rene Préval, needed to show leadership in the crisis, and the United States leaned forward to support him. Thus, *Confidence* was ordered to the scene to conduct the search for and recovery of those who had been lost. Within a short time of *Confidence*'s arrival on the scene, US Navy divers from a mobile dive salvage unit reported aboard to use *Confidence* as their base of operations. The ship supported the divers with our small boats, which transported the divers to and from the sunken vessel and moved the bodies ashore as the divers recovered them.

Onshore, distressed family and friends engaged in ritual wailing and grieved around the clock. They expressed anger that the bodies of their loved ones weren't being recovered more quickly. The task was overwhelming, even for the expert Navy salvage divers. Operating in one hundred feet of eighty-five-degree water, they struggled to remove bloated bodies from deep within the sunken ship. They became exhausted, physically, mentally, and emotionally.

As the days passed, tensions ran high on board *Confidence*. We worked around the clock, with many of the crew taking turns performing exhausting and gruesome body recovery and delivery to shore. We were running low on food and, more importantly, water. Our operating area was a few hundred yards offshore, directly across from where a river used by both cattle and humans emptied into the sea. To make fresh water, we would have to run the shipboard evaporators while on scene in those contaminated waters. Some in the crew became concerned about the prospect of making fresh water under those conditions.

Ships are required to be at least three miles offshore when making fresh water to distance themselves from contaminants. The commanding officer, focused on the high profile of the mission, was willing to forgo the regulation given the operational exigency. No one knew for sure if the contaminants would be removed in the evaporation process. As the ship's safety officer and medical officer, I wasn't willing to risk the well-being of the crew.

I presented my case against making fresh water to the commanding officer and firmly held my ground that we couldn't risk the health and safety of our crew given the circumstances. I prevailed in convincing the commanding officer to not make fresh water on the scene. Instead, we steamed offshore to a safe distance to run the evaporators for a few hours. Still, we were compelled to double-down on water use restrictions. We explained the situation to the crew, to reassure those who had been worried about making water and to ensure they all understood the reason for the austerity.

To maintain order amidst the tumult, clear, concise communication was essential. *Confidence* had almost no extra berthing to accommodate the Navy salvage divers, and living conditions deteriorated for everyone. I directed that the Navy salvage divers, who started their work first thing each morning, go to the head of the line for breakfast. At one point, I got wind of a complaint from some in our crew that the divers were eating all the eggs, resulting in a shortage for the permanent crew.

I mustered the crew and explained that we were one team. This wasn't "us" and "them." It was a joint US Coast Guard-US Navy unified effort on an operation of international significance. I reminded the crew what those divers were going through all day, underwater in the bowels of that sunken ferry. Our mission was to support them and ensure they had everything necessary to do their gruesome duty. That included the eggs they needed to fuel their bodies. It wasn't easy to find a balance, because many of our crew were also working hard all day. My goal was to unify the crew around our purpose by shifting their focus away from the day-to-day activities inside the ship to the mission.

To succeed, I had to nip in the bud any drama that could divide them.

Pressure from ashore increased the sense of urgency on board *Confidence.* We learned that in the voodoo religion, which many of the Haitians in that region practiced, burial rituals are considered crucial to both the society's welfare and an individual's afterlife. Hence, it was of great social and political significance to recover and return all the bodies to the waiting families. Further complicating matters, there was also significant unrest among the families over the belief that *La Fierte Gonavienne* was sunk by a voodoo curse placed by a competitor. Angry mobs burned a competitor's ferry in retaliation. The situation ashore was getting out of control.

Confidence was directed to host President Préval at the scene of the disaster to provide him a platform to demonstrate command presence and build trust with the people. We hosted a press conference on board the ship, providing him a highly visible communications platform. Although his words sounded strong and reassuring if you heard them, it dawned on me that getting the message out to the masses was a major problem. The disaster occurred in an impoverished region in the days before smartphones and social media; I doubt if President Préval's words were heard by those who most needed his reassurance.

In due time, we completed our mission and were released back to patrol. The mood on board the ship was somber for days afterward as crew members reflected on the tragedy they had experienced. Although we endured some bad days at sea during that patrol, we grew and learned more about crisis response and leadership—particularly the value of communicating to build trust—than could ever be taught in a classroom or experienced in an office. In the end, we knew we had made a difference, and that was satisfying. Yes, a bad day at sea is always better than a good day ashore.

Circling back to the importance of passion and purpose, I've been asked what kept me motivated to persevere in my career for forty years. I've given that question a lot of thought. There were times when I became frustrated and tempted to quit. Yet I persevered. I found the answer in my commitment to lifelong learning, which opened my mind and renewed my spirit as I progressed up through the ranks.

The Kellogg Business School gave me frameworks for problem-solving, empowering me to better prepare alternatives and defend arguments. The Massachusetts Institute of Technology Seminar XXI program broadened my perspective on national security and foreign policy. Later, the National War College at the National Defense University provided me the opportunity to examine the workings of government at the strategic level.

The knowledge gained through professional development and education at each step in my career led to a deeper understanding of, and excitement for, my purpose. Focusing on the greater meaning helped me look beyond the tyranny of the present to all the promises and possibilities the future might hold. Discovering my passion and purpose at each stage of my career provided me new energy and the motivation needed to persevere and succeed over the longer term.

★ CHAPTER FOUR ★

LEARNING TO LEAD

The only source of knowledge is experience.

—Albert Einstein

LEADERS OF CHARACTER GROW through real-life experiences, learning equally from failures and successes. Although learning *how* to lead starts at the entry level, you are never too senior to learn. I continued learning more about leadership as I moved up in the Coast Guard to the executive level. The following principles apply to learning to lead at every level:

Leading at Every Level

- Commit to lifelong learning
- Practice what you learn
- Improve by applying lessons learned
- Learn from and become a good mentor

Commit to Lifelong Learning

As they progress to the next levels in their organizations, where more is expected, leaders of character must commit to lifelong learning to continue growing and maturing. Many executives inspire their workforces to pursue professional development by promulgating annual reading lists. Such lists are likely to include volumes that prescribe leadership theory, along with those from which a reader must derive the leadership lessons.

Although prescriptive, how-to books can be useful, I prefer the more nuanced way to learn leadership, which is to derive the lessons from good literary fiction. The classics, biographies, memoirs, and other forms of literature are replete with leadership lessons waiting to be discovered.

I attribute a significant portion of my leadership development to a lifelong fascination with books and love of reading. Growing up, television held little interest for me. While the rest of my friends and family watched programs, I sequestered myself in my room with a good book. I devoured Thornton W. Burgess nature stories. They captivated me with adventures of animals that, despite their different needs and personalities, lived together sharing the forest, meadows, streams, and sky. Those stories imbued in me a lifelong appreciation and respect for the outdoor world and its inhabitants.

When I reached young adulthood, contemporary literature featuring the coming-of-age theme captured my imagination and inspired me to search for greater knowledge and understanding. *The Chosen* by Chaim Potok and *Siddhartha* by Herman Hesse gave me insights into different cultures and showed how people of all backgrounds and origins share common struggles in their search for truth and purpose. In *The Chosen*, Reuven and Danny, two teenagers belonging to different Jewish communities in Brooklyn, New York, struggle to meet the expectations of their fathers. I admired Reuven for eschewing convention and reaching beyond the boundaries to discover the stimulating world of western literature, leading him to break from tradition and choose his own path. His story helped me remember to be true to myself when faced with complex choices. Likewise, by following Siddhartha's quest for enlightenment, I learned to believe in myself and look within to find wisdom.

At the Coast Guard Academy, one of the courses that impacted me most was an elective, The Tragic Hero in Literature, offered in the humanities department. In *Hamlet* by Shakespeare and *Oedipus* by Sophocles, I witnessed the insidious effect of hubris on the heroes. Both men fell not only because of their hubris but as a result of their failure to recognize the flaw within themselves. I learned from Aristotle, who postulated, "A man does not become a hero until he can see the root of his downfall."[2] The tragic hero course taught me the importance of self-awareness. I came to understand the need to search inward to recognize and address my flaws and strive to make good choices.

Over time, I turned to books exploring the nature of man as my mainstay. I've found books of this genre particularly useful in my role as a leader because they help me understand the motivation behind how people act and interact. In turn, that skill has helped me be a better leader, both of individuals and of teams. My personal experience was validated when I learned about Theory of Mind, which I think of as the ability to understand how others think and why they behave the way they do. Theory of Mind research shows that reading challenging literary fiction with complex characters enhances leadership skills. People learn how to navigate ambiguity by inferring what others may be thinking and interpreting what might drive their actions.[3]

Having spent a career at sea on ships, I relish *The Caine Mutiny* by Herman Wouk—a case study for Theory of Mind. The infamous Captain Queeg viscerally taught me what not to do as a leader of character. The book is set in the waters of the vast Pacific Ocean during World War II. Captain Queeg, a tyrant, commands the USS *Caine* with a heavy hand. Strictly by-the-book, his dogged focus on minutia blinds him to the bigger picture of the mission. Many notorious "incidents" cast a pall on Captain Queeg's ability to effectively lead.

The target-towing incident is one of the most instructive. In it, the *Caine* has been ordered to tow a target to be used for shooting practice by other navy warships. During the operation, Captain Queeg gives the helmsman a rudder command to turn the ship. He then fixates on reprimanding a watchstander for a uniform discrepancy, losing situational awareness as the ship makes a slow, giant circle. The helmsman notices the problem but is reluctant to say anything out of fear of the captain. Consequently, the *Caine* cuts her own towline, leaving Captain Queeg completely baffled and looking for someone to blame. Captain Queeg cultivated a hostile command climate, stifling the teamwork and communication necessary to operate a warship.

Practice What You Learn

I applied the lessons learned from *The Caine Mutiny* when I commanded *Katmai Bay*. Operating in the narrow Saint Mary's River, the helmsman was instrumental to safe navigation. We trained our helmsmen well and, with no margin for error in the narrow waterways, empowered them to question a command if they believed it would send the ship into harm's way.

Our best helmsman was Seaman Mike Weyhrauch. A big, strapping young man with a personality to match, his skill at the helm was unparalleled. I could rely on him to safely maintain the ship's position in the shipping channel without ordering specific courses. A typical order might be, "Steer on the navigational range," or "Steer down the middle of the channel." Seaman Weyhrauch stood a little taller with the new responsibility. He taught me the importance of cultivating a positive command climate—to believe in your people and trust them to perform beyond expectations.

Leaders desiring to inspire their people should be prepared for the question, what book are you reading? Or what podcasts do you listen to, and what would you recommend? Leaders serve as role models and must set the standard for continuing education in the workplace. Throughout my career, I've enjoyed both consulting my mentors for book recommendations and, in turn, recommending books to my subordinates.

A piece of classic literature can be as meaningful to a junior person as it is to a senior leader, offering timeless relevance connecting different people across generations. For those interested, I've included a reading list with some of my favorite books in appendix one. There are leadership lessons to be discovered in each volume.

Leaders must get out of their office or workspace and put into practice what they learn about leadership. In the sea services we call this "deck plate leadership," which means getting out and walking the decks of the ship. Too many leaders are well read yet ineffective because they fail to execute what they learn. When I was a junior officer on board *Clover*, my commanding officer recommended *The One-Minute Manager* by Kenneth H. Blanchard. The primary message, "to catch someone doing something right,"[4] was refreshing. What a positive perspective! Throughout my career, I followed that advice and made it a point to look for and recognize people's contributions instead of focusing on their shortcomings.

Upon reporting aboard *Katmai Bay*, I got to know the crew by getting out of my stateroom and walking the decks of the ship. I wanted to recognize people who had done a good job, as a way of breaking the ice, so to speak. Of the sixteen or seventeen crew members under my command, some were senior leaders, including the chief petty officer in charge of the deck department or the chief warrant officer in charge of the engineering department. Others were very junior personnel who worked for one of those department leaders.

One evening, I decided to walk through the ship before heading home. My travels took me down to the engine room. At that time of day, only a couple of junior crew members remained on board the ship standing duty. I came upon a very young fireman, sitting alone on the deck plates engaged in some routine equipment maintenance. I cannot recall his name, so will refer to him as Fireman Jones.

I asked Fireman Jones what he was doing. He told me, in a somewhat despondent voice, "Ma'am, I'm just cleaning this dirty oil filter." He thought it minor, thankless work.

I squatted down next to him and said, "Can you show me what you're doing and how that piece of gear works?"

Fireman Jones looked a little surprised but then brightened right up and told me all about that piece of gear. I didn't understand much of the technical explanation, but that didn't matter. I told Fireman Jones what he was doing helped keep the ship running and how pleased I was with his work.

The next morning, while sitting in my stateroom, I heard a forceful knock at the door. Bang, bang, bang! It was my chief engineer, Chief Warrant Officer Mike Smith. Chief Warrant Officer Smith was a dedicated leader who took a lot of pride in his duties. He had been incredibly supportive and had stood up for me in my new role. I felt very fortunate to have a leader of his experience and character as my chief engineer.

Chief Warrant Officer Smith, who supervised Fireman Jones, was in a huff. He declared with indignation, "I guess you don't need me since you're getting your information from Fireman Jones."

Come to find out, Fireman Jones was ecstatic to be recognized for his mundane task. He had spent the morning making sure his shipmates knew "the captain said what I was doing is the most important job on the ship."

Once I explained the situation to Chief Warrant Officer Smith, he understood. He still expressed displeasure with my having been down in his engine room talking with junior people in his absence. I had unintentionally taken him by surprise and disempowered him in front of his subordinates. From then on, I strived to communicate better with my senior leaders. By getting out and walking the deck plates, as taught in *The One Minute Manager*, I learned from my experiences and grew as a leader of character.

Improve by Applying Lessons Learned

Leadership development entails exhibiting the discipline to reflect and analyze performance after significant events or undertakings. Good leaders consult with their teams to identify lessons learned and then apply those lessons for continuous improvement.

The Coast Guard requires a formal risk assessment to be performed before a major operation, like getting the ship underway. Normally, a team of crew members who will be involved in the operation, including the command cadre, or senior leadership, conducts a collaborative risk assessment. Elements considered include the weather, the condition of the crew (whether they are well rested or fatigued), and complexity of the operation. They adjust the plan as necessary to mitigate risk. Later, when the operation is completed, the same team objectively reviews or "hotwashes" the events, using the exercise as a learning experience. This disciplined process produces a cycle of continuous improvement.

One wintery day while I was serving as executive officer aboard *Confidence*, we were preparing to get underway for a six-week patrol. We had been in port for a long maintenance period, which meant newly repaired machinery, along with new crew members. Consequently, we were out of practice for underway operations.

The day was blustery and unseasonably cool. Blowing strong from the north, the wind pressed *Confidence* hard against the pier. We conducted our standard getting-underway risk assessment and decided to modify our plan. We realized we needed help pulling the stern of the ship away from the pier so we could back out without being set down on the ship moored behind us. Calling for a tugboat would have taken hours, so we asked the Coast Guard small boat station, located adjacent to our ship's berth, for help. The station sent a small boat, which passed over a line we secured to the ship's stern. The small boat then pulled the ship's stern away from the pier, giving us clearance to get underway.

The technique worked well, but it took time for the small boat to get underway and in position. It was also an uncommon evolution, new to the ship's crew, which interjected additional, unnecessary risk. Everyone had to quickly adapt to the change, from leaders on the deck force responsible for securing the tow line to leaders on the bridge responsible for getting the ship underway. The change of plans delayed our departure. That, in turn, inconvenienced the operations manager of the busy shipping port, who had many ship movements to deconflict in the restricted waterway.

In the hotwash discussion following, we all agreed we should have anticipated the weather ahead of time. We could have planned for the Coast Guard station to stand by to assist, or we could have arranged for the services of a tugboat. That day, we did not live up to the Coast Guard's motto, *Semper Paratus.*

Leaders of character demonstrate the courage to admit when an operation for which they were responsible did not go as planned. They address the situation by objectively critiquing performance, adherence to policy, procedures, standards, and other relevant factors. Those who lead with character create a workplace culture that values feedback and promotes frank discussion to ensure continuous improvement.

Learn From and Become a Good Mentor

Mentors can help others recognize their talents and abilities, develop goals, work through problems, improve weaknesses, and leverage strengths. Leadership development becomes a virtuous cycle when leaders deepen their learning by seeking mentors, then give back by mentoring others in turn.

Leaders at all levels can serve as mentors. Contrary to what many may think, mentoring isn't limited to the conventional senior-to-junior relationships. Peer-to-peer mentoring is powerful and indicative of healthy respect between coworkers. Turning the paradigm upside down, some of the best mentoring I experienced as a senior leader came from those junior to me. Younger people offered me a valuable perspective that helped me better lead at their level.

Mentoring works best when the relationship happens naturally, or even spontaneously. People who take the initiative to seek advice and guidance from others at all levels around them will gain the most from the process. Effective mentoring requires active engagement by both juniors and seniors. Although senior leaders will often reach out their hand to juniors, it is incumbent upon juniors to initiate reaching out and up for mentoring.

Throughout my career, I've benefited from a diverse array of mentors, each of whom uniquely enriched my personal development. Mentoring is truly an *art*, not a *science*. There are many interpretations and some common misperceptions that can mislead both mentors and mentees. To get the most out of mentoring, leaders at all levels must recognize and beware of these three misperceptions:

Mentoring Misperceptions

- Mentors must look like you
- Mentors must be senior to you
- A mentor will make you successful

MISPERCEPTION #1:
MENTORS MUST LOOK LIKE YOU

None of my mentors looked like me. Since I was one of the early female officers to serve in the Coast Guard, most of my colleagues were men. I was the first, and for a time the *only*, woman to serve on three of my six ships. I consider myself extremely fortunate to have been mentored by men dedicated to helping me advance and succeed as an officer in the Coast Guard—not as a female officer.

A misperception has surfaced that people cannot succeed in an organization unless they see someone above who looks like them. I don't subscribe to the "you've got to see one to be one" myth. It is self-defeating. It's like Neil Armstrong's believing that since there had never been a man on the moon, he may as well not try to be the first. My experience has taught me that people limit themselves more than they are limited by others. You must look beyond what you can see and dream of, then reach for, what you imagine.

Certainly, organizations should include people at every level who reflect the diverse society they serve. That does not mean members should exclusively choose mentors who look like them or mistakenly believe a mentor who looks like them will assure their success.

On the contrary, those who desire to lead and succeed in ever more diverse organizations should actively seek people who *don't* look like them. Doing so will serve them well. They will glean a valuable perspective and expand their network. Diversity is all about different perspectives. Individuals who surround themselves with people who look and think the same will restrict their professional development. The best mentors are those with strong character and core values, who are a good fit regardless of gender, race, or ethnicity.

One of the best mentors I ever had was Secretary of Transportation Sam Skinner. He taught me lifelong lessons on leadership and one of its core components—followership. Dedicated to providing opportunities to top performing women and minorities, Secretary Skinner created a highly visible job to enhance my professional development. I accompanied him to his meetings and events, ensuring any action items arising out of those engagements were completed.

I will never forget the secretary's first gathering of all the modal administrators, which occurred early in his administration. The modal administrators were the transportation agency heads—the senior-most leaders in the department. They included the Coast Guard commandant, along with the heads of the other transportation modes, including the Federal Aviation Administration, Federal Highway Administration, and Federal Railway Administration.

The new senior leadership team was still forming. People did not yet know each other well, and most weren't accustomed to their roles. During the introduction phase of this inaugural meeting, the secretary looked at me, the only junior person in the room, and stated, "This is Lieutenant Stosz, my military aide. She will attend all my meetings and follow up directly with you on action items. When she speaks, you'll listen, because she's speaking for me."

I sunk a little lower in my chair as the eyes of the commandant of the Coast Guard fixed icily upon me, conveying the warning, "We'll see about that!"

The other modal administrators, civilians accustomed to working with younger people in responsible positions, thought nothing of the secretary's proclamation. Shortly after the meeting, I discovered I'd already been christened with a new nickname, "Lieutenant Follow-Up." The moniker stuck and followed me for years afterward.

Although Secretary Skinner empowered me with significant responsibility and ensured I had the necessary authority, I started out as an unknown quantity to the senior leadership team. I quickly learned the secretary's confidence in me wasn't enough. I needed to build trust with and earn the respect of the senior leaders. Being a good follower meant learning how each modal administrator operated, then working with him or her to best serve the secretary. Most of the modal administrators mentored me in navigating the department and understanding politics.

Astonishingly, the hardest modal administrator to work with was my own commandant. Coast Guard leadership was very skeptical of a junior officer in a prominent role with such close access to the secretary. Instead of embracing the opportunity and leveraging it, the Coast Guard resisted and made it difficult for me to adequately follow up on items for the secretary. According to the chain of command, the information I needed would have to be pushed down from the commandant to a much lower level in the Coast Guard, then over to the secretary's office.

Eventually, the information made its way to me through the secretary's military adjutant, then-Commander Jeff Hathaway (who retired years later as a rear admiral). I found, in Commander Hathaway, yet another superb mentor. Secretary Skinner couldn't have chosen a better officer to serve on his personal staff. Commander Hathaway was both well-liked and well-respected. A gregarious person with high emotional intelligence, he masterfully navigated the intricacies of the relationship between the Coast Guard and the department. Commander Hathaway and I were the only two Coast Guard officers assigned to the secretary's personal staff. He dedicated himself to helping me succeed. He did more than mentor me; he stood up for me.

One day, Commander Hathaway called me into his office and informed me, "A senior advisor to the commandant called, and the commandant is concerned about your appearance."

As members of a civilian staff, military officers were supposed to wear civilian clothes when in the office. When accompanying the secretary to an external event, we donned our military uniforms.

Commander Hathaway pressed the commandant's senior advisor for more details on the perceived problem that needed to be corrected regarding my appearance. The senior advisor hesitated, then answered, "Well . . . I guess she just looks too good."

After the initial surprise and consternation, Commander Hathaway and I both had a good laugh. He explained, "I had to tell you because I told the commandant's senior advisor I would. But don't worry about it, there's nothing you need to do differently."

Understanding that first impressions matter, I took great care in how I presented myself in the new job. Dressed in business suits with knee-length skirts, I conveyed a conservative appearance by any civilian standard. To maintain a professional decorum, I kept my hair up in a bun and never wore makeup. At the time, few women served in the Coast Guard, and even fewer were detailed outside the Service. Senior leadership couldn't reconcile the image of a young, female lieutenant looking so different in civilian clothes. The incident taught me the importance of opening my mind to judge people by their performance, not by their appearance.

Thanks to having a superb leader of character in Commander Hathaway to help me navigate and lead in those uncharted waters, I could focus my efforts on serving Secretary Skinner. I accompanied him to his meetings, including those held outside of the Department of Transportation. I had the privilege of sitting in on personal one-on-one engagements and significant discussions with senior government officials and transportation chief executive officers.

I traveled to Capitol Hill with Secretary Skinner in 1989 to meet with Senator Ted Kennedy. Senator Kennedy wanted to discuss the Americans with Disabilities Act, a piece of new legislation he was sponsoring. Senator Kennedy wisely brought in every senior government official whose department would be impacted to answer questions and achieve buy-in for the new law. Secretary Skinner expressed concern regarding the significant problems, like cost, service disruption, and the like, that the necessary accommodations would pose for all transportation modes.

Senator Kennedy was prepared for such questions. He assured Secretary Skinner appropriate consideration would be given to retrofitting existing capital assets and facilities to minimize the burden on public and private transportation systems. He clearly articulated his vision of the far-reaching positive impact the new law would have on society and demonstrated how the benefits would be well worth the investment.

From that meeting, I learned a couple of lessons on the power of humility that served me well throughout my career. First, for a significant new initiative to succeed, you've got to consult with stakeholders upfront to build trust and garner support. Second, to achieve an outcome fundamentally acceptable to all, you must understand and respect others' concerns and be willing to compromise.

In high-level meetings like the one with Senator Kennedy, I captured the key issues and action items. I then informed the appropriate senior leaders, assigned tasking, and followed up. It was an enormous responsibility to entrust to a junior officer.

By placing such trust in me, Secretary Skinner won my intense loyalty and undying respect. I didn't want to let him down or fail him in any way and gladly put in the significant hours the job required. In addition to trusting me, Secretary Skinner truly believed in me and recognized my potential even when I did not. He asked about my career aspirations and advised me to continue seeking opportunities to advance in the Coast Guard.

Secretary Skinner made it a point to introduce me to senior leaders, even though I held the lowly position of military aide. The highlight came when he presented me to President George H. W. Bush during a reception hosted on board the *Eagle*. I had the distinct honor of conversing with President Bush and having my picture taken with him. What a thrill for a young officer!

Long after being reassigned from his office to my next position, Secretary Skinner continued to reach out to mentor me. He flew to Sault Ste Marie, Michigan, to preside at the ceremony when I assumed command of *Katmai Bay*. Later, he wrote a letter of recommendation supporting my application to the Kellogg Business School. And, in keeping with his commitment to lifelong mentoring, he flew to Washington, DC, to share in my retirement ceremony thirty years after my assignment as his military aide.

Looking back, my fortuitous assignment as Secretary Skinner's military aide connected me with two lifelong mentors. Secretary Sam Skinner and Commander Jeff Hathaway both devoted themselves to mentoring a young woman, helping me overcome obstacles to achieve my full potential. In turn, I committed to doing the same for others as I advanced in my career.

MISPERCEPTION #2:
MENTORS MUST BE SENIOR TO YOU

When people think of what it means to be a mentor, they may envision a typical senior to junior relationship. Yet, if you explore a little deeper, you'll discover superb mentors outside of the standard paradigm. Some of my best mentors were peers and subordinates.

My assignment as captain[ix] of the *Katmai Bay* created a human-interest news story since I was the first woman to command a ship of any type on the Great Lakes. I will be forever grateful to the male officer I replaced. Lieutenant Craig Bennett was a Coast Guard

---

ix   In the Coast Guard, the term captain is another word for commanding officer; it applies to the position regardless of rank. There is also a rank of captain, which is a level of seniority not to be confused with the position of commanding officer.

Academy classmate and a humble, selfless leader. He served as an awesome peer mentor when I most needed one. In addition to helping me prepare to take command, he paved the way in advance of my arrival by managing the crew's expectations. He assured them I was well-qualified and capable of doing the job, stressing the significance of professional competence over gender.

Craig also managed the local news personnel, who came looking for a story even before I arrived. They wanted to interview the crew for reaction on the prospect of having a female captain. Reading the crew's responses made me so proud. One of the quotes went something like, "The ship is still 140 feet long, and we're still going to get underway every day to break the ice." In other words, it would be business as usual, regardless of gender.

In contrast to the positive backing and mentoring from the current captain, the higher-ups in the chain of command acted the exact opposite. Looking back, I was very naïve. When Secretary Skinner informed me he planned to fly in to attend my change of command, I was thrilled. I honestly believed the Coast Guard would be, too. How awesome for the Coast Guard service secretary to dedicate time to participate in a Coast Guard activity, at an operational unit!

I didn't anticipate the extremely negative reaction of senior Coast Guard leadership. It annoyed them the secretary had chosen to participate in a junior officer's change of command. Since the secretary would be there, the admiral in charge of the entire geographic region felt obligated to come all the way up from Cleveland, and he didn't appear pleased.

There was no warm welcome for me from anyone in my Coast Guard chain of command. My new supervisor, a gnarly old sailor, rose through the enlisted ranks, commissioned as an officer, and attained the senior rank of captain. He greeted me gruffly, forewarning, "You're nothing but Secretary Skinner's fair-haired golden girl, and I'm going to test you in every way I can to see if you're really up to the job."

I was thunderstruck. The command screening panel selected me based on my extensive icebreaking experience, not for what I was or who I knew. My new boss had it in for me regardless, and I braced for what might come.

It wasn't easy being a new commanding officer reporting to a senior officer who didn't think I belonged in the job. The ship's crew soon realized something was amiss. The harassment adversely impacted them too, creating uncertainty as my supervisor openly hassled me. I kept doing my best to earn the trust and respect of the crew and knew I was making headway. Yet I couldn't help but feel continually stressed. It bewildered me not to be given a fair chance to succeed, solely because of my gender. Command is lonely, and it would have been easy to quit right then and there. Instead, I hung on.

My strongest support came from an unexpected source. Chief Petty Officer Dave Foley, the chief boatswain's mate, led the deck department with competence and good humor. A big, burly boatswain, he tolerated no nonsense and commanded everyone's respect. Despite his imposing physical presence and force of personality, he nonetheless understood when to use compassion in leading his workforce. Keenly aware of my troubles, he stepped up to mentor me, helping me learn the ropes, so to speak, in my new role.

I've always had the highest respect for chief petty officers, the senior enlisted leaders on whom both the officers and crew rely for technical expertise and sage advice. Therefore, I was thankful for Chief Foley's support. Although junior to me, he served as a sage mentor when I needed one most given the troubles with my supervisor. I found out later Chief Foley also stood up for me with the crew, not all of whom accepted a female captain.

After a while, I noticed, miraculously, my supervisor had suddenly backed off his harassment. What a relief! I reveled in the newfound freedom. Later, when I got to know Chief Foley better, he shared with me a remarkable story about what caused the change. Becoming exasperated with my supervisor's behavior, the chief had marched up to his office, requested permission to enter, and then shut the door. He told my supervisor his behavior toward me was inappropriate, and he needed to back off. To my supervisor's credit, he respected Chief Foley for taking a stand. He decided if the chief supported me, that was good enough for him.

A few months later, after my supervisor retired, we met one evening at a Hiawathaland Law Enforcement Officers Association meeting. He put his arm around me and exclaimed to some of the attendees that he had been very hard on me—to test me—and I'd passed all his tests and succeeded in proving myself. He told them he was proud of me. I was stunned. I learned people can change for the better, and it often takes patience and perseverance to survive difficult situations.

In Chief Foley and Lieutenant Craig Bennett, I witnessed shining examples of leading with character. They selflessly demonstrated the courage to stand up for me, risking adverse consequences to their careers. Who says mentors must be senior to the person they are mentoring? Chief Foley and Lieutenant Bennett debunked that misperception. Chief Foley (who achieved the rank of chief warrant officer) continued to serve as one of my most trusted mentors and advisors for my remaining twenty-eight years of service in the Coast Guard. Likewise, Lieutenant Bennett (who joined the ranks of the federal Senior Executive Service) advised me over the years as we both rose to the senior executive ranks of the Coast Guard. You're never too senior to be mentored!

MISPERCEPTION #3:
A MENTOR WILL MAKE YOU SUCCESSFUL

Although I'm a strong advocate for mentoring, both up and down the chain of command, I worry when I see young people competing for senior, influential mentors. During a mentoring session I once attended, I heard someone senior advising a group of junior people how to succeed. He told them they had to find the right senior mentor, then "get in the elevator with her or him and ride it to the top." I was dismayed to hear a senior person utter that statement in front of impressionable young people. He could not have been more wrong.

Unfortunately, I've witnessed junior people who put too much weight on a mentoring relationship with a more senior leader, thinking they have it made. Then hubris creeps in, often accompanied by a haughty attitude and sometimes a decline in performance. They lose the respect of those around them and rely on their proximity to their mentor as a crutch. Inevitably, when the senior leader retires or moves on, they're left without support and must learn to stand on their own. Those individuals are unlikely to succeed.

Contrary to what some may believe, a mentor's role is not to use their influence to give mentees an advantage over others. Rather, it's to help their mentees reach their full potential. That's where near-peer mentoring comes in. Mentors who are one or two paygrades or levels above their mentee offer a more relevant perspective.

As a senior leader, I agreed to mentor many junior people. Those were valuable relationships for both them and me, but junior mentees often posed tactical questions better suited for a near-peer. Also, it can be hard for junior people to envision themselves as a senior officer. They rightly focus on the next job and the next paygrade and need strong role models and mentors who are succeeding in those next-level jobs. Ideally, people should cast a wide net and seek mentors at all levels of the organization. A broad and diverse perspective is most likely to help you succeed.

Having mentored many leaders, I believe what they need most is timeless advice on how to approach obstacles, confront challenges, and recognize opportunities. While serving as executive officer on board the *Confidence*, the operations officer, Mark, reached a key decision point and approached me for career advice. He had been selected for promotion and would rotate into a new job the next summer. Mark and I sat down after the normal workday to discuss his career options. He began by asking my thoughts on what follow-on assignment he should pursue to best advance his career. I let him know we needed to consider other factors in evaluating what he should do next.

During my years working in the officer personnel management system counseling hundreds of officers, I discovered advising another person is an art, not a science, and requires getting to know the mentee on a deeper level. The advisor must first fully understand the mentee's status and goals. Important points to consider include whether the person is on active duty or in the reserve, how many more years he or she has until retirement, the timing of the next promotion point, whether he or she has earned an advanced degree, and other pertinent career and personal information.

To aid in our discussion, I turned to the computer and started up a spreadsheet to capture Mark's assignment history matched up with his past and prospective promotion points, including retirement eligibility. The timing is important to understand because certain career milestones must be attained at or by certain paygrades. For instance, as a surface afloat operator, Mark needed to plan on competing for an executive officer assignment in his next paygrade.

The career discussion tool provided us a means for reflecting and projecting to develop different scenarios based on Mark's long-term personal and professional desires. Since he desired to pursue his career as far as possible, we evaluated scenarios prioritizing professional development geared toward the senior ranks of the Coast Guard. We compared options, discussing the upsides and risks each posed for his career progression.

In the end, Mark still had to make tough choices, but his choices were much clearer and better informed. He didn't need my advice on what to do; he needed me to help shape and focus the alternatives so he could make a sound decision. I knew Mark was exceptionally sharp and analytical; therefore, I tailored my mentoring to his personality and specific needs.

My advice to mentors is ask mentees where they see themselves in ten, twenty, thirty years and at retirement. What is their vision of success? Do they want a steady income and time at home with family, or do they want to compete to make it to the top of the organization? People need to look beyond the present to consider the future because where they see themselves finishing will influence the career and personal choices they make along the way.

My advice to mentees is actively seek a diverse set of mentors who will offer a broad perspective. You shouldn't hesitate to ask for mentoring and should continually seek chances to grow and learn from others. Mentees should clearly convey their career goals and objectives and ask a mentor for help in shaping and evaluating alternatives. But you should never expect your mentor to pave the way for a plum job. Regardless of all the benefits that can flow from a mentoring relationship, you are responsible for your own success or failure.

CHAPTER FIVE

A FORMULA FOR SUCCESS

There is no secret ingredient.

—Kung Fu Panda

NOTHING IS MORE REWARDING than working with young people and watching them grow as leaders of character. My many interactions with students over the years have had a common theme: young people want to find the secret to success, be it a secret ingredient or, better yet, an app!

Although there is no secret ingredient, there are useful tools. I developed a formula to help leaders succeed. It's comprised of what I call the Three Ps for Success—preparation, performance, and perseverance. One of my favorite leadership movies, *Kung Fu Panda*, uniquely illustrates the formula. Though an animated film associated with the younger generation may seem like an odd choice, this gem of a movie appeals to a broad audience and adds humor to an otherwise serious discussion. The themes presented in this movie can teach leaders at all levels about diversity, inclusion, and equity; mentoring; core values, and more.

Kung Fu Panda tells the story of a novice with a passion and purpose who, under the leadership of his mentor, prepares, performs, and perseveres to reach his goal. The unlikely hero of the story is Po, a giant panda who secretly dreams of becoming a Kung Fu warrior. Po is a sympathetic figure. Overweight and clumsy, he is working in an unfulfilling job as a waiter in his father's noodle shop. Through a series of unlikely events, Po is chosen by a mystical power to become the fabled Dragon Warrior, destined to save his village from extermination by an evil foe.

Po begins training with the five Kung Fu warriors who have been preparing their entire lives to defend the village. They are all studying under Master Shifu, the preeminent Kung Fu warrior trainer. Po has no apparent talent or self-esteem, and despite intense training, he is nowhere near skilled enough to face the evil foe. He seems like a lost cause.

Finally, there comes a time when Master Shifu realizes he has done all he can to train and prepare Po. He leads Po to the palace where Po will take possession of the mysterious Dragon Scroll. According to legend, the scroll contains the secret to victory over the evil foe. The only individual who can read the scroll is the Dragon Warrior.

As the scroll is brought down from its place of reverence high in the ceiling of the palace, the assembled Kung Fu warriors and Master Shifu all look on with keen anticipation. Po eagerly unfurls the scroll only to scream and jump back; instead of the secret to success, Po sees nothing but his big, fat face reflected from the mirrored page of the scroll.

At first, everyone is confused and fearful, as the scroll was supposed to contain the secret ingredient needed to beat the much stronger evil foe. It becomes clear there was never any need for a secret ingredient for Po to succeed as the Dragon Warrior. Po had only to look within himself to find the strength and determination to defeat the evil foe; he had it inside him all the time waiting to be discovered. Po unlocked his power by transforming what had appeared to be weaknesses into strengths, defeating his opponent and saving the village.

The story of the *Kung Fu Panda* illustrates there is no secret ingredient. My formula, the Three Ps for Success, will help leaders reach deep within themselves to draw on their inner strength and find the answers they need to become their very best:

THE THREE PS FOR SUCCESS
Preparation + Performance + Perseverance = Success

Preparation

Although everyone's passion and purpose will likely change with growth and maturity, one constant is preparation. Admiral James Loy, one of the Coast Guard's most accomplished commandants, set forth a seminal tenant in his guidance to the organization: preparation equals performance. He later teamed up with the noted author Don Phillips to memorialize the concept in their book *The Architecture of Leadership: Preparation Equals Performance.*[5]

Preparation equals performance stuck with me throughout my career. I greatly admired and trusted Admiral Loy and sought to emulate him. Since he placed preparation in such high esteem, I made it a component of my formula for success. Over time, I discovered a continuum of preparedness. It starts with the individual but requires the next level of unit readiness. The most complex component is organizational readiness which, as demonstrated in the continuum below, is the sum of individual and unit preparedness:

PREPAREDNESS CONTINUUM
Individual Preparedness + Unit Preparedness =
Organizational Readiness

At the individual level, I learned the power of preparedness from personal experience. Although never the most talented or gifted person in the workplace, I leveled the playing field by putting in the time and effort to prepare myself. That helped me succeed.

In my early years as a junior officer serving at sea, my primary duty was standing the watch as the underway officer of the deck. During my four-hour watch, or shift, I was responsible to the captain for keeping the ship and crew safe. Those duties and responsibilities applied whether the ship was engaged in a major operation, such as a search and rescue case, or merely in transit.

Before relieving the watch, it was essential to prepare intently. Arising early, I spent twenty to thirty minutes making a thorough round of the ship, both below decks and topside, which means both inside the ship and out on deck. I visited the galley to see what equipment was in use and the engine room to determine the machinery status. Topside, I checked to see what evolutions might be in progress and to notice if everything was secure on deck. Only then would I make my way up to the bridge, the place where watchstanders are responsible for the movements of the cutter.

As the officer of the deck, I was responsible for all the other watchstanders. To prepare, I arrived one-half hour early to apprise myself of the status of operations, equipment, and machinery, and to adapt to the darkness, if necessary. When sufficiently prepared to assume the duties and responsibilities of the officer of the deck, I approached the captain, if he was on the bridge, and asked permission to relieve the watch. Then and only then, when fully prepared, would I offer my relief and step into that position of extreme responsibility and complete trust.

When my watch ended, the preparation started all over again. My collateral duties included running the ship's store, a fifty-thousand-dollar retail operation. With no accounting experience, I took the initiative to learn the business while provisioning for a five-month deployment to Antarctica. I had to stock the store with the right products and quantities to serve 170 people for five months, with limited storage space.

I needed to know and understand my customers, who were also my shipmates. My responsibilities included discovering what products they needed and desired to see them through the deployment.

Reaching out to individuals recognized as leaders among their peers, I received enthusiastic feedback. I learned an important lesson to lean on throughout my career—it always pays to include the customer in the decision-making process.

The learning didn't stop there. I discovered my customers wanted canned sardines, of all things, and became well versed in the many varieties on the market. I couldn't even imagine eating a salty little fish with the ship rolling in heavy seas. I had to learn which candy bars were most popular, what kind of razors and soap people liked, and what kind of drinks to put in the soda machines.

What a lesson in diversity! Soap and soda might not sound like a big deal, but imagine what would happen if, three months into a five-month patrol, the ship's store ran out of shaving cream, candy, sardines in mustard sauce, or any one of many products considered vital to hygiene and morale.

As my career progressed and I moved up in the organization, the importance of preparation was repeatedly driven home. I learned that individual preparation, like getting ready to stand a watch, is only part of the equation. Preparation at the unit level is crucial. In the case of a ship, equipment must be properly maintained. Drills and training must be conducted and inspections passed. Administrative matters need to be in order. Shipboard preparedness requires an adaptive culture ready to meet emergent circumstances. It requires using the right people for the task at hand and empowering them to collaborate across boundaries to pursue innovative solutions.

On November 20th, 1997, the cutter *Confidence* got underway from its homeport in Cape Canaveral and headed south for a six-week patrol in the Caribbean. In my position as executive officer, I put the crew through the normal underway drills, and everyone was adapting to being at sea after a long in-port period. As we approached Miami, a radio call came in directing us to interdict a migrant vessel overloaded with passengers. It was unstable and in imminent danger.

Below decks, Lieutenant Junior Grade Craig O'Brien was lying in his rack (a shipboard bed) resting up before assuming the underway officer of the deck watch. He felt *Confidence* turn sharply and come up to full speed. He knew the ship must have been called to respond to something big, and he was right. *Confidence* arrived on the scene to find a true disaster in the making. We had been told to anticipate under one hundred people on the migrant vessel. We encountered a much graver scenario. Sadly, the small vessel had been dangerously overloaded with literally hundreds of people who had left Haiti trying to reach the United States. People had been crammed into the approximately sixty-foot boat far beyond its capacity, causing it to wallow in the gentle waves. The passengers were in obvious distress. We knew we had to save them—and save them quickly— before nightfall and before the weather deteriorated.

We weren't specifically prepared for the crisis we confronted. It was, after all, our first day underway. Nevertheless, our people had trained well, and the ship was ready. I assigned our best boarding officer, Lieutenant Junior Grade O'Brien, to lead a team to assess the situation. He was experienced, capable, and had demonstrated exceptional leadership ability as a junior officer. Although Lieutenant Junior Grade O'Brien had no training in mass rescue operations, I knew he could be depended upon to make good decisions and take appropriate actions to manage the crisis.

Upon arriving at the migrant vessel, Lieutenant Junior Grade O'Brien climbed over the rail with his boarding team members, Chief Petty Officer Thompson and Boatswain's Mate First Class Jennings, right behind him. They were met by a nearly impenetrable sea of distressed humanity. They squeezed their way through the throngs to the vessel's bridge, where they met the boarding officer from a smaller Coast Guard vessel. He was overwhelmed. His small team had managed to start a dewatering pump, but it was not keeping up with the flooding. Lieutenant Junior Grade O'Brien and Chief Thompson locked eyes as the gravity of the situation set in. The grossly overloaded, flooding vessel could roll and sink without warning. Lieutenant Junior

Grade O'Brien knew it was imperative to get another pump running and start offloading people from the vessel to improve stability.

Back on board *Confidence*, we anxiously awaited the boarding team's report. The news was worse than we expected. Lieutenant Junior Grade O'Brien informed us people were packed into the vessel so tightly some could barely breathe. The boat had left from Haiti about a week earlier, and the people had been given little food or water. The human trafficker who had likely taken their money for the voyage had no concern for their welfare. On the migrant boat, Lieutenant Junior Grade O'Brien saw the news helicopters overhead and promised his team that the evening news would tell a story of a compassionate Coast Guard rescue, not a fatal tragedy at sea. Then they got to work.

Upon hearing Lieutenant Junior Grade O'Brien's report, we set the ship's migrant recovery bill, an official procedure we had prepared for and practiced in the past. The crew surged competently to carry out their assigned duties. We lowered both small boats with experienced teams to begin transferring people off the wallowing migrant boat onto the decks of *Confidence*. They kept coming and coming. We brought aboard one hundred, then another hundred, and another, and another, until we had 421 people crammed on to the decks of our 210-foot cutter.

Many people at the bottom of the migrant boat were unconscious from dehydration and suffocation. We brought twenty to thirty of them to the fantail of the ship, where our independent duty corpsman administered intravenous fluid to revive them. Our corpsman discovered a few nurses among the migrants, which greatly relieved him; he would need all the help he could get. Although Haitian people speak Creole, to my astonishment, we easily communicated with them by other means such as hand motions and facial expressions during the crisis. The Haitian nurses set about administering IVs and treating patients, and we worked in harmony. I was so relieved to see the unconscious people start to move.

Lieutenant Junior Grade O'Brien and his boarding team toiled for hours executing an extended evolution that exemplified cohesive teamwork. The team finished their duties as the sun set over nearby Miami. Lieutenant Junior Grade O'Brien noted the bold Miami skyline peacefully dotting the darkening shoreline. The migrant vessel had almost made it yet had almost sunk in its desperate attempt to reach our shores. There were no words for what they had experienced that day. Lieutenant Junior Grade O'Brien and his boarding team simply stared at each other in relief before climbing down the boarding ladder to depart the empty vessel. They were filled with the sense that they, supported by *Confidence*, had pulled off something much greater than themselves that fateful day and evening. It had been the epitome of teamwork. All the drills and preparation had spurred innovation and fostered a sense of calm in the face of disaster.

But unloading the distressed migrant vessel was just the beginning of the saga. With 421 upset, starving, thirsty and, in some cases, angry people on board, the ship could have been in chaos. Instead, the calm and competent engineer officer took charge on deck, directing efforts to provide each migrant a blanket, to keep family units together, to set up and construct bathroom facilities, and to start preparing food. The ship carried supplies for this purpose, but the sheer number of migrants overwhelmed us. To the best of my knowledge, 421 is the most migrants ever taken aboard a 210-foot cutter. Normally, there would be only a few dozen.

Although the engineer officer and I coordinated the overall effort on deck, many of our enlisted personnel surprised and pleased me by stepping up to lead, regardless of their rank. Some of those crew members had previously experienced migrant operations, having served on board other cutters. They employed their personal and professional power to develop and implement the innovative solutions we direly needed.

With the migrants somewhat settled in on deck, the operational commander directed us to proceed to Haiti to repatriate them.

As the ship got gingerly underway, the crew tried to resume the normal routine. The atmosphere was charged with an undercurrent of intensity and emotion. The events of the day had exhausted everyone. Many had put their safety at risk, managing the crowd and conducting dozens and dozens of small boat trips to safely transfer the migrants, a few at a time, to the cutter. Members of the crew felt deep compassion for the migrants, so desperate for the promise of a better life that they would risk their lives for the chance. I'm certain everyone on board went to sleep that night thankful for the privilege of living in the United States.

The next day, we learned another cutter would rendezvous with *Confidence* to relieve us of some of the migrants. Strained to the maximum to care for, manage, feed, and secure so many people, that was good news. Although relieved to see the other cutter, it also meant another risky day of small boat operations to transfer already stressed people.

Upon completing the transfer, the remaining migrants realized they were going back to Haiti, not to the United States. Hugely disappointed, given what they had endured, some became agitated. We had to separate those whom we thought might pose a threat and place them under guard.

The situation only got worse. On top of the unrest, one of the migrants informed us she was pregnant and needed medical attention. Our corpsman recommended we evacuate her. Night had fallen. The Coast Guard sent a helicopter, and we had to clear the flight deck of over 250 remaining migrants and their gear in a short period.

Conducting flight operations on the deck of a 210-foot cutter is dangerous under any condition, to say nothing of what we faced that night. In my opinion, there are no better helicopter pilots than Coast Guard aviators, and the mission to medically evacuate the pregnant Haitian woman succeeded.

Within a couple of days, both cutters arrived in Port-au-Prince, and we repatriated 420 migrants to the Haitian authorities. I watched the Haitians leave the ship with mixed feelings. I felt good about rescuing them from the distinct possibility of perishing at sea. On the other hand, it saddened me to see them right back where they started, without hope, in a tragically impoverished land.

Confidence succeeded in this demanding mission because the ship and crew had built a solid foundation of preparedness, enabling us to rise to any occasion. We also placed our best leaders in key positions and called upon the crew for innovative solutions to manage the unprecedented influx of people.

True to its motto, *Semper Paratus*, Coast Guard people and units are a model of preparedness. Its deeply ingrained culture of preparedness sets the Coast Guard apart from other organizations, serving as a model of excellence. Anyone who aspires to lead and succeed will necessarily be responsible and accountable for people, resources, programs, and operations. Leading with character means understanding the obligation to be prepared—always—for everything from the daily norm to contingencies and crises.

Performance

Although working hard and preparing thoroughly are necessary to succeed, you're evaluated on results achieved. Both supervisors and subordinates play an important role in setting and meeting performance expectations.

Good supervisors set high expectations, then coach subordinates to raise their performance and stretch themselves to meet those expectations. Supervisors should require frequent counseling and feedback sessions as a tool for communicating directly to keep their subordinates on track.

Leading with character means supervisors must demonstrate the moral courage to give honest evaluations. They should be sure subordinates know early on where they need to improve. Subordinates should never learn they're falling short by seeing the problem for the first time on their performance evaluation. Supervisors must appropriately document substandard performance, provide opportunities for the person to improve and, if necessary, remove a poor performer from the workplace.

Responsible subordinates focus on meeting their supervisor's expectations and achieving required results. They must guard against the temptation to focus on what they want to do, instead of what their supervisor needs them to do. To ensure alignment, subordinates must seize the initiative and request periodic, routine discussions with their supervisor to ask for specific performance feedback. Counseling sessions also provide an ideal opportunity for subordinates to make specific requests for training, professional development programs, increased responsibility, benefits, or accommodations.

High-performing organizations create a culture of excellence, with motivated members giving their very best effort in every task assigned. During my tour of duty as executive officer on board *Confidence*, we received a new group of ensigns (junior officers) every summer. We set high expectations for the ensigns, to whom we assigned important duties and responsibilities. As developing leaders of character, they were expected to act as models for the crew in their roles as division officers.

One of the new ensigns reported aboard with great enthusiasm and performed superbly in his primary duty as a watchstander in the engine room. An engineer officer in training, he traced out engineering systems, learned to operate the machinery, and led firefighting teams. He enjoyed working at the deck plate level and got along great with the crew. He was incredibly talented, reliable, and dependable. In fact, in his first year on board, we recognized him with a performance award for his outstanding efforts running a major maintenance and repair contract.

Entering his second year, the ensign advanced to the division officer level. The new position of greater responsibility took him away from hands-on tasks to managing people and programs, which is the normal progression for an officer. Most junior officers are eager to move up to more demanding leadership roles, but this ensign showed no interest. He didn't like attending to all the details required to prepare for a big event like an administrative inspection.

It happened that the ensign's increase in responsibility coincided with the ship's formal biannual readiness assessment. Preparing the ship for that major event was his primary duty, but he failed to take it seriously. Despite repeated counseling and intervention by his direct supervisor, the ensign's performance did not improve. By his indifference, he put the ship at risk and let down both the command and the crew. He lost the trust of the commanding officer and was subsequently relieved of his duties.

Unfortunately, the ensign fell victim to what I call "selective obedience," choosing to perform well at duties he enjoyed and neglecting those he did not. Self-serving behavior breaks the trust that binds the crew of a ship. Leading with character means doing what's required, putting the ship's interest above your personal interests, and performing to the best of your ability—always.

Professionalism goes hand in hand with performance. As our society shifts to more casual workplaces, I've noticed a general decline in people's professional presence and interaction. It may be a consequence of social media, which encourages people to "friend" or otherwise connect informally with each other. In this new environment, communication is more one-sided and does not require personal interaction with others. It is an entirely new, informal way of communication filtered by a machine, resulting in a substantial loss of critical, nonverbal signals.

To succeed in the workplace, leaders must understand the difference between being friends and being professionals. The two are not the same. Friendship invites a certain familiarity that can interfere with the appropriate level of decorum required to convey a professional presence. Finding the appropriate balance can be tough, but you must do so, particularly in senior-subordinate relationships. My rule of thumb is, in the workplace, you should strive to be respected, not to be liked.

People always ask me, "Wasn't it hard being the only woman on a ship?" There were certainly some unique challenges, as I discovered on board *Polar Star*. I found it possible, though, to influence how people treated me by maintaining a professional demeanor.

Upon reporting aboard *Polar Star* as the first woman ever assigned, I learned my place in the crew, my role, and the expectations for my performance. I endeavored to earn my shipmates' respect by working hard, performing to the best of my ability, and caring about the people in the crew. I asked a lot of questions, seeking to learn as much as I could. I recognized people when they performed well but, as importantly, held subordinates accountable to the high standards I expected.

Assigned the role of assistant navigator, I led a division comprised of four or five petty officers in the quartermaster rating. The division was supervised by a master chief petty officer, the most senior enlisted grade in the Coast Guard. The quartermasters were responsible for the ship's navigation, including laying down tracklines, or courses, on the nautical charts, which are like maps for the maritime domain. Underway, the ship followed the tracklines to safely reach its destination.

My first encounter with the master chief was a memorable one. Eager to get to know my people, I wanted to learn more about him and start building a relationship so we could work together. He epitomized the image of an old salt, complete with the graying hair, weather-worn face, and a look of quiet competence.

He studied me skeptically, sizing me up, and slowly rolled out a question. "How old are you?"

I was feeling experienced, with a year of polar icebreaking aboard *Glacier* already under my belt. Hence, I responded with a degree of newfound confidence that I was twenty-three.

The master chief gave me a cool stare and stated matter-of-factly, "I've got more years at sea than you have on this planet."

What a warm welcome! The master chief was making it known in front of the troops that he would be the one who was really in charge of the navigation division. Thus began my leadership predicament.

The master chief was, without question, incredibly experienced and competent. I discovered, nonetheless, that he suffered from overconfidence in both himself and his navigation team. On our first patrol together, *Polar Star* embarked upon the Arctic Winter West mission, requiring us to navigate some of the most treacherous waters in the world.

I was responsible for the navigational tracklines the ship would follow from its homeport in Seattle, Washington, up across the Gulf of Alaska, through the Aleutian Islands, and into the frigid Chukchi and Bearing Seas below the Arctic Circle. The navigation petty officers were assigned to map our course and lay down the tracklines for watchstanders to follow.

I'd learned during my first year at sea aboard *Glacier* to follow a trackline across the chart with my finger before relieving the watch as the underway officer of the deck. I carefully scanned for any hazards that might have been missed. Before the ship deployed, I asked the master chief if he had verified the tracklines for our journey. He seemed a little put out and told me he trusted his petty officers. They knew their jobs.

I pressed him, saying, "Well, just take a look to be sure and let me know when you're confident the nautical charts are all ready for deployment." He reluctantly complied.

Once the ship got underway for our three-month deployment, the tracklines understandably changed with the ship's mission. When the time came to navigate through the Aleutian Islands, the quartermasters laid down fresh tracklines. Given the danger of transiting the narrow passes, or straits, between the islands, I again asked the master chief if he had checked the tracklines. At that point, checking the tracklines had become a contest of wills between us. He stood stubbornly by his belief that his petty officers were capable and didn't need oversight. I stood my ground wanting him to do his job and "trust, but verify," giving me the assurance I needed.

Frustrated, I went up to the bridge and traced the tracklines myself. I needed to be confident in my evening report to the commanding officer verifying our courses for the night. To my astonishment, as I traced the trackline through a narrow pass, my finger crossed a very small shoal with a depth a foot or two shallower than the ship's navigational draft. The course took the ship into danger, and we could have gone aground. I wanted to storm down to the master chief and give him an earful, regardless of who might be listening. Instead, I took a deep breath, went below, and asked him to come up and look at the chart with me. I didn't need to say anything.

Although the master chief never admitted he had been wrong, from then on, I received reports that the tracklines were safe. Although frustrating, the experience taught me many lessons. I observed a powerful example of the need to trust but verify when empowering subordinates. I learned how to hold a very experienced professional accountable in a respectful manner that preserved dignity. I understood the need to guard against overconfidence and to value the vigilance that often comes with inexperience. And I learned the power of a professional demeanor grounded in giving and earning respect.

Perseverance

Many people leave their jobs due to dissatisfaction with leadership, specifically their first-line supervisor. While commanding the cutter *Katmai Bay*, struggling under the supervisor who made my life miserable, I was eligible to resign my commission . . . and almost did.

On my worst days, I felt very alone, which can happen to anyone in command. I allowed my emotions to get the better of me and developed tunnel vision regarding my situation. As a result, I sat down, pulled the Coast Guard Personnel Manual off the shelf, and drafted my letter of resignation. I printed it out and kept it where I could go back to read it when I felt emotionally down. I could tell myself each day, "All I have to do is drop this letter, and it'll all be over."

Thankfully, I found the fortitude to keep persevering. The day came when I received word my supervisor would soon be retiring. I took solace in the fact that he hadn't been selected for continued service, which renewed my faith in the Coast Guard. It also gave me hope that one of the darkest periods of my professional life would soon end and brighten into a fresh start.

Realizing all it took to restore morale was a change in work conditions struck me as a major inflection point. I'd allowed myself to become overly consumed with frustration about things beyond my control. I should have pushed the frustration aside to make room for the positive experiences and not permitted one negative influencer to consume my thoughts. I failed to realize my exasperation was but a moment in the timeline of a career.

Later, I used my experience to encourage others never to quit but to persevere through periods of darkness. My analogy featured the term for transferring to a new job. In the armed forces, we call it a permanent change of station (PCS) move. PCS is used as a verb, as in "I'm going to PCS to a ship." I advised people experiencing a formidable work environment to stick it out because "this too will PCS." In other words, this too will pass. That simple phrase resonated and never failed to elicit head-nodding and laughter.

Looking back, I'm thankful I didn't act on my impulse to take the easy way out and quit because the going got tough for a while. The Coast Guard is an amazing organization with great people and missions, and I had no desire to leave. Had I resigned my commission, that toxic supervisor would have won, so to speak, while I would have ended up the loser by giving up my exciting career. Although I regret allowing one person to get to me, I'm glad I found the courage to persevere.

Following this powerful formula that *preparation, performance, and perseverance* lead to success helped me level the playing field and succeed in a demanding environment among more naturally talented or gifted peers. I discovered there is no secret ingredient; everything you need to succeed can be found within. Natural talents and abilities may be an advantage, but there is no substitute for the Three Ps for Success.

★ CHAPTER SIX ★

THREE PS OF POWER

Nearly all men can stand adversity,
but if you want to test a man's character, give him power.
—Abraham Lincoln

WHILE SERVING AS A young ensign aboard the cutter *Glacier*, my supervisor Lieutenant Dale Thompson imparted a life-long lesson that guided me throughout my entire career. One day I found myself struggling with how to manage a junior enlisted person under my supervision. He wasn't producing the results I needed to complete a task. I sought out my boss to report my dilemma and ask his advice. Lieutenant Thompson looked me in the eye and told me, "There are three types of power, and you need to learn how to use them if you want to succeed." Here are the three Ps of power that helped me succeed:

The Three Ps of Power
- Personal Power
- Professional Power
- Position Power

Lieutenant Thompson advised that the best leaders rely on personal and professional power and reserve position power for rare cases when it's absolutely necessary. That resonated with me. I'd approached my subordinate without much consideration, simply ordering him to do the work. I went back to the crew member and considered the circumstances. He was performing extra duty, as punishment for not meeting expectations, and his heart wasn't in the task.

I took a different tack and lowered my guard to come across in a more personable manner. I explained the importance of the job he was assigned. Although he didn't miraculously transform into a motivated worker, he got the job done. The Three Ps of Power model taught me there are far better ways to lead than to give an order, and I was eager to explore them.

Personal Power

Exceptional leaders, at any level, tap their personal qualities to create a positive, enthusiastic workplace environment. They are motivational leaders of character who people choose to follow. They are approachable, genuinely interested in the people around them, even-tempered, consistent, and they probably even have a sense of humor.

Leaders with strong personal power take their work seriously but make it a point to not take themselves too seriously. They put the welfare of their people and mission performance above their own ambitions. They make tough workplace decisions in a firm, fair manner. Perhaps most importantly, they earn the respect of those under their supervision and build trust in the organization. In summary, leaders with strong personal power are servants who follow the age-old Golden Rule, "Do unto others as you would have them do unto you."

The Coast Guard builds superb leaders of character, and I had the good fortune to learn from many who chose to lead with personal power. One of the most impactful was Captain Bill Simpson, a senior naval engineer and project manager for the Coast Guard's polar icebreaker acquisition program. A tall, lanky man, he moved around the workplace with a sense of purpose that belied his calm, cool demeanor. Captain Simpson's reputation as a highly respected naval engineer served us all well because people trusted him; hence, they believed in the program.

I reported in to work for Captain Simpson in the summer of 1989 as the operations technical manager on the project staff. I was the junior member of the team and, as usual, the only military woman. The highly visible project was in the early stages of development. The need for a new icebreaker had to be justified before the project could be approved and funded.

One day, we learned we would be presenting a significant decision briefing to the commandant of the Coast Guard and subsequently to Congress. We started working enthusiastically on the brief we presumed the project manager would give. Captain Simpson had another idea. He surprised us all by selecting me.

It was a highly unusual, if not unheard of, decision. Normally, the project manager himself would be the one to present such a significant briefing. Captain Simpson took a measure of risk in assigning the task to a junior lieutenant. He was a truly humble senior leader who looked beyond the conventional way of doing business. He saw an opportunity not only for me but for the project.

Captain Simpson wanted the most effective briefer, regardless of position or rank. Although the junior person on the team, I had recent, relevant experience with icebreaking in the Arctic and Antarctic aboard the *Glacier* and *Polar Star*. I would, therefore, bring credibility, which could potentially advance the project to achieve approval. There was just one problem . . . I was terrified at the prospect!

My six years at sea had offered very limited public speaking experience, and I wasn't a naturally gifted speaker. Nonetheless, the project team rallied around me, helping write the presentation and preparing the slides. Team members encouraged me, offering advice, and building my confidence. After much preparation and support, I was ready and able to deliver an impactful presentation.

Captain Simpson didn't have a big, outgoing personality, but he had big personal power. A quietly competent leader, he employed a dry sense of humor that would lift us up and keep us grounded on the tough days when we felt like we could make no progress. He earned our deepest respect by trusting us and truly empowering us to explore creative solutions. Everyone felt comfortable speaking with him and hashing out the tough issues. We all loved working for Captain Simpson and enthusiastically supported him in advancing the project. It was eventually approved and funded, and in 1999, the polar icebreaker *Healy* was commissioned for service in the Arctic.

Leading with character means leveraging your personal power to inspire and motivate others. The best leaders draw upon the power of their emotional intelligence to attain a deeper understanding of themselves and others, enabling them to better relate and empathize. Those leaders succeed by inspiring people to reach their full potential and add value to the organization. Renowned emotional intelligence expert Dr. Daniel Goleman proposes five components of emotional intelligence:[6]

Components of Emotional Intelligence

- Self-awareness: Ability to recognize and understand one's moods, emotions, and drives, and their impact on others
- Self-regulation: Ability to control or redirect disruptive impulses and moods; the propensity to suspend judgment or to think before acting
- Motivation: Passion to work for reasons beyond money or status; a propensity to pursue goals with energy and persistence
- Empathy: Ability to understand the emotional makeup of other people; skill in treating people according to their emotional reactions
- Social Skills: Proficiency in managing relationships and building networks; an ability to find common ground and build rapport

To me, emotional intelligence is a measure of a leader's *softer* skills, whereas intellectual intelligence is a measure of a leader's *harder* skills. Since hard skills are more tangible, intellectual intelligence has long been the predominant measure of one's ability. In recent years, the concept of emotional intelligence has been gaining more attention, as people better understand its value in the workplace. I came to realize my emotional intelligence quotient (EQ) was more instrumental than my intellectual intelligence quotient (IQ). Although never the smartest leader in the room, I possessed a common-sense ability to read people and perceive risks and opportunities. Those skills gave me an advantage over more analytical leaders who hesitated to make decisions because they did not have every piece of information. Leading with character requires a degree of emotional intelligence and is something everyone can, and should, strive to improve.

I learned an important lesson about the value of emotional intelligence while embarked on an educational trip to Southeast Asia. One of the highlights was a trip to Yogyakarta, the major cultural center of Indonesia. Our group journeyed into the countryside, a patchwork of rice paddies, to observe the ancient art of kris making. A kris is an asymmetrical dagger that, in ancient times, adorned men of power or influence.

The elderly kris maker with whom we met obviously had a passion for his craft. He gladly shared his knowledge and recounted the story of the kris. The art of kris making is passed down by apprenticeship and takes years to master. Each kris starts with the highest quality metal that's heated to a specific temperature, then precision shaped. Most fascinating of all, the kris maker informed us each kris had to be tailored specifically to the individual customer. The kris maker had to get to know the prospective owner well enough to craft a kris that would fit his personality and spirit.

Leading with character means making the effort to understand your people well enough to discover what motivates them and how they learn. Walking around and talking with people, sitting down with each subordinate to develop a performance plan, and organizing office outings are some of the many methods leaders can use to get to know people better. As the Indonesians believe each kris must be fashioned to fit its prospective owner, so should leaders tailor their style to best serve each subordinate.

Professional Power

Professionalism has no substitute in the workplace. It's a hallmark of character. Leaders of character build trust and earn respect by demonstrating competence in their profession, living their core values, and holding others to the same high standards. They foster a culture of respect, enabling all people to pursue their career aspirations.

Every time I reported to a new operational unit as the first or only female, inevitably, some questioned whether a woman could do the job. The antidote to that bias was to demonstrate competence through performance and professional presence. I looked for early opportunities to build trust and earn respect.

When I reported aboard the cutter *Confidence* as executive officer, I was again the first woman to serve in that position. The ship was scheduled to get underway a couple of weeks later. Although I'd spent eight years at sea on board four different ships, I'd never set foot on a 210-foot medium endurance cutter. I had no idea how the ship handled and hadn't gotten familiar with the people, the port, or the nuances of how the ship conducted business when getting underway.

The time came to get the ship underway. I reported to the bridge to oversee preparations. The quartermaster of the watch piped, "Now, set the special sea detail," over the ship's announcing system. All seventy-five crew members hurried to their watch stations. One of the officers of the deck had been assigned to get the ship underway. Since this would be my first underway evolution, I looked forward to the opportunity to observe and learn.

For those who have never been on the bridge of a military vessel, the atmosphere is electric. The relatively small space is filled with people energetically manning their watch stations, breaking out gear, giving and taking orders. Electronic equipment is being lit off, or started up, and machinery is being tested. People are talking on the radio, getting updates on shipping activity in the port, and gathering information. To me, it always felt like "organized intensity."

Amidst all the activity, I walked around, trying to stay out of the way while observing the process. Imagine my shock when the commanding officer turned to me and directed, "Lieutenant Commander Stosz, why don't you get us underway?"

In a heartbeat, I had to switch my frame of mind from relatively passive to intensely active.

Following protocol, I informed the commanding officer of my plan for pulling the ship out and started taking reports and giving commands. The bridge of the ship is one place where I've found it necessary to raise my voice to be heard, and that afternoon, I made sure it resonated.

Later, the commanding officer told me he decided I should get the ship underway to build credibility and prove myself with the crew. That way, there would be no question as to my competence with ship handling and navigation. He was right. People respect professional competence. It builds trust and earns you a measure of respect.

Although being put on the spot was very uncomfortable, the only way to grow is to get out of the comfort zone. Once safely underway and out of the port, I was thankful for the opportunity. I succeeded during my tour of duty aboard *Confidence* and for the rest of my career, because in the Coast Guard, I was judged not by gender, but by my professional competence and presence.

Position Power

Unfortunately, some leaders rely on position power like a hammer as the go-to tool to get a job done. You don't need to. There is almost always a more precise instrument in the toolbox. People who choose the hammer do so because they lack something needed in a leader of character. The shortcoming could be a dearth of confidence, poor professional competence, low emotional intelligence, or limited imagination. Such leaders may try to make up for their shortcomings in personal and professional power by exerting power in the only way they know how—through their position.

Reporting aboard my first ship, the cutter *Glacier*, I joined a cadre of a dozen junior officers at the ensign and lieutenant junior grade level. The wardroom also included a smaller group of second tour junior officers, lieutenants, with a little more seniority and experience. Some of the officers had graduated from the ninety-day Officer Candidate School program while others, like me, had matriculated through the four-year Academy program.

The difference in leadership styles exhibited by my peers was profound. Some had mastered leveraging their personal and professional power while others deferred to their rank. One lieutenant struck me from the start as a model leader of character. George DuPree reported aboard *Glacier* as a second tour junior officer who entered the Coast Guard through Officer Candidate School. He served as the ship's navigator, among other duties. George had worked for a few years before joining the Coast Guard and demonstrated more maturity and wisdom than the rest of us.

Fittingly, George hailed from Georgia, and his gracious southern manners enhanced his professional presence. With his laconic drawl and common-sense attitude, he lowered the stress level during risky evolutions, such as scuba diving operations in the icy waters or maneuvering the ship alongside a pier. A master of his profession, he earned the reputation as the best shiphandler and officer of the deck among us. Everyone—both officers and enlisted, subordinates, peers, and superiors—trusted and respected Lieutenant DuPree. A young, inexperienced, and impressionable new ensign, I looked up to him as the perfect role model.

On the other side of the leadership divide was another lieutenant, a very knowledgeable and technically proficient Coast Guard Academy graduate. Although undeniably skilled in the performance of his duties, he lacked emotional intelligence and didn't seem interested in the people around him. He wasn't a bad person, just a weak leader.

The workforce this lieutenant helped lead encountered constant stress trying to keep up with never-ending maintenance on old, unreliable equipment and machinery. The overworked crew members faced immense pressure to keep the ship operating. Tensions ran high. The workforce desperately needed an engaged, motivational leader who could build trust and improve morale. Unfortunately, the lieutenant was unapproachable and not the right person to meet the leadership challenge. Since he lacked the necessary leadership qualities, people viewed him through the lens of his rank and position. The lieutenant was an officer to be obeyed out of necessity, not one whom people chose to follow and emulate.

Comparing the effectiveness of the two leaders, I watched the people serving under Lieutenant DuPree thrive, while those serving under the other lieutenant merely survived. Lieutenant DuPree inspired everyone around him. He led with humility and good grace, building trust and earning respect.

As testimony to the differences in leadership, Lieutenant DuPree went on to complete a very successful career, retiring at the rank of Commander. The other lieutenant didn't succeed in advancing his career. Leading with character means motivating and inspiring your subordinates to draw out their best performance. Such leaders create an innovative workplace climate encouraging creativity, imagination, and expression.

Leaders serving in positions of power and influence over others must constantly guard against the insidious effects of position power, which can lead to hubris and a sense of entitlement. The antidote to hubris is humility. As they become more senior and powerful, leaders cannot merely talk about humility; they must live that virtue every day. I've learned to beware of leaders who make inferences about how humble they are. They're often the ones who are the least humble and who have the biggest egos.

Ego can invade a person's mind, pushing aside reason. Sometimes leaders with unchecked egos perceive they're entitled to executive privilege, an alternative reality in which they are all-powerful and untouchable. They convince themselves they can get away with inappropriate behavior or eschewing responsibility for their actions due to their position or status. This is particularly true regarding a ship at sea, which, with a toxic commanding officer, can become the last bastion of totalitarianism.

There have been commanding officers in the Coast Guard who have taken liberties by engaging in prohibited romantic relationships with junior crew members. Some have lashed out at their crews in fits of rage. Others have wrongfully accepted gifts. Sadly, I recall some cases of criminal misconduct. Those leaders lost their way as a result of the hubris that can accompany position power. As with the tragic hero in literature, the personal flaw they failed to recognize led to their demise.

Leaders of character must understand when and how to use the three types of power—personal, professional, and position. The Golden Rule is the north star that can guide leaders in applying the most appropriate type of power to a given situation. Leaning on personal and professional power will keep leaders humble and focused on serving others, not themselves. Leaders will be judged by how they chose to apply their power, with the final measure being whether subordinates follow because they willingly choose to or because they must.

★ CHAPTER SEVEN ★

SUSTAINING WELLNESS

*Wellness is like a three-legged stool that depends upon
balancing and integrating the mind, body, and spirit—
only then can one achieve a state of well-being.*

—Sandra Stosz, Vice Admiral, US Coast Guard (ret.)

ACHIEVING A SUSTAINABLE LEVEL of wellness of the mind, body, and spirit is instrumental to building a successful career and achieving happiness at work and at home. It requires deliberately balancing work and life priorities to minimize stress and reduce tiredness. Today, people struggle more than ever to keep up in a world driven by globalization and social media. Tiredness, caused by a variety of stressors, has become pervasive. It even has an acronym TATT, "tired all the time." If ignored, tiredness can progress to the next level on the continuum—fatigue. Absent intervention, it can reach the most destructive level—exhaustion. Here's a model to help you recognize the erosion of wellness:

CONTINUUM OF EXHAUSTION
Stress => Tiredness => Fatigue => Exhaustion

If not recognized and addressed, exhaustion can result in burnout or lead to destructive behaviors, including overeating, alcohol or substance abuse, and domestic violence. Cases of burnout or destructive behavior amongst coworkers often come as a surprise to others. Up until the point of collapse, someone may have been the star performer on the team, exuding energy and enthusiasm. Such is the insidious nature of exhaustion.

The impact of exhaustion isn't only devastating to the individual but is also harmful to the organization, as illustrated by Russell Cropanzano and his colleagues, who conducted two field studies on emotional exhaustion. The studies indicated exhausted employees demonstrate lower performance, organizational commitment, and citizenship behaviors[7] along with higher absence rates and turnover.[8] Helping people balance their lives to achieve wellness should be every leader's goal.

I found myself routinely exhausted throughout my career, which can happen as one advances into higher visibility, impactful positions. During my assignment as commanding officer of the Coast Guard cutter *Reliance*, I had the opportunity to learn more about exhaustion and how to counteract it. In the wake of the terrorist attacks of September 11, 2001, the ship's operating tempo was unusually high, leaving me and my crew tired and depleted. How, I wondered, could we achieve and sustain wellness?

I'd long desired to visit a holistic wellness spa and seized the opportunity during a rare in-port period. I invited my mom, and we ventured to Canyon Ranch in the Berkshires. During the retreat, a bevy of wellness programs enlightened me. I learned that avoiding exhaustion and achieving wellness are two sides of the same coin and should be considered together. The four components of wellness/exhaustion I discovered are:

Components of Wellness/Exhaustion
- Physical
- Mental
- Emotional
- Spiritual

Understanding the different components of wellness/exhaustion and the interaction between them helped me recognize and manage exhaustion before it could degrade my wellness. Most people mistakenly think of exhaustion in the most simplistic terms of the physical component, yet they may be suffering from mental, emotional, or spiritual exhaustion or a combination of those. When one or more of the four components of exhaustion is high, the others should compensate to regain wellness. If a person experiences exhaustion in two or more of the above components at the same time, the effect can be debilitating. To best manage exhaustion, you must understand the four components and how to address them individually and as an interrelated system to achieve wellness.

Physical Exhaustion

Physical exhaustion occurs when people reach a state of being worn out from exertion and don't get enough sleep or rest to recover. Prolonged activity, such as laboring in a machine shop, serving customers all day, or deploying on a ship for weeks at a time, can lead to decreased vitality and performance.

Recovery can be relatively simple; resting the body usually cures the symptoms. People respond to different forms of rest. For some, a daily nap or a break restores energy and staves off exhaustion. Others may find a good book or movie engages the mind while allowing the body to recover. Whatever the preferred method, you must make the necessary time to recover.

Mental Exhaustion

Mental exhaustion is caused by extended and/or intense periods of cognitive activity, including concentrated, sustained effort applied to research, problem-solving, decision-making, and human interaction. In some cases, the causal factor of physical exhaustion is mental exhaustion. A systematic review of eleven studies in 2017 showed how mental exhaustion made daily tasks and/or exercise more difficult by causing a higher perception of exertion.[9]

A partial antidote may be a healthy dose of exercise. Physical exertion releases chemicals called endorphins that trigger positive feelings, which can improve both mental as well as physical health. A common example is a runner's high, the state in which you experience less pain, more energy, and a clearer mind as a result of the endorphin flow.

My best ideas come when I'm in the state of mental relaxation brought on by intense physical activity. The thoughts and themes for my numerous speaking engagements often materialized during my one-mile morning swim. I arrived at the office with renewed enthusiasm, refreshed and ready to perform.

Personality type can also influence your state of mental exhaustion. During graduate school, I took a personality test revealing my nature as an introvert. I had never really understood what that meant. Mistakenly, I thought an introvert was someone quiet who enjoyed time alone. For the longest time, I couldn't figure out why many of my peers seemed to thrive in high-intensity social environments that left me depleted. I counted it as another one of my weaknesses.

Then, I discovered the fuller definition of what it means to be an introvert. Unlike an extrovert who builds energy during social and public engagements, an introvert is often drained by such activities and needs downtime to recharge. For me, that meant going home to a quiet house after a social engagement, not searching out the after-party. By understanding this truth about myself, I learned to cope and succeeded despite my limitations.

Emotional Exhaustion

Emotional exhaustion is perhaps the least understood, and most impactful, type of exhaustion. I see it as the depletion from stress caused by overwhelming thoughts and feelings about problems in a person's work life, home life, or both. The problems might be significant, emerging from major life events. For instance, financial hardship, divorce, death of a loved one, moving, dealing with a medical condition, caregiving, or coping with other challenges can all cause the feeling of losing control that characterizes emotional exhaustion.

Not all problems are associated with major life events. There are other, less obvious, causes of emotional exhaustion. The steady accumulation of seemingly small day-to-day aggravations may be what emotionally pushes a person to the breaking point. People suffering from such stress can be overlooked, appearing normal to their family, friends, and coworkers but falling apart inside. Leaders must detect signs and symptoms of emotional exhaustion, particularly when the cause isn't obvious as it might be in the case of someone experiencing a major life event.

Few people are comfortable opening up to others about feelings of hopelessness and helplessness. Reaching out in a kind manner may be all that's needed to break the spell afflicting someone seized by emotional exhaustion. Burnout isn't the only adverse consequence of this type of exhaustion. Unfortunately, it can, in extreme cases, lead to suicide. Changes in behavior that appear to be rooted in stress should be a call to action for leaders of character to engage with and understand their people.

When people become emotionally exhausted, they can lose hope, and with it, their ability to look beyond the immediate stress to envision a brighter future. They become focused on their stress to the point that it dominates their mind, excluding reason. Although there are many fine intervention tools and programs available in most organizations, engaged leaders can create a supportive workplace climate that helps people manage exhaustion before they need formal intervention. Engaged leaders who walk around asking people how they're doing might be surprised by what they hear. In the armed forces, senior enlisted leaders excel in this regard, as their unique position enables them to operate at all levels, up and down the chain of command.

I once served with a senior enlisted leader who personified engaged leadership. Master Chief Petty Officer Shane Hooker never missed an opportunity to reach out to others with a spirit of genuine concern. Unflappable and enthusiastic, he filled a room with energy. His leadership style served a worthy purpose one day when he stepped into an elevator with a junior enlisted member. Never one to miss an opportunity, Master Chief asked the member how he was doing, expecting the standard response, "Everything's going well, Master Chief."

Instead, the junior member said to him, "Master Chief, I'm having problems."

Long after the elevator reached its destination, Master Chief Hooker continued listening empathetically as the junior member poured out his worries. It didn't matter that Master Chief Hooker couldn't solve the member's problems on the spot. What mattered was that someone at the top of the organization genuinely cared and took the time to listen.

Sometimes, what people under emotional stress need is an outlet—someone to reach out and listen and perhaps give them a ray of hope. Master chief petty officers and sergeants major in the armed forces do this better than any other cohort of leaders. Leading with character means getting to know your people, understanding their struggles and stressors, and knowing how to encourage and inspire them to work through and overcome exhaustion.

Spiritual Exhaustion

Weariness of the inner being, or soul, can be a major detriment to overall wellness, yet people often don't know how to address spiritual depletion. Since spirituality is commonly associated with religion, this aspect of exhaustion can be awkward for some to discuss. The spiritual component of human beings has long been acknowledged, whether based on God or other intrinsic beliefs of a greater power or purpose. The spiritual component of wellness is so important that the armed forces employ chaplains to minister to the spiritual needs of service members.

Looking back on my career, I experienced the most profound spiritual exhaustion as a first-year cadet, or freshman, at the Coast Guard Academy. My class was participating in the rigorous "boot camp" portion of the summer program designed to initiate new cadets to Coast Guard life and values. Being away from home for the first time with no communications and no family or friends lowered my resilience. Enduring the daily stressors of cadet life exhausted me physically, mentally, emotionally, and as I discovered, spiritually.

On a Wednesday evening after a particularly exhausting day, I noticed my roommate Amy preparing to leave our barracks room. Since we were restricted during training, I grew concerned and asked about her intentions. Amy told me she was heading to the chapel for vespers, an evening praise and worship service held each Wednesday to serve cadets and others in the Academy community.

I'd never heard of vespers, but having grown up in a church, my faith was very important to me. I accompanied Amy to the chapel. During the service, a wave of relief swept over me. It was deeper than escaping the stress of the barracks; I'd embraced the beginning of my spiritual renewal. The breakneck pace of the initial training regimen had consumed me and left a spiritual void.

The chaplain delivered an inspiring message, filling the emptiness inside me. The Academy's two devoted chaplains, Chaplain Saeger and Father O'Keefe, were kind, understanding men who knew how to minister to stressed-out cadets. At vespers, they helped me find comfort and renewed energy to cope with the tribulations of day-to-day life as a cadet.

Those enlightening vesper services inspired me to attend Sunday worship services and to sing in the cadet chapel choir. I also joined the Officer Christian Fellowship affinity group. My daily encouragement came from the *Bible*, and I posted a particularly motivational verse above my desk. It gave me hope and guided me in making the many tough choices I faced over the next four years.

Trust in the Lord with all thine heart and lean not unto thine own understanding. In all thy ways acknowledge Him and He shall direct thy paths.

—Proverbs 3:5-6

Through participation in chapel activities and renewing my commitment to God, I found the balance I needed to sustain my wellness even when otherwise exhausted physically, mentally, and emotionally. That balance brought me a deep wellspring of inner peace, joy, and strength that powered me to persevere with spiritual wellness for the next forty years as I rose from cadet to admiral.

Signs and Symptoms of Exhaustion

Although each of the four components of exhaustion is unique, signs and symptoms of depletion can appear very similar. Depletion in any one area may adversely impact behavior, thinking, performance and relationships. Some of the signs and symptoms to look out for in yourself and others include:

Signs and Symptoms of Exhaustion
- Decreased focus or concentration
- Lower resilience to everyday stressors
- Impaired decision-making
- Extremely low energy and level of alertness
- Depression and/or anxiety
- Lowered sense of esteem or self-worth
- Mood swings, including frustration and shortness of temper
- Feeling deeply overwhelmed
- Forgetfulness

- Decline in performance
- Increased and/or sustained sickness

Although far from a perfect checklist, the above indicators can help identify when exhaustion starts to take a toll on wellness. I've observed that certain people are more at risk than others of succumbing to the continuum of exhaustion. Those with a Type A personality who strive for perfection and who are overly demanding of themselves may never make enough time for rest and recovery. Sometimes, they're the same people who have not formed a strong family or social network upon which they can rely. At-risk people also include those with poor coping mechanisms, who may neglect their health or turn to destructive behaviors.

Often, people don't realize when they're stressed. Nor do they recognize signs of exhaustion in themselves and others, particularly if they accumulate over time. As a rule of thumb, someone who exhibits two or three of the above indicators may require intervention by coworkers and/or family members.

Finding Balance to Achieve Wellness

Those who perpetually travel the continuum of exhaustion will find themselves out of balance and unlikely to realize their life's goals and objectives. To achieve and sustain wellness, you must search for and find a healthy balance when managing priorities at work and at home. Doing so isn't easy for anyone and is incredibly difficult for many of us. Human nature often leads people to overwork in pursuit of their goals and objectives, particularly if they feel pressure to "have it all."

While working too hard can result in the undesirable outcome of exhaustion, not working hard enough can result in the equally undesirable outcome of idleness. So how do you achieve balance? The ancient philosophers, whose wisdom remains relevant, have a lesson to share. Aristotle proposed the concept of the "golden mean," which is the desirable middle between the extremes of excess and deficiency.[10] Balance to achieve wellness is the golden mean between idleness and exhaustion.

Balance, in the context of managing physical, mental, emotional, and spiritual wellness, is the result of moderation in all your efforts to achieve the ideal proportions of work-life and homelife. You must find the right proportion of effort to apply to each priority; there is no secret ingredient. Sustaining a healthy balance requires ongoing effort, shifting focus as necessary between the four components of wellness. For instance, if you're emotionally depleted from a contentious personal relationship, you may seek spiritual renewal. If you're mentally depleted from a surge of effort at work, you may find balance through physical exercise.

Finding the golden mean is difficult because people fail to recognize when adjustments are needed to avoid exhaustion. They must possess the emotional intelligence to understand the causes and effects of their exhaustion on themselves, their co-workers, and their families. Techniques I've used to achieve the golden mean of wellness include:

Techniques to Achieve Wellness
- Engage in sensory stress relief through aromatherapy, mood lighting, relaxing music, massage therapy, a warm bath, or better yet, a combination of these
- Create energy by trying something new; master a piece of music, write a poem, cook a different dish, or start a workout routine
- Connect with another person by making a new acquaintance or reaching out to check in with a friend or relative
- Make a list of desired activities, then schedule them to be sure recreation is prioritized
- Acknowledge that most taxing situations are temporary and will come to an end by taking one day at a time
- Practice mindfulness

Of all the above, I've found practicing mindfulness to be the most beneficial in balancing priorities. The discipline of willing yourself to return to the present moment with a spirit of contentment is the essence of mindfulness. That means refusing to dwell on the past or worry about the future. It means living a full, rewarding, satisfying life by focusing on the positive. To navigate the uncharted waters of life's journey, you must learn how to address the obstacles and opportunities encountered along the way. To that end, mindfulness is a powerful tool, if you know how to use it.

Mindfulness is different than meditation. It involves using external stimuli to achieve inner peace. My life-changing mindfulness journey started when I recertified in scuba diving while attending graduate school. The heavy academic load, and self-imposed pressure to do well, left me feeling stressed and tired. I needed something to help me cope. A friend invited me to accompany her over spring break on a week-long scuba diving trip to Bonaire.

Upon arrival, I took a refresher course and learned something I didn't expect—how to control my buoyancy and breathing underwater. Buoyancy is how much you move up and down underwater, and the desired state of neutral buoyancy can be achieved by proper breathing. Breathing and buoyancy control required extreme focus and engaged my spirit of mindfulness. The more slowly and deeply I breathed, the better I could maintain buoyancy, giving me a powerful feeling of control and freedom.

I imagined myself as part of the system of life on the coral reef. The sun's rays penetrated the water layers, highlighting the underwater paradise as sea turtles glided gracefully past in slow motion. Brightly colored fish darted about, scintillating as they turned and caught the filtered light of the sun. What an otherworldly experience! Scuba diving fully restored me. By focusing on the present and filling my mind with so much positive energy, there was no room left for worry.

During my visit to the wellness spa at Canyon Ranch, I engaged in yoga as a stress management activity. I found a familiar pattern of mindfulness with the solace of deep, steady breathing and concentration on the present. Holding each pose for a set amount of time demanded a level of concentration that kept the stressful thoughts of home or work at bay. My yoga practice introduced me to a sturdy three-legged "wellness stool" model that I call the "mind-body-spirit" stool. It fosters physical, mental, emotional, and spiritual strength and resilience and has helped me balance my priorities to achieve wellness over the years.

Going back to the cutter *Reliance*, I used the three-legged stool analogy to help find balance among the competing mission demands. Operations were intense during the months following the terrorist attacks of 9-11. The crew was stressed and frustrated. No matter how hard they worked, they couldn't accomplish everything that needed to get done while underway on patrol. Exhaustion, a huge risk factor, began to emerge.

Based on my newfound experience with mindfulness, I mustered the crew and talked about balance. I informed them we needed to accept the fact we wouldn't be able to do everything in a twenty-four-hour day. I wasn't going to put that pressure on them. From thenceforward, we were going to balance the three priorities needed to succeed in our mission: operations, training, and crew rest.

The crew rest component was critical, as that was the one most likely to be pushed aside and to slip out of balance. There would be days when operations dominated, during a high-interest vessel boarding, for instance. In those cases, the next day would include the crew rest needed to recover. Planned training would be rescheduled, if necessary. By focusing on the balance between the three priorities, instead of trying to maximize each one every day, we succeeded in achieving and sustaining the crew wellness needed to perform during six grueling weeks of high operating tempo at sea.

Those striving to find the balance to achieve wellness should first pause to look beyond the tyranny of the present and reflect on what's most important in the long run. Recently, I attended a moving memorial service held during my Kellogg business school twenty-five-year reunion. We had the privilege of honoring and eulogizing classmates who had passed away. Every speaker focused on the character, values, and virtues that defined the individual, even after death.

When the service ended, the audience remained silent. Everyone contemplated the monumental difference between "resume virtues," which seem so important while people are alive, and "eulogy virtues." We palpably perceived that eulogy virtues are, in the long run, what matters. Focusing on the character, values, and virtues for which you hope to be remembered may help you achieve the balance Aristotle presented through the golden mean.

To address the challenges posed by a more complex world, leaders of character must learn how to recognize physical, mental, emotional, and spiritual exhaustion in themselves and others. Helping members of the workforce manage exhaustion and achieve wellness is becoming an increasingly important requirement for a leader. Discovering balance through the principle of the golden mean will help leaders of character manage stress and sustain a healthy state of wellness for themselves and their people.

★ CHAPTER EIGHT ★

THE CONTROL PARADOX

What consumes your mind controls your life.

—Anonymous

EARLY IN MY CAREER, working overtime to earn my qualifications and perform my many duties left me stressed and exhausted. One day, a package arrived in the mail. On opening it, I found a beautiful plaque inscribed with an inspirational verse known as the Serenity Prayer.[11] "God, grant me the serenity to accept the things I cannot change; the courage to change the things I can; and the wisdom to know the difference."

A dear friend sent me the plaque, hoping the verse would help me manage frustration with things beyond my power to change. He knew I'd become unduly focused on gaining more control, mistakenly believing that would make work and life better. The paradox was that rather than more control, I needed a better understanding of control, as the Serenity Prayer taught me.

I kept the treasured Serenity Prayer plaque on my wall for years, through many military change-of-station moves. It inspired me to loosen my grip and let go instead of holding on. I learned sometimes the internal state of being content, or serene, is more important over time than is the surface state of being happy.

Happiness is elusive. Those who pursue happiness as an end will likely meet with disappointment. There will always be something seemingly better lying temptingly just out of reach. Although you may not always be happy, you can achieve a state of serenity by understanding and accepting natural forces that cannot be controlled. In this example, serenity, or contentment, is the golden mean between happiness and worry.

As the years passed and I found myself counseling others on how to cope, I developed a model to address the control paradox. The model imagines span of control in three equal parts that together make the whole. The first two elements—make good choices, and work hard and persevere—are within an individual's power to control. The third element—accept luck/fate/God's plan—is outside an individual's power to control. The model is designed to help people frame the paradox and visualize where to best apply their energy. Here's how to achieve a healthy state of serenity:

Addressing the Control Paradox
- Make Good Choices (within our power to control)
- Work Hard and Persevere (within our power to control)
- Accept Luck/Fate/God's Plan (outside our power to control)

Make Good Choices

Each day presents a series of choices. Some are relatively small and insignificant, such as what to have for breakfast. Others are monumental, requiring tough, trade-off decisions between competing options of significant consequence. Sometimes there are too many choices, leading to indecision or procrastination. Regardless, choosing cannot be delegated. We must make our own choices, and leaders bear the responsibility to choose wisely, guided by their moral compass, at each stage of a process or chain of events.

Ancient philosophers, from Plato to Socrates to Aristotle, pondered the complexities of making decisions. They explored how people's choices are influenced in the context of virtues and ethics.

How leaders make choices and deal with the consequences of their choices says a lot about their character. Leaders of character take full responsibility for the choices they make and the associated outcomes, however undesirable. They don't blame someone or something else. They succeed because they choose fortitude over fragility, victory over victimhood, execution over excuses, and merit over mediocrity.

Those discussions of the ancient philosophers remain highly relevant to today's generation. I once encountered a group of young Coast Guard students, about twenty years of age, preparing to pose for a photo. One of the young men deliberately put aside his cup of water before joining the group.

Noticing my quizzical gaze, he explained, "Ma'am, when a photo gets posted to social media, no one knows what's in that red plastic cup; even if it's only water, the perception may be that you're drinking alcohol."

I was astonished and impressed one so young would act with such maturity. Although demonstrating an overabundance of caution, the young man took control and made a wise choice, eliminating the potential for an undesired outcome.

Fortunately, most people aren't alone when it comes to making choices. Mentors, particularly an accountability mentor, can help you set—and more importantly, maintain—a straight course leading to positive outcomes. When in doubt, individuals should reach out to a trusted mentor. Leaders of character also develop networks of responsible friends and coworkers, keeping good company and looking out for each other, both personally and professionally. Friends, teammates, and coworkers should actively engage as necessary to help each other make good choices.

Personal responsibility is integral to building the strong civil society and resilient organizations people need to succeed. Character development always involves choice, and temptation provides the opportunity for people to either diminish their character by succumbing to a bad choice or elevate their character by making a good one. By making good choices and accepting responsibility, you can avoid, and help others avoid, risky behavior and the undesirable, and sometimes irreversible, outcomes that inevitably follow.

Hard Work and Perseverance

Working hard and persevering to achieve your goals and objectives requires the virtue of willpower to stay the course and never give up. In the immortal words attributed to Winston Churchill, "Continuous effort—not strength or intelligence—is the key to unlocking our potential." There will always be someone who's a better scholar, athlete, musician, or artist, and there will always be someone born with more opportunity. There is no substitute for hard work and perseverance. Together they help level the playing field of life.

The character of the individual is what matters most. Hard work and perseverance distinguish the person who will become successful from the one who is merely more gifted or privileged. Perseverance is the operative word. To achieve your goals, you must find the willpower to keep going and resist the urge to quit despite the odds and obstacles. And that is never easy.

Many times, I contemplated quitting and making a fresh start. Then I discovered the power of perseverance. This story starts at the Coast Guard Academy in 1980 when I was a twenty-year-old rising second class cadet, or sophomore. I was participating in a summer training program at the Coast Guard Aviation Training Center in Mobile, Alabama, where cadets learn the basics of flying. I loved operating helicopters. A couple of days earlier, we had the chance to practice copiloting a helicopter and even got to help land it on the water. In those days, the H-52 helicopters were equipped with skis to allow for water landings.

Even though I knew the pilot could take control at any time, I still felt incredibly empowered by the awesome opportunity to help handle the helicopter. When I pulled up on the collective and felt the helicopter lift, the power of that formidable machine surged through my entire body like an electric current. The experience energized my inner being and boosted my self-confidence. Topping off that awesome opportunity, we cadets jumped out of the helicopter like rescue swimmers[x] would do, splashing into the warm water of Mobile Bay.

One night during training, we attended a mandatory social function. The two of us women wore our military uniform pants to conform with our male peers. Someone in authority informed my friend Julie and me that we should have worn our skirts. We were unaware of any such requirement.

We expected to be in trouble and worried as we went to bed that night. The next morning, an orderly came to curtly inform me to pack my bags. The executive officer of the Aviation Training Center, Commander Bob Wehr, wanted to see me and I was being sent home. I was told nothing more. My world seemed to fall apart right then and there. Stressed to the max, I envisioned my career ending before it even started, all because I'd worn pants instead of a skirt. A duty driver transported me to Commander Wehr's office, where I braced for the bad news. And the news was far worse than I expected.

The kind executive officer compassionately conveyed to me that my seventeen-year-old brother had been killed overnight in a tragic automobile mishap. My heart stopped, and my mind went blank for an instant before a flood of emotions surged through my brain as it tried to compute what he had said. Wait a minute. I was supposed to be getting sent home for not wearing a skirt. For one perverse moment, I felt glad not to be in trouble.

But then it started to sink in. *Did he say my brother is dead?* That couldn't be right. My brother Tom couldn't be dead before he even graduated from high school. The executive officer must be wrong. The words I didn't say kept ringing in my head. *No, this isn't true. I want to go home because I didn't wear a skirt. My brother can't be dead.*

---

x   In the Coast Guard, a rescue swimmer is an enlisted person in the aviation rating who is trained to enter the water from a helicopter. Once in the water, the rescue swimmer retrieves the person in distress and prepares him or her to be hoisted to safety in the helicopter.

Commander Wehr put me on his private office telephone with my mother, and I found myself in the tough position of having to comfort her amidst my own grief. She told me how strong I was, and I reassured her. "Mom, I'm strong, but you're so much stronger than I am. I know you'll get through this fine."

Commander Wehr consoled me as best he could and gave me a pocket-sized *New Testament* before sending me home on emergency leave. I kept that little book close for years afterward, and it gave me the spiritual power I needed to persevere. In the following years, I often thought about the kind and caring executive officer, with great appreciation for the compassion he showed that fateful day. Commander Wehr set the standard for me on what it means to lead with character.

Less than a year later, in the spring of 1981, the offshore sailing squadron had mustered down on the waterfront at the Coast Guard Academy. We were preparing to get our two large, donated racing yachts underway for an afternoon of practice. I had raced aboard the Academy's Swan 39, *Mareva II*, the previous summer and was assigned to the same boat again for the current summer. No ordinary sailboat, *Mareva II* was a fast, stripped-down racing yacht. I'd been a member of the crew that delivered the boat to the Academy when it was donated the year before and had learned its many peculiarities.

My friend Julie also participated with the offshore sailing team. She was the same person who had been with me at flight training in Mobile, Alabama, when we thought we were in trouble for wearing pants instead of skirts. Julie and I were as different as night and day. She excelled as an athlete and a student, and it seemed to me she breezed through the Academy's tough programs. I wished I could be more like her. A beautiful person, Julie got along with everyone and was loved by all.

Having sailed on another yacht the prior summer, Julie wanted to try something different. She asked if I would swap boats with her so she could be part of the *Mareva II* crew. I consented.

Mareva II left the pier first that fateful afternoon, while we continued to rig the second boat. The wind had increased on the Thames River, kicking up whitecaps. Shortly after getting underway, *Mareva II* came screaming back to the pier in obvious distress. Julie had been hit in the head with the boat's huge boom, the spar responsible for holding down the bottom of the mainsail. She died instantly.

We were all in shock. This wasn't supposed to happen to a cadet; a young, vibrant woman with her Coast Guard career ahead of her shouldn't be dead before she even graduated. I kept asking myself why I let Julie take my place. *Why did Julie die and not me?*

I knew that boom was low and had learned to duck when it came across. If I'd refused to trade boats with her, Julie would still be alive. That regret haunted me. Learning to let it go took years. By maturing as a leader, I embraced there were going to be things in life, like Julie's death, over which I had no control. Letting them build up would overwhelm me with stress and cause me to fail. I knew I needed to break the cycle. I learned to let go of the guilt by returning to my Christian roots and giving it up to God. With the burden thus relieved, I was able to refocus my efforts on the part of the control paradox model I could influence—working hard and persevering through adversity.

In the nine short months between my brother and Julie dying, I experienced three other traumatic deaths. First was my maternal grandfather, Archie Malette, who instilled in me a fondness for the sea during my summer visits to Cape Cod as a young girl. Grandpa died of cancer, and his death marked my first loss of a grandparent. I felt a deep void with his passing as if a link in the chain was now missing.

Second was the sitting superintendent of the Coast Guard Academy, Rear Admiral Malcolm Clark, who died suddenly. What a blow to the entire corps of cadets and Academy community. Senior officers seldom die on active duty in a staff position, and young people generally have limited exposure to death, making it harder to endure. The cadets all liked and admired Rear Admiral Clark; he impressed us as a leader of character and a decent man.

Third was the famed World War II hero, General Omar Bradley. Although I didn't know General Bradley, I participated with the contingent of cadets sent to Washington, DC, to march in his funeral procession. I recall marching across the Memorial Bridge heading to Arlington National Cemetery, the hallowed final resting place holding the remains of so many heroes. It was a solemn day. During the entire procession, I pondered all those I'd lost in the past year, people who had been vibrant and alive one day, and in a cemetery the next. It dawned on me how little control we had over life.

It felt surreal, participating in the funerals of each of the five people whose deaths impacted me. I delivered the eulogy at Tom's and Julie's funerals. In each case, I stood in front of churches packed to capacity, doing my best with the hopeless task of finding a way to capture the lasting impact of a life well-lived juxtaposed with the tragedy of a life cut far too short. I sang in the Academy chapel choir during the funeral service for Rear Admiral Clark. My emotions welled up inside me as we remembered him with that hauntingly serene song "Amazing Grace." Finally, I attended my granddad's funeral and marched in honor of General Omar Bradley.

The hardest time I ever faced was those nine months from 1980-1981 when I experienced such losses. I turned even more inward and upward to God and gave my mind over to much internal reflection and soul-searching. The losses I experienced matured me and awakened in me a keen awareness of the precious and fleeting nature of life. I learned to value each moment and each individual.

The Academy's institutional system couldn't appreciate that context. It valued the processes and procedures that governed cadet life; it didn't value the cadets for who they were as people.

I resented some of the leaders with power over me, people who didn't express any interest in my welfare. They were people who always sought to criticize or punish, never trying to understand their subordinates or look for behavior to praise. I swore never to become like any of them.

Astonishingly, others would assure me, "Oh, you'll be just like them when you move up and it's your turn. That's what people do."

Those words incensed me. Then and there, I resolved to defy the predictions and lead with humanity and humility when my turn came.

It was emotionally draining to have endured so many personal losses on top of the many other hardships of Academy life. To help me cope, I read inspirational material and wrote poetry. One day I came across a passage that captured my imagination and deeply inspired me when I most needed it. The passage came from Thomas Paine's *The American Crisis*, written in 1776, while our aspiring nation waged war to win freedom from England.

> *These are the times that try men's souls. The summer soldier and the sunshine patriot will, in this crisis, shrink from the service of their country; but he that stands by it now, deserves the love and thanks of man and woman. Tyranny, like hell, is not easily conquered; yet we have this consolation with us, that the harder the conflict, the more glorious the triumph. What we obtain too cheap, we esteem too lightly: it is dearness only that gives every thing [sic] its value. Heaven knows how to put a proper price upon its goods; and it would be strange indeed if so celestial an article as freedom should not be highly rated.*[12]

Thomas Paine's passage from over 200 years earlier may as well have been written for me. His observation "what we obtain too cheap, we esteem too lightly" gave meaning to the hardships that tried my soul at the Academy. I could relate to the struggle for freedom, in my case, from the bonds of the Academy. Thomas Paine's inspirational words gave me much-needed hope to persevere through my conflict to the glorious triumph that would be graduation and commissioning into the Coast Guard.

Spiritually refreshed and renewed, I couldn't wait to trade the frustrations of the Academy training environment for the satisfaction of the "real" Coast Guard. To achieve that goal, I drew upon willpower to get through each day. To honor the five people who had died, I remained true to my purpose of serving in the Coast Guard. Quitting would have let them down, leaving victory to those uninspiring leaders who would be only too happy to see me give up. I couldn't let that happen, and I persevered with the words of Thomas Paine as my guide.

Luck/Fate/God's Plan

Although two-thirds of the control equation consists of elements within a person's control, there remains a vital one-third representing what cannot be controlled. I call this luck, fate, or God's plan. People tend to expend a disproportionate amount of effort trying to influence things they can't control. The tragedy of the control paradox is that worrying about what they can't control distracts people from focusing on what they can control. The result is a sure path to exhaustion and failure.

At some point in their work and/or home lives, most people will encounter an overwhelming hurdle that presents problems totally out of their control. Perhaps it will be an illness or death of a loved one. If you don't have the tools to cope, the frustration and stress can lead to destructive behaviors. During the most trying circumstances, all the hard work and perseverance in the world will be of little use. Those are the times when you must draw strength from within and look outward for support from friends, family, mentors, and others.

I've learned to embrace the things I can't control, drawing inspiration from heroes like Vice Admiral James Stockdale. During the Vietnam War, he endured angst and torture in the infamous Hanoi Hilton for over seven years. To survive, Vice Admiral Stockdale looked to the ancient philosophers of the stoic genre to inspire him to focus beyond the day-to-day misery he couldn't control to the things he could control—his own feelings and attitude. My go-to coping mechanism is prayer, as I lift my concerns to God. I remind myself to put my circumstances in perspective and to be thankful that none of my problems compare to what Vice Admiral Stockdale endured.

Recognizing and accepting the part of life over which you have no control inspires a healthy dose of humility, a necessary virtue in a leader of character. I cringe to see people take credit for an outcome made possible by luck and being in the right place at the right time. Leaders of character recognize when they have been fortunate or succeeded as a result of someone else's efforts. Leading with character means putting ego aside and recognizing those whose hard work at the lower levels contributed to organizational excellence.

Ambitious leaders search for hidden opportunities in the one-third of the equation they cannot control. They ready themselves to recognize possibilities and take advantage of circumstances regardless of the situation. Some of the best chances to excel arise in times of tragedy or crisis, when faced with leading in uncharted waters.

Admiral Thad Allen, who served as commandant of the Coast Guard from 2006 through 2010, led the nation's response to both Hurricane Katrina in 2005 and the Deepwater Horizon oil spill in 2011. Both of those crises rose beyond the power of any individual to control. Nonetheless, Admiral Allen succeeded because he recognized the opportunities and knew which competencies to apply. His favorite definition of leadership reflects his bias for action and innovation. "Leadership is the ability to reconcile competency and opportunity."

Admiral Allen lived by those words every day, whether leading organizational change or leading in a disaster. He moved rapidly to harness opportunities before they could slip away. For the Hurricane Katrina response, he made personal phone calls to assemble a small team of highly capable leaders. Each possessed a well-honed competency needed to manage the response. Admiral Allen directed them to get to New Orleans, by whatever means they could, as soon as they could, and find him, wherever he might be.

As Admiral Allen seized the opportunity to reach out to them, those leaders recognized and seized the opportunity to participate. Without knowing what awaited them on the scene, the assembled team prepared for what would be weeks that turned into months of uncertainty and sustained effort. By answering the call to serve, they led with character, helping a devastated population recover from one of the largest natural disasters ever to impact the nation. Later, Admiral Allen proudly coined the leaders on his team "dogs that hunt," as a tribute to their ability to recognize, then leverage every opportunity, delivering results amidst the chaos.

Today, rapid advances in technology require organizations to empower leaders to adapt and move adroitly to take advantage of emergent opportunities. Twelve years after Hurricane Katrina devastated the Gulf Coast, the region was slammed by Hurricane Harvey. The slow-moving storm dumped over fifty inches of rain on Texas, submerging much of Houston.

Technology had raced ahead during those twelve years, providing not only opportunities but associated challenges. First responders still relied on traditional communications networks to coordinate rescuing tens of thousands of people trapped by rising water. Their efforts were stymied when the national 911 emergency telephone system became overwhelmed.

Stranded people started posting their distress calls unofficially on social media. The Coast Guard began receiving hundreds of plaintive cries for help on its Facebook page and other social media spaces. A family had been separated by the floodwaters; an elderly person was weakening; a baby needed formula; someone requiring dialysis had reached extremis. The postings were desperate and heart-wrenching.

Unfortunately, there existed no national emergency call system for the social media realm. Coast Guard watchstanders couldn't channel incoming requests for help to the on-scene rescuers. The commandant of the Coast Guard Admiral Paul Zukunft was notified of the crisis. Immediately addressing the problem, he boldly led by promising, "No call to the US Coast Guard will go unanswered."

Admiral Zukunft called for innovative solutions, and the workforce responded. At Coast Guard Headquarters, the command center set up an impromptu call center where watchstanders responded day and night to social media posts and tweets relaying distress. At the Coast Guard Academy, cadets eagerly joined the effort. They took the initiative to get involved and harnessed the power of geolocating. Employing the geospatial tool used by the government of Texas, the cadets helped the Coast Guard Command Center prioritize requests for help and push the information back to the local Incident Command Post in Texas.

At first, advanced technology seemed to thwart the Coast Guard's ability to locate those in crisis when the legacy national distress telephone system failed. Leaders seized the opportunity to harness the untapped power of the new technology. Amidst the mass confusion, the Coast Guard adapted to meet surging demand. The commandant empowered people to innovate and make decisions at the lowest reasonable level, all the way down to cadets at the Coast Guard Academy. High-performing organizations create an innovation culture encouraging leaders to exercise initiative in seeking ways to manage complexity.

Leaders of character seek balance for themselves and their people. They accept, with serenity, there are some things they cannot control. They apply their effort to making good choices then working hard and persevering toward their goals. During tumultuous times, they lead in uncharted waters, determined to reconcile competency, in both themselves and others, with opportunity to achieve positive outcomes.

PART TWO

Leading Programs and Making Policy

If your actions inspire others to dream more, learn more, do more and become more, you are a leader.

—John Quincy Adams

Leaders at the middle to senior level of an organization are ideally positioned to significantly influence people, programs, and policy. Unlike leaders at the executive level who are often distanced from the workforce, middle- to senior-level leaders can directly impact morale and motivation. Leaders at that pivotal level must understand and embrace their responsibility to advance the programs and policies that support their people and the organization.

A recent Gallup analysis of the future of work found having a rewarding job ranked first among people's priorities. Results also indicated the degree to which employees felt engaged and valued at work depended upon the leadership ability of the organization's managers. The analysis showed over thirty percent of employees are highly engaged at work. In high-performing organizations, the statistic is nearly seventy percent.[13] The survey results infer the significant impact engaged middle-to senior-level leaders can have on employee satisfaction and, hence, organizational success.

It's incumbent upon middle to senior-level leaders to take a strategic pause and consider how they can best use their influence to achieve positive outcomes. Because they're responsible for implementing programs and policies, they must broaden their perspective and seek to understand the complex interaction between a society, its organizations, and its people.

At the highest level, society must devise laws and policies that open the door to all who desire to participate. Next, organizations are responsible to implement cultural change, so each member feels engaged and valued. Rounding out the model, individuals must actively participate and demonstrate personal resilience. It is the middle- to senior-level leaders who will integrate between the society, organizations, and individuals to enable success at every level.

★ CHAPTER NINE ★

CHANGING COURSE

I can't change the direction of the wind,
but I can adjust my sails to always reach my destination.

—Jimmy Dean

THE COAST GUARD CUTTER *RELIANCE*, homeported in Kittery, Maine, was embarked on a six-week patrol in the North Atlantic Ocean. As luck would have it, we were scheduled to be underway over the Thanksgiving holiday. I had been assigned as commanding officer the previous year. During that time, we had spent most of our time away from homeport due to increased security requirements following the terrorist attacks of 9-11. The crew hadn't seen much of their families.

Fortunately, we obtained approval for a mid-patrol break over Thanksgiving. I was pleased the crew would be able to join their families at home for the holiday. After being on patrol for a few weeks, everyone was tired, as the weather is rough that time of year (recall the legendary Perfect Storm that ravaged New England in late October 1991).

My family drove an hour and a half to pick me up for Thanksgiving dinner. Shortly after arriving home, we sat down to enjoy a nice, big turkey with all the fixings. We said grace, each of us offering thanks for something in our lives. I was thankful to be home for Thanksgiving! The first forkful of moist, delicious turkey was on its way to my mouth when, as if on cue, the phone rang.

The duty watchstander on the ship notified me, "Ma'am, we've been recalled for a search and rescue case, and we've been ordered to get underway as soon as possible."

After making sure underway preparations were in order, I hung up the phone, let out a sigh, and informed my family I had to get back to the ship. That infamously interrupted Thanksgiving dinner is now a part of a great sea story, but at the time it was deeply disappointing for my entire eighty-person crew and their families. Nevertheless, we all joined the Coast Guard to serve a greater purpose. Saving lives was what we did, regardless of holidays or special occasions that went on without us.

Back at the ship, we got underway into the teeth of a storm coming up from the south. Our mission necessitated steaming hundreds of miles offshore in the North Atlantic Ocean to rescue a small sailboat disabled and adrift with only one person on board. Small sailboats aren't supposed to be out in the middle of the ocean during storm season, but the Coast Guard is *Semper Paratus*, even when mariners are not.

During my few precious hours at home for Thanksgiving, I'd seen the story being covered on television. Reporting focused on the amount of money the Coast Guard had spent over the past couple of days flying planes out to support the sailboat. I should have realized *Reliance* would be the next resource applied to the rescue.

Given the urgency of the situation, a life-and-death matter for the small sailboat owner/operator, we proceeded out to sea at our best possible speed under the conditions. With the seas building and hitting us on the starboard quarter, our stern lifted, and the ship rolled and surged down the waves in an unsettling manner. We had been underway for only a few hours when the power suddenly went out, the engines stopped, and we started rolling wildly in the trough of the waves. We immediately sounded the general emergency alarm, and the crew rushed to man their stations.

When the report came in from the engine room, the story unfolded featuring a huge toolbox that had been bolted to the deck. The force of a heavy roll broke the toolbox loose and hurled it across the room. During its unintended flight, the wayward toolbox struck a small valve on one of the main engines, causing fuel to gush out like water from a showerhead.

For those who are unfamiliar with the nature of ships at sea, this caused great alarm, as the next likely event was a main space, or engine room, fire. Fortunately, a watchstander flung himself to the engine and shut it down before combustion could occur. That junior person saved the day.

Although thankful for the crew's exceptional response, it concerned me that the toolbox had broken loose. The likely cause was neglect to maintain the bolts holding the box in place, which had sheared as a result of fatigue and degradation of the metal. Such a small thing as a bolt had almost caused catastrophe. I knew the engineers were dedicated to maintaining the engine plant and had checklists for all the machinery, but who was checking the bolts?

The entire crew learned a compelling lesson on the vital importance of the seemingly most insignificant parts and people. Because of a small piece of hardware, a junior watchstander ended up in the spotlight that fateful day. Leaders must reflect on each casualty, gleaning lessons to improve future outcomes.

Rolling in the heavy seas without power motivated us to recover quickly. We cleaned up the spilled fuel, repaired the valve, and resumed our mission. After a couple of relatively uneventful days, we arrived on the scene with the disabled sailboat. Its sails had been blown out during one of the routine winter storms that battered the area where the cold air meets the warm water of the Gulf Stream as it heads over to England. We pulled alongside the drifting sailboat while awaiting better weather for a rescue. A day, and then two, went by. We drew further and further from the United States and closer to England as the strong Gulf Stream swept us relentlessly across the Atlantic.

The sailboat drifted out of helicopter range, leaving *Reliance* as the sailboat operator's only hope for rescue. The weather was too rough to launch a small boat to retrieve him, and we watched for a window of opportunity. Instead, the forecast became ominous. Yet another winter storm approached. The disabled sailboat wouldn't likely survive such a storm, packing winds over fifty knots driving the seas up to over thirty feet.

Drawing on the diverse experiences and perspectives of the crew, we devised a plan to take advantage of a very short weather window that arrived in front of the pending storm. We intended to lower our small boat, precariously retrieve the operator, get the sailboat in tow, and head back before the storm hit. Although I approved the final plan, the rescue was an extraordinary team effort. The crew all knew their jobs, and we set about the necessary tasks.

Our small boat maneuvered alongside the sailboat to recover the operator and safely transfer him to *Reliance*. In the same evolution, one of our boatswain's mates went aboard the sailboat to make up the tow. Thereafter, the seas began to build quickly. By the time the boatswain's mate had completed his task, the sea was churning.

We directed the boatswain's mate to jump overboard, where the small boat crew expeditiously retrieved him. Remarkably, that unconventional tactic was safer than trying to position the small boat alongside the pitching sailboat. The boatswain's mate had his lifejacket on, and the decision was sound given the exceptional circumstances.

What a relief to get the small boat with the crew and the distressed sailboat operator on board the ship just in the nick of time! We soon discovered our journey had only begun as we turned back toward the United States. Our destination now lay several hundred miles away, and we steered directly into the fury of the winter storm.

Never before, or since, have I experienced such a maelstrom. My mind locked onto Joseph Conrad's captivating novella *Typhoon*, in which the protagonist, Captain MacWhirr, must face a raging storm in the South China Sea. Darkness fell and the night lasted forever. The wind-driven rain and sleet forced the lookout to stand watch inside the bridge. We ordered the crew to stay inside the ship to keep them safe from the risk of being washed overboard. I spent a restless night on the bridge. Looking back at our stern, I never saw the sailboat on the towline behind us.

As expected, the seas rose to thirty feet. The less-experienced bridge watchstanders looked at me with big, trusting eyes, tentatively asking if this type of weather was normal. I told them rough weather was to be expected, and the ship was designed to ride out storms. I did a good job of hiding my apprehension. In all my years at sea, I'd experienced winds that blew and winds that howled. Until then, I'd never heard them shriek. At a mere 210 feet, the ship felt rather small battling the shrieking winds and bucking the mountainous seas.

That night, I would have liked to seek advice. But, like Captain MacWhirr, I couldn't. As the saying goes, "When the captain looks over her shoulder, no one is there to ask." The privilege, and perhaps burden, of command comes with a massive responsibility for the safety of the ship and crew. The weight was mine and mine alone to carry.

When the day finally dawned, we observed, between the tempestuous seas, the sailboat miraculously riding on the towline behind us. The towline must have been set at exactly the right length and catenary[xi] to place the sailboat in perfect cadence with the rise and fall of our ship. Like the tow, the crew's efforts were synchronized, and they performed harmoniously in the face of the storm. Individual crew members, with different backgrounds and personalities, had demonstrated resilience and pulled together as a team, accomplishing the mission in the most adverse conditions.

A couple of days later, the storm abated, and we made it safely to the shelter of Cape Cod Bay, where a commercial vessel came to relieve us of the sailboat and the man we had rescued. At our parting, the grateful survivor thanked me profusely and offered to repay me by, of all things, taking me on a sail! I bit my tongue to keep from laughing out loud.

---

xi Catenary is the balance between tension and slack in the line used to tow a boat.

Later that year, *Reliance* was assigned to a six-week patrol off the coast of New York City. The nation remained in a heightened state of alert, and port security had significantly increased. The high operating tempo exhausted the crew. We weren't following our normal patrol routine, if there was such a thing. Rather, we had been assigned a new, homeland security mission. On top of everything else, the North Atlantic winter storm season started up.

Before getting underway on patrol, we meticulously covered our securing for sea protocol, given the importance of lashing and stowing all gear during storm season. As the patrol wore on and people became fatigued, routine tasks occasionally took second place to operations. After an extended vessel boarding or damage control drill, equipment had to be lashed and stowed, then checked by watchstanders making rounds to ensure all was secure about the decks. All it takes is one oversight to invite disaster.

Midway through that six-week patrol, a severe nor'easter battered the ship, pushing us toward shore. During the storm, we relied on our propulsion machinery to keep us positioned safely offshore. We had to be near enough to perform homeland security duties but far enough away to avoid shoal water.

Sometime during the night of the storm, while beset by gale-force winds and pounding seas, the officer of the deck called. When the captain of a ship is awakened at night, it generally means bad news. The officer of the deck informed me one of our two propellers was fouled and therefore inoperable, cause unknown. With the storm driving us toward shore and only half of our propulsion system available to counter the intense force, the casualty caused significant concern. I hoped and prayed nothing would happen to disable our second shaft, which would leave us adrift, at the mercy of being driven aground by the storm.

In the morning, the engineer officer and I discussed the situation and speculated about the cause of the problem. We thought it might be a lobster pot—the typical culprit—wrapped around our propeller.

As the storm subsided, we walked the decks topside, checking for loose gear. Proceeding aft toward the fantail, which is the stern, or back, of the ship, I noticed an empty reel that had held one of our fifty-foot, damage-control fire hoses.

I looked at the engineer officer and said, "Do you think it's possible? Could our fire hose have broken free, gone overboard, and wrapped around one of our propulsion propellers?"

Although astounded, we both acknowledged the possibility.

The casualty rendered the ship not fully mission capable, requiring us to transit into New York City for repairs. After mooring at Stapleton pier on Staten Island, contract divers went down to inspect the propeller. They verified our worst fears. Sure enough, our fire hose had disabled our vessel, giving new meaning to the saying, "We have met the enemy and he is us."

We never found out who or what caused the fire hose to break free from its station. Given the punishing operations tempo combined with the heavy weather, the fire hose could have gradually loosened over time. Nonetheless, the damage control personnel responsible for maintenance, or an alert watchstander, should have noticed the problem. Even the best teams are put to the test under stressful conditions. Like the ship's anchor chain, the crew is only as strong as its weakest link. It is the commanding officer's duty to create a climate of excellence that inspires crew members to perform at their very best to ensure mission success.

A bad day at sea is, indeed, better than a good day in an office. In my view, there is no more rewarding experience than commanding a ship, conducting exciting and meaningful Coast Guard missions with a superb crew that's like family. Going to sea gets into your blood and becomes a way of life. It was hard to leave *Reliance* when the time came for my change of command.

Completing twelve years at sea marked yet another career inflection point. Upon being selected for promotion, I had cause to re-examine my passion and purpose, which theretofore had been executing the mission at sea. The next logical step, given my afloat career track, was to ask for command of one of the largest Coast Guard ships, a 378-foot, high-endurance patrol cutter. An inner voice caused me to pause and question my purpose. Did I really want to continue my career at sea? I found myself contemplating what I enjoyed so much about serving on a ship. Was it the sunrises, the sunsets, the excitement of the mission? My answer surprised me.

My passion wasn't the adventure of being at sea. People were my deeper passion, specifically the young people who made up the backbone of the ship's crew. I thought about the times I'd stood on the bridge wing of *Reliance* while moored at the pier, watching the happenings below as the crew went about their work. From time to time, newly minted recruits reported in fresh out of recruit training, or boot camp. They presented themselves in their dress uniform and approached, in a very hesitant manner, the brow, which is the gangway leading from the pier to the ship.

The recruits understood they had to salute the national ensign upon reporting aboard but had forgotten whether it was located on the bow or the stern, which is the front or back, of the ship. Sure enough, the recruits would raise their right hand and, with trepidation, salute the bow, which was the wrong end. They were then immediately met with a not-so-warm welcome from their first-line supervisor.

My inspiration came from watching the rapid progression and integration of the new crew members. Within a couple of weeks, I saw them pulling on a line to help lower a small boat, acknowledging commands with confidence. Such a scene always made me swell with pride in our Coast Guard people.

The Coast Guard brings in young people from across America, developing them from individuals into a team with a shared purpose in service to the nation. What an honorable, impactful mission! I wanted to become a part of it. The time had come for me to move on from operational sea duty. Having matured as a leader, I'd progressed from the tactical perspective to the strategic and felt the pull of what

I considered to be a greater calling. It was time for me to step up to lead major Coast Guard programs and to make policies that would move our service forward.

I made the incredibly tough decision to send in a written notice declining to participate in the screening process for command of another ship. Although filled with self-doubt and emotionally stressed with the thought of relinquishing my sea-going profession, I responded to that inner voice. I changed course and requested command of the Coast Guard's boot camp, the Recruit Training Center in Cape May, New Jersey. Discovering a new passion and purpose later in my career set me on a path to giving back to the organization I loved.

I recognized that leading a major Coast Guard training center would be much different from command at sea. I was excited and a little bit apprehensive. The mission—to train and prepare the next generation of the Coast Guard's 40,000-person enlisted workforce—was vitally important. I needed to tap every resource I could to succeed.

Prior to reporting in as commanding officer, I experienced a major event in my personal life. The time was right to get married. Bob and I met in the Coast Guard and had known each other for a few years. We're the same age, and neither of us had ever married; we were both too busy deploying aboard ships. Although I'd served an impressive twelve years at sea, Bob beat me out with fourteen.

Bob worked his way up through the ranks from his start as a machinery technician in the enlisted corps to become an officer. While I attended the Coast Guard Academy, Bob undertook boot camp, right there at the recruit training center I would lead. Upon graduating from our respective accession sources, we both served at sea on icebreakers.

Remarkably, we'd been shipmates for about two weeks on board the cutter *Polar Star* back in 1983. I had reported in from the cutter *Glacier*, and Bob was finishing up his first tour of duty aboard *Polar Star*. He remembered me as the first woman ever assigned to the ship, but I didn't remember him. While I had to recognize hundreds of male faces, the rest of the crew had but one female face to know.

Bob advanced to chief petty officer very quickly, then rose through the ranks from chief warrant officer to lieutenant, then to lieutenant commander. Finishing up his career in Coast Guard Headquarters as the Service's environmental engineer for naval engineering, he retired after twenty-seven years. We moved to Cape May to begin our married life together, while I started a new job in command.

At the recruit training center, Bob helped me bridge the gap, or chasm, between a senior officer and the junior enlisted people. He helped me understand, for example, how awkward it could be for enlisted members when a senior person entered a small space, like a lobby or an elevator. The appearance of the senior officer would silence all conversation on the spot.

Bob advised me to reach out and put junior people at ease through simple conversation, perhaps by asking them about a ribbon on their uniform. Ribbons represent personal performance awards, so the question not only started a conversation, it allowed the junior person to show pride in an accomplishment. Those small, personal interactions helped me get to know my people and build trust with them. I'm very thankful to have had Bob as a practical expert to advise me whenever the need arose.

I soon found how hard it could be to manage and lead a large, diverse organization. It was akin to serving as mayor of a small town, with all the associated politics and personalities. It perplexed me, of the hundreds of people assigned to the command, so few took the initiative to explore ways to improve the processes. Unfortunately, many expressed contentment with maintaining the status quo. That disappointed me, because as a newcomer, I saw so many possibilities for improvements to make the training center even better.

I discovered we had issues to resolve with both the organizational culture and the curriculum comprising the recruit training program. Surprisingly, the eight-week curriculum contained very little physical fitness. A staff member told me the decision had been made to eliminate most of the fitness activities because recruits got hurt when they worked out, resulting in higher attrition, particularly of women, a cohort we strongly desired to retain.

Ill-fitting shoes contributed to many of the injuries, so we started using a scanner to accurately measure each recruit's foot. I also submitted a proposal to switch to a better running shoe. Quite logically, we changed our processes and equipment to reinstate physical fitness, an essential element of recruit training. Morale and performance immediately increased among the recruits and their trainers.

As I walked around and watched the training, I looked for ways we could add new, relevant blocks of instruction. I'd been warned there was no more room in the curriculum to add new material. Although I hadn't been trained in curriculum development, I knew a good program had to be flexible and accommodate necessary changes.

One day, I walked by the seamanship training platform. I noticed recruits being taught to use sound-powered phones and asked the instructor to tell me about his lesson. He proudly informed me each recruit received eight hours of sound-powered phone training. I was stunned. Since I'd recently served on a ship, I knew those ancient phones had been pretty much replaced by handheld radios.

Having discovered that plenty of room could be made in the recruit training curriculum for more relevant material, I set my team to work. Within the year, we materially changed the curriculum, which hadn't been reviewed for ten years. We replaced the outdated sound-powered phones and other elements with exciting new activities like pugil stick training that introduced the recruits to the concept of self-defense.

We put together a diverse, cross-functional team to implement the changes, but it wasn't easy. Members of the training center who felt threatened, particularly those who had been there for many years, resisted the changes, making a hard job more difficult. Despite the opposition, the change effort created a lot of excitement and built momentum.

Thankfully, my supervisor Rear Admiral Cindy Coogan gave me her full support. She believed in me. Her confidence meant a lot to me personally and it also sent a strong message to the training center. Leaders at all levels came together to change the culture from one of inertia to one more forward-leaning, leading to better outcomes for the recruits and the Coast Guard.

★ CHAPTER TEN ★

THE MEANING OF SUCCESS

Success is not final, failure is not fatal;
it is the courage to continue that counts.

—Winston Churchill

AMERICANS LIKE TO WIN, and they venerate success. From an early age, people are urged to excel at everything they do, both personally and professionally. Be it in academics, sports, relationships, or work, those who succeed are rewarded, while those who fail are not. Failure, however, is a necessary component of the journey.

Success is a complex concept. Inspirational posters boldly proclaim captivating interpretations of the word. They all sound good, but success means different things to different people. Leaders must turn inward to discover their interpretation of success, while guarding against prevailing societal pressures. Unfortunately, success is often associated with wealth, fame, social standing, or other material, and sometimes temporal, types of status.

In her impactful book, *Quiet,* Susan Cain discusses the attributes of introverted people—like me. The lure of material possessions has never motivated me, but I'm keenly and curiously aware that for many others it does. Susan Cain explains the "reward system" in a person's brain that influences desire and how it often produces a lesser response in those who are introverts.[14]

I once knew a colleague who drove a fancy car that meant the world to her. I asked why. She enthusiastically proclaimed, "I went all-in for this car because the person with the most toys when they die wins!"

Her answer truly baffled me. I couldn't conceive of someone feeling so strongly about material possessions. Even after reaching the executive level in the Coast Guard, I still drove my nearly twenty-year-old 1999 Ford Escort. I take great satisfaction in applying the money saved to support worthy causes. Although I don't need a new car to make me feel accomplished, I respect the other person's interpretation of success—that's real diversity.

Success and its companion, failure, are part of the progression of everyday life, and both should be embraced. Individuals should heed the advice, "You're going to fail, so make sure you fail forward."

In other words, fail reaching for a goal, not while standing still or hesitating, allowing the smallest force to cause a backward fall. A rich, rewarding life includes periodic failures, along with the small but meaningful triumphs we often take for granted.

Learning from failures while celebrating life's victories, however small, can fuel you day after day, bringing joy and satisfaction from the ordinary things. In his masterpiece *Don Quixote*, Cervantes captures this perspective well, advising, "The road is better than the inn," or in more modern language, "Life is about the journey, not the destination." Those with the wisdom to adopt that outlook will discover satisfaction through contentment in everyday living.

Looking back, the road to success on my life's journey was paved with failures. They weren't huge failures, but persistent, nagging failures sometimes leading me to question my choices. Reporting to the Coast Guard Academy straight out of high school, I could hardly wait to learn how to sail. Growing up near Annapolis, Maryland, I'd always dreamed of sailing, but my family lacked the means. I knew sailing at the Coast Guard Academy would be a dream come true.

One of the first cadet leadership experiences during swab

summer[xii] indoctrination training is sailing in the intercollegiate dinghies. I remember thrilling to the core as we marched down to the waterfront and prepared to set sail for the first time. I had a vision, based on witnessing sailboats blissfully gliding along on the Chesapeake Bay, of a wonderful, inspiring experience of freedom in harnessing the wind. I could almost feel the wind in my hair and the cool sea spray on my face. I could see myself earning a spot on the intercollegiate dinghy team.

My dreams were shattered from the moment I first stepped gingerly into my dinghy and sat down on the gunwale. I grabbed for the tiller in one hand and the sheet, which is a line to pull in the sail, in the other, and the dingy seemed to slip right out from under me! I started drifting aimlessly down the river.

My situation worsened from there. To my chagrin, I spent the entire training session stuck "in irons." With a mind of its own, the boat defeated my efforts to control it, pointing triumphantly up into the wind. There it stalled, sails luffing vigorously, causing the boom to swing wildly from side to side. I, the would-be sailor, was left crouching helplessly in the cockpit, trying to survive and decide what to do next.

The boom bonked my head continuously as I tried in vain to impose my will on the stubborn little boat. When I finally figured out how to pull on the sheet and catch the breeze, the boat rebelled by rounding up on one side and unceremoniously surrendering to the sea. Continuing its unbounded momentum, it turned completely upside down, leaving me drenched, gasping for breath, and clinging to the slippery bottom for dear life. Feeling conspicuous, I hung there, unglamorously, in the middle of the Thames River with the sailboat "turned turtle," or upside down. To add insult to injury, I was left with the conundrum of figuring out how to right the blasted thing and get it back to the dock.

---

xii   Swab is the term used at the Coast Guard Academy to describe newly reported first-year students, while they're participating in the boot camp-style summer training program that includes physical fitness, leadership, and a cruise on EAGLE.

I wanted to quit right then and there, after my first escapade in a sailboat. Then I noticed other cadets capsizing their boats; it wasn't only me. I bucked up and kept trying, although I became convinced the boat had it in for me. After countless failures over the ensuing weeks, my perseverance paid off, and I finally mastered that darned sailboat. Then I realized my dream and made the intercollegiate dinghy team.

Although I initially thought success meant making the dinghy team, I was wrong. I felt like I'd achieved far more through the journey of learning how to master the wind and feeling the deep satisfaction that comes from persevering through failure to achieve a goal. Exactly as depicted in *Don Quixote*, making the dinghy team was merely the manifestation of the journey. What a powerful life lesson!

The small failures I experienced while learning to sail and engaging in other cadet activities helped instill in me the confidence and competence I needed later in my career when I graduated from the Academy and went on to serve in ships at sea. No one reports to their first ship as a new junior officer knowing how to handle the vessel safely alongside a pier. There are little failures as you learn under instruction, and the sailboat had taught me not to quit. I started my career as a seagoing officer with the mental preparation and nautical skills I needed to succeed, based on working through and learning from my failures in the sailboat.

When I wanted to quit, I drew inspiration from historical figures who started with failure, like the famous Marine Corps General Chesty Puller. General Puller held the distinction as the most decorated Marine in American history, earning more medals and awards than any other Marine. Yet success didn't come quickly or easily for him.

Puller began his professional journey during World War I at Virginia Military Academy in 1917. Eager to enter combat action, he quit after the first year. He completed the Army's Reserve Officer Training Corps camp in Plattsburgh, New York, but was too young for an Army commission. He enlisted in the Marines after discovering he qualified by age for a commission in that service.[15]

Filled with passion and purpose, in 1919, he attended Officers' Training Camp at Quantico, Virginia. He performed well enough to earn a commission, but that event coincided with the drastic drawdown from World War I. A mere three days after commissioning, Puller was transferred to inactive reserve status. What a blow to a motivated young man who wanted to fight! The indomitable Chesty Puller resigned his reserve commission and enlisted all over again as a private to get on the front lines.[16]

In 1921, Puller was issued orders and reported to the Marine barracks at the corner of 8th and I streets in Washington, DC, to attend the newly established Candidates School. This time, he didn't fare well in his quest to earn a commission. On top of failing five of eleven subjects, he went before a summary court-martial for being late and wasn't recommended for a commission.

After serving admirably in Haiti, he was offered another chance to attend the Candidates School. Finally, he earned his commission as a second lieutenant in 1924. Seeing opportunity in the new field of aviation, young Chesty Puller attended Marine Corps Flight School in Pensacola in 1926, but once again, he failed.[17]

Given his aspiration to become a Marine Corps officer, it must have been incredibly frustrating for Chesty Puller to spend his first seven years seeking to earn his commission. Undeterred, through hard work and perseverance, he achieved his goals, serving valiantly as an officer in World War II and the Korean War. Despite his many failures, General Puller retired as one of the most accomplished and revered Marine Corps officers and leaders of all time.

General Puller probably never envisioned the place he would claim in history, but he had a vision for what it meant to him to succeed at each level of his journey through the ranks. Everyone should emulate General Puller and construct a vision to achieve their goals, both in the short term and looking ahead. Although few will follow General Puller's path, some universal tenets can help leaders of character shape their vision regardless of their profession. Leaders of character follow these principles:

Principles of Success

- Embrace failure and keep on persevering
- Strive to reach your full potential
- Motivate others to reach their full potential
- Live your core values
- Earn the trust and respect of those around you
- Leave your organization and community a better place
- Make the very most of your God-given abilities

The Menu Analogy

People tend to associate success with winning, achieving fame or recognition, or making it to the top of their profession or organization as General Puller did. In addition to getting ahead in the workplace, members of a multi-tasking society expect the same level of achievement in every dimension of their personal lives.

Individuals, particularly women, face incredible social pressure to "have it all" or risk feeling like underachievers. Visiting a favorite social media site confirms the high expectations. Friends, family, and coworkers post photos of their adorable kids, amazing vacations, satisfying jobs, awards, and recognition. In those pictures, people are smiling and looking happy. Social media could convince a woman to believe everyone else is completely satisfied and fulfilled while she's being unfairly left behind.

Everyone must confront reality and carefully consider what matters most when envisioning success. I once heard a wise saying, "You can have *anything* you want, but you can't have *everything* you want." That inspired me to create what I call a "menu analogy" to help people work through what "having it all" means to them.

Say you're eating out at a restaurant. The waiter hands you one of those extra big menus, with a dizzying array of choices. It's impossible to try everything. Even choosing between comfort food and healthy alternatives is hard. Then you've got to address the serious question of whether to leave room for dessert. Even if you want to, you can't have everything on the menu, at least not all at once. You must choose between many good alternatives and select *anything* you want, but you can't select *everything* you want.

Those who think they want to try as many items as possible on the menu of life must contemplate a timeline to sequence the events. For instance, perhaps they spend the first ten years working hard to advance their careers. Then the time might be right to start a family or pursue other interests. Part-time employment or working from home are components of an expanding array of workplace options that can provide flexibility, enabling people to add more to their plates.

Another possibility applicable to couples is for spouses to work out a plan harnessing the power of two people who support each other in a shared purpose. They should create a vision of what success means to each of them as individuals, to them as a couple, and to them as a family. Discussions should include visions for the future, not merely the present. For instance, do they want to raise children while they're younger and still working, or later in life when they've matured? Are they willing to alternate between career-enhancing jobs, or does one plan to support the other's career? Today, it's possible to select jobs that allow one or both to work from home.

There are many options to help enterprising women and men manage their work-life choices. Driven people who desire to experience as much as possible on the menu of life can do so if they're willing to make, and live with, the tough, trade-off decisions required.

I never desired to have it all, which caused people to judge and pressure me. From a young age, I focused on pursuing a career, not a family. That didn't deter well-meaning people, who thought they knew best, from trying to convince me I wouldn't be fully satisfied until I married and had children.

I assured the influencers I didn't need to create a family of my own. After all, I had my Coast Guard family. They would continue to press, warning, "Your clock is ticking, and you just don't know it yet."

They would smile knowingly at my protestations, fully suspecting, in time, I would come to my senses.

I didn't have the capacity to add a family commitment to my pressure-filled career, nor did I want to. I was confident in my belief God had called me to serve as a trailblazer, breaking a path as would an icebreaker, for those who would come behind me. Later in life, having set my course and fulfilled many of my goals, I married my husband, Bob. Looking back on my choices, I couldn't be happier and am thankful I remained true to myself along life's journey.

Many years later, I mentored a young female lieutenant who was going through an experience like the one I had at her age. Like me, she enjoyed her career and had worked hard to advance. Still single, she had many friends but wasn't dating anyone.

She told me, "Ma'am, I'm so happy with the Coast Guard and love my life. But every time I open my social media sites, there's a picture of a friend with her new baby or another one getting engaged. It feels like a lot of pressure and makes me question my happiness."

I gave the lieutenant advice from my *Kung Fu Panda* leadership lessons. Like Po, she needed to pursue her passion and purpose and most of all, to believe in herself. I told her my experiences mirrored hers. I wondered why men didn't seem interested in me; did something about me turn people off? I advised her to be confident; sometimes it can be lonely when you're a strong, competent woman. The same qualities that make a woman like her stand out can intimidate others, both women and men.

For a long time, I also wondered if my choices caused me to miss out on something important. Thankfully, a strong circle of friends, Coast Guard family members, and caring mentors kept me grounded. As I was mentoring her through this trying time, so others had mentored me. And I persevered. Later in my career, my personal and professional lives came into balance when I met my husband. I assured the young officer she needed to be true to her interpretation of success, and as with me, her personal life would evolve when the time was right.

Several years later, I got a note informing me how well she was doing, both personally and professionally. After completing a high-visibility assignment, she was attending graduate school and cultivating her personal life. She found a wonderful place to live, made new friends, took up a new hobby, and met a nice person to date. It pleased me to learn the young woman I mentored dared to stay true to herself, despite the societal pressures to have it all.

Be True to Yourself and Don't Judge Others

I came across a great book that ardently illustrates the importance of being true to yourself. Bronnie Ware, a palliative nurse caring for patients in the last twelve weeks of their lives, wrote *Top Five Regrets of the Dying* after listening for years as people expressed regrets on their death beds. The top regret she recorded was, "I wish I had the courage to live a life true to myself, not what others expected of me."[18]

Unfortunately, people are pressured to conform to certain expectations and risk being judged if they don't comply. Remarkably, mothers are impugned if they decide to raise their children instead of working outside of the home. Likewise, women who work outside of the home are judged if they dedicate themselves to their job and forgo having children.

At times throughout my career, some women colleagues suggested I needed to back off on my work ethic. They complained it wasn't fair for someone like me, who chose not to have children, to work harder and perhaps advance faster than they did. I've never been a competitive person and didn't know what to make of those comments. My commitment to the oath of office—not getting ahead—motivated me to perform to my best ability. Unfortunately, women find themselves in the conundrum of being judged regardless of the decisions they make.

Society is rife with altogether too much judging and not enough acceptance, limiting people's ability to succeed. Not only are people judged by others or by their organization, some even judge themselves.

Throughout my career, I experienced the harm of judging in all its forms. Consequentially, I tried to avoid judging others and to build the confidence of those who were too hard on themselves. Individuals who judge themselves too harshly risk failing to achieve their goals and objectives. As a person who struggled to build my self-confidence, I had to work hard to avoid being my own worst enemy. I've noticed that others fall into the same judgment trap.

A few years ago, I attended a leadership event sponsored by a women's advocacy group. The keynote speaker was a remarkably accomplished woman who had risen to the executive level in her organization, raising three children along the way. I recall a woman stating during the question-and-answer session how much she admired the keynote speaker because she, the questioner, only had one child!

I was dumbstruck. The questioner extrapolated that the woman with more children must be more accomplished, regardless of the quality of parenting or any other factors relevant to a rational analysis. At the reception following the keynote, I visualized each attendee looking around the room at her accomplished peers, her self-confidence strained as she compiled the best parts of every other woman's resume, combined all those qualities in her mind, and lamented falling short.

Although I was often the first or only woman in the workplace and expected to be judged, the manner of judging almost always surprised me. Hearkening back to my assignment as commanding officer of the cutter *Katmai Bay*, I experienced judgment in an unexpected place in the community. On the first Sunday in my new hometown, I attended a local church service with some older relatives. Word of my being the first woman to command a ship on the Great Lakes had made the news, so many people recognized me.

On the way out of church, we joined the rest of the congregation in line to greet the pastor, an elderly person. When our turn came, the pastor looked me in the eyes and said, "Don't you feel bad taking the job some young man needs to feed his family?"

My jaw dropped, and I froze in consternation. My cousins pulled me along, explaining with mortification that the pastor grew up during the World War II era when things were different.

During the war years, women entered the workforce, in many cases as members of the armed forces women's reserves, to backfill for men shipped overseas to serve. They performed both administrative and operational duties. Others, like the famous Rosie the Riveter, filled the factory jobs of men who left work to serve. They were incredibly admirable women on whose shoulders I stand. Tragically, most of them had to leave their jobs and return home when the men came back from the war. They did so without thanks or recognition, and sadly, most of their stories remain untold.

I had the good fortune to hear one of those amazing stories. One evening during my time on *Katmai Bay*, I attended a reception honoring veterans. There, I met a remarkable, elderly woman. I regret not remembering her name, as she made a deep impression on me. We struck up a conversation. She had served during World War II with the Women Air Force Service Pilots (WASP). Still fit, lively and vivacious, I could picture her in the cockpit of a fighter plane. She told her story, and I listened attentively.

The WASP recounted how she had grown up an adventuresome young woman. When the call came for women to step up to serve their nation, she volunteered. She described her momentous role as a test pilot for newly produced fighter planes. Incredibly, she and other women like her flew those planes to work out the bugs, then delivered them to their destinations for the men to fly in combat.

After a group of WASPs had delivered some fighter planes, she learned of an amusing story. A male pilot watching the planes land said to someone standing next to him he wasn't ready to trust getting into the cockpit of one of those mass-produced planes. No one realized that women piloted the planes until they landed and the WASPs stepped out. Seeing the women flying brand-new combat aircraft was precisely the incentive the hesitant male pilot needed to change his mind!

Members of the WASP were federal civil service members, not military members. As such, they left their jobs after World War II without much recognition and, most importantly, without veteran status. Finally, in 1977, after years of effort, Congress passed legislation recognizing the WASPs as veterans.

I was struck by how matter-of-factly and how enthusiastically the WASP told of her adventures. She inspired me deeply, causing me to feel a little bit small in her presence. She was the real pioneer, not me.

I expected to be judged in my early years as a junior woman. It surprised me that the judgment, like being the first woman to lead in different roles, followed me throughout my career. At least twice as a senior officer, I was nominated for a significant position but almost *not* selected due to judgment based on something other than my qualifications. In both cases, the organization expressed concern that a senior woman without children wasn't the desired role model for younger women.

Although I was selected for both positions, it was disconcerting to have my suitability called into question based on personal factors unrelated to work. It never occurred to me that my choice to dedicate myself to the Coast Guard would be held against me as a liability. It astounded me, decades after entering the Coast Guard as one of the first women, I experienced the most palpable discrimination as a senior officer, simply because I didn't meet someone else's interpretation of success. I doubt if a man would have been held to the same standard.

Leaders must find the confidence to be true to themselves and not feel pressured to conform to someone else's beliefs. Judging has no place in a civil society; people should respect each other's choices and support them in achieving what matters most to them. Leaders must also accept that the road to success will include failures. The key is to fail forward, while stretching to achieve a goal. Recovering from failures and celebrating the small, day-to-day wins make life's journey rewarding and deeply satisfying.

★ CHAPTER ELEVEN ★

SUCCEEDING IN AN ORGANIZATION

Success comes from knowing that you did your best to become the best that you are capable of becoming.

—Coach John Wooden

THE NEXT LOGICAL STEP beyond exploring what success means to an individual is understanding how that vision translates in an organization. The model below, Succeeding in an Organization, recognizes several interdependent elements necessary for someone to lead and succeed at every level.

Success requires more than individual effort and personal resilience. Despite how hard someone might work and persevere to achieve established goals, there are mitigating factors beyond one's power to control.

Looking back over my journey progressing up the ranks in the Coast Guard, I realized there are fundamental societal and organizational elements necessary to provide the foundation for motivated, resilient individuals to succeed. I drew inspiration from legendary basketball coach John Wooden, who led the University of California Los Angeles basketball team to ten NCAA championships.

Coach Wooden developed his success pyramid depicting personal qualities he believed necessary to succeed.[19] His model gave me the inspiration and foundation for my own model, Succeeding in an Organization, to portray my theory of what it takes to lead and flourish at every level.

Since I first joined the Coast Guard forty years ago, society has steadily progressed. Many barriers have been broken down and opportunities presented to help more people realize their dreams. There is much to celebrate, and I'm so pleased to see young women and minorities today taking advantage of the rich spectrum of options afforded them.

Expectations have risen at an even faster pace than the progress made. I attribute this phenomenon to the internet and the speed of technology. The United States has come a long way as a fair and just society, and today, the nation is a far better place than it was forty years ago. It is not yet, however, where it needs to be. More work is required of our government, organizations, and individuals to enable all people to reach their full potential. My success pyramid model can help leaders of character advance that goal.

SUCCEEDING IN AN ORGANIZATION

Stage One: Access and Opportunity (Societal) / Law and Policy

I have a dream that my four little children will one day live in a nation where they will not be judged by the color of their skin, but by the content of their character.

—Martin Luther King, Jr.

The first stage in enabling individuals to reach their full potential is to provide equal access and opportunity for all. Laws and policies must be implemented to open doors and eliminate barriers to participation. Access and opportunity can range from physical (Americans with Disabilities Act), to participation (Voting Rights Act), to education (*Brown v. Board of Education*), to employment (repeal of combat exclusion policies opening military jobs to women), to critical information services, such as the internet.

Legislation and policy changes have been opening doors granting access and opportunity to women and minorities in America for many years. The 1970s brought a sea change of empowering legislation providing me options unavailable to women of my mother's generation. As a result, I attended the Coast Guard Academy and graduated in 1982. Almost thirty years later, I had the distinct honor and privilege of returning to serve as superintendent of my alma mater. It pleased me to see how far women had advanced in the intervening years. In my days as a cadet, women made up a mere five percent of the cadet corps. By the time I became superintendent, the number had risen to over thirty-six percent, higher than any other armed forces service academy.

Although I benefited greatly from legislation enacted during the 1970s, the real story to celebrate is the achievements of the young women who make up today's generation, who are in line to replace me one day. Many of them are young women I mentored along the way, and in the end, their success is in great part how I measure my own.

As one of the first female line officers in a military service, I had to earn trust and respect through my performance and accomplishments and never wanted to be singled out because of my gender. Yet it always made news when I was the first woman assigned to a position. I came to realize and accept that people were genuinely interested in seeing women advance. I tried to turn what I perceived as adversity for myself into an opportunity for the Coast Guard by making every effort to refocus the media engagements on our amazing people and missions.

During my assignment as commanding officer of *Katmai Bay*, I spoke at many venues around the Great Lakes. At the time, it was a novelty for a woman to command a vessel. One evening during a talk at a meeting of the Upper Great Lakes Captains Association, I ended by declaring, "I'll be glad when the day comes when I'm seen as the seventh captain of *Katmai Bay*, not the first female captain." The audience cheered.

Little did I know that twenty-one years later I would be installed as the first female superintendent of an armed forces service academy, and history would repeat itself. In my inaugural speech, I expressed hope that one day I would be seen as the fortieth superintendent of the Coast Guard Academy, not as the first female superintendent. In all my forty years, I couldn't outrun being labeled "the first" many times over.

On baseball great Frank Robinson's death, I heard a previously recorded interview on National Public Radio. It instantly caught my attention when I heard him say, "Everywhere I went, it was, how does it feel to be the first black manager? I just wanted to be looked upon and thought of as a major league manager."[20] Frank Robinson spoke for many of us women and minorities who struggle to be recognized for our success as leaders, not singled out for becoming "the first woman or minority" leader.

Although perhaps well-intentioned, labeling defines people in terms of their gender, race, or ethnicity. It leaves the door open for others to assume they got ahead because of those innate traits, rather than by their accomplishments and performance. Those who are members of less represented groups want to be recognized, like everyone else, for what they have done, not for what they look like.

Despite the challenges associated with being "the first," I'm eternally grateful for the legislation that opened doors and removed barriers. It provided me the opportunity to pursue a rewarding career, moving up the ranks in the Coast Guard from the entry-level to the executive suite. Since there is always more work to do in advancing a just society, I tried to pay it forward by pursuing law and policy changes to provide more access and opportunities for the leaders coming behind me.

Stage Two: Cultural Change (Organizational) / Diversity, Inclusion and Equity

It's not about dredging the river that runs between us, it's about building a bridge to connect us.

—Sandra Stosz, Vice Admiral, US Coast Guard (ret.)

Even when opportunities become available for people to pursue their passion and purpose, barriers to advancement remain in some form in many organizations. Once the door is opened, cultural change must follow. Barriers must be broken down to ensure all those who aspire to participate are welcomed, included, and valued for who they are and what they have to offer. At the heart of cultural change are the elements of diversity, inclusion, and equity.

Those three loaded words must be clearly understood if progress is to be made. They mean different things to different people, and the meanings morph over time. Throughout my forty years in the workforce, efforts to ensure organizations represent the richness of society matured. The narrative progressed from a commitment to diversity, then to diversity and inclusion, then to diversity, inclusion, and equity. Building on a thought by cultural change strategist Verna Myers,[21] I find the following construct useful: *Diversity* is being invited to the party, *Equity* is ensuring everyone has transportation to get there, and *Inclusion* is being asked to dance.

WHAT IS DIVERSITY?

The word diversity has its origin in the Latin word *diversus*, meaning differences or "turned different ways." As with many words, the context of the word diversity has changed over the centuries. Today, it can trigger either positive or negative associations, depending on the audience. While one person or cohort may perceive opportunity provided, another may imagine opportunity lost.

Since diversity implies different, the differences between people and the meaning of those differences must be considered. Cultivating such an understanding requires breaking down barriers limiting the definition of diversity to differences in skin color and/or gender. That narrow perspective sells people short by failing to recognize and value what makes them truly unique—their experiences and their thoughts.

Fortunately, diversity is far richer than skin-deep factors or physical appearance a person can't control. Understanding this complex element of identity, experiences, and thoughts is foundational to individual, organizational, and societal success. For cultural change to be embraced, people on all sides of the spectrum need to broaden their perspectives to *include* and *unite*, not narrow them to *exclude* and *divide*. My broader, more inclusive, construct of diversity breaks down this characterization of differences between individuals into three categories: Demographic, Experiential, and Cognitive.

Demographic Diversity: Race, Gender, Ethnicity, Age

People are all partly defined by their outward appearance, be it race, gender, ethnicity, age, or other characteristics. Sometimes, human nature causes people to stereotype others based on their appearance, presuming members of specific groups are all the same. That is inaccurate and robs people of their individuality and uniqueness.

It always annoyed me when someone presumed I thought or acted a certain way solely because of my gender. During my early years in the Coast Guard, women would intentionally avoid sitting together at gatherings. We didn't want the men to imagine we were all alike or only comfortable with other women. We were determined to integrate and be treated like everyone else, not differently.

Many years ago, when assigned as the first and only woman on board the icebreaker *Polar Star*, I found myself serving alongside 150 men. The ship's senior leadership, the commanding officer, and executive officer wanted me to succeed. They expressed concern about me being "alone" and set about the task of having another woman assigned. Although well-intended, their plan wasn't a panacea. The ship's senior leaders mistakenly believed gender mattered most, and therefore, any woman assigned would solve what they perceived as a hardship for me.

Despite insisting I felt very comfortable and confident I was fitting right in with the rest of the crew, I couldn't change their minds. They had fallen into the trap of thinking all women must be the same, presuming another woman would be company for me, thereby helping me succeed. That presumption made me feel like senior leadership didn't believe in me. It also made me feel guilty and frustrated as if I was causing a problem they had to solve. Never had I yearned so strongly to be looked at as just another Coast Guard member, not a female Coast Guard member. Despite my agitation, I respected my supervisors for acting in good faith. They meant well and thought they were helping me.

Within a month or so, Betty reported aboard. From the start, she was put in a tough position. Betty, a lieutenant-junior grade, was senior to me, but I was more experienced. While I'd spent four years training at the Coast Guard Academy, she entered the Coast Guard from a civilian college through the three-month Officer Candidate School program. Likewise, while I'd already deployed on *Glacier* and earned my watch standing qualifications, Betty had never served at sea or held an operational position. I felt sorry for Betty, as she unknowingly walked into a prickly situation.

The awkward circumstances set us up to feel like we were competing. People couldn't help but compare the two of us. I felt like I should somewhat hold back on my performance to avoid inadvertently outdoing Betty. Unfortunately, the arrangement contrived by the ship's leadership didn't account for these factors, resulting in a situation unfair to both of us. Betty and I became friends, but not because we were both women. Rather, we bonded because we were shipmates with a shared purpose, who respected each other and helped each other succeed.

There are several lessons to be learned from this case study. First, people assigned as part of a productive team must possess the right skills and qualifications. They shouldn't be selected because they meet someone's criteria for the desired gender, race, or ethnicity.

Second, people must be careful to not presume others need special considerations or help because they're in a less represented group. A book that adeptly illustrates this concern is *Please Stop Helping Us* by Jason L. Riley, an African American.[22] In it, he discusses the unintended adverse consequences of some well-intentioned social programs. Such programs can disempower the individuals they're meant to help and, as in my case, inadvertently send a signal that the organization doesn't believe in them.

Third, a positive workplace should ideally support a critical mass of women and minorities. Although there is no absolute definition of what constitutes critical mass, it means having enough of the less represented voices to resonate at all levels in the organization. In turn, the organizational culture must respect and value the voices in the less represented groups. Having been part of many newly integrated units and teams, I believe critical mass is unique to each situation. A good rule of thumb is "you know you have it when you can see it and feel the impact."

On board *Polar Star*, the two junior female officers in a crew of 150 most definitely did not constitute critical mass. There were no senior female officers (supervisors) above us, nor any female enlisted members (subordinates) below us. Although far from ideal, an organization must start somewhere. It takes time and commitment to achieve a critical mass of women and minorities in any workplace, and during that process, everyone must do their part to make the change.

Beyond race, gender, and ethnicity, a much-overlooked demographic diversity trait is age, which reflects significant and important generational differences. Young people, regardless of other physical attributes, have entirely different perspectives than older people. Take parents and their children, for example. A group of teens of different races and genders who hang out together in high school are likely to have far more in common with each other than with their parents.

Unfortunately, many organizations are overrepresented with older workers, particularly as a result of the aging baby boom generation. For instance, the average age of a civilian employee in the US Government is close to forty-eight years, with only about six percent of the workforce under thirty years of age.[23] Such an imbalanced age representation deprives an organization of valued voices and perspectives.

As I became older and more senior in rank, some of my most impactful staff members were the young workers always at my side who kept me grounded. Prominent among them were my military aides, all women and/or minorities under thirty.

The perspective I desired most from my aides related to their age, not their race, gender, or ethnicity. Since I often appeared in front of young, mostly active duty military audiences, I relied on my military aides to help me understand those service members and the issues most important to them.

Likewise, there were times when I was surrounded by senior leader peers and found myself leaning on the knowledge and experience of the younger generation. I once brought my military aide, the youngest member of my staff, to a classified briefing on cybersecurity. At the end of the briefing, comprised of senior leaders, I asked for her thoughts

. . . and she captivated the audience. Although her knowledge of the cybersecurity topic impressed the audience, how she thought about the topic and her ideas on what it could mean for the Coast Guard were what captured their attention.

The Coast Guard, like the other armed forces, must include more young people in its decision-making processes. Due to the nature of the military chain of command, junior personnel are often marginalized in the presence of senior leaders. Those who want to succeed as leaders must step up to lead the cultural change needed to include the extremely relevant, fresh voices of the younger generation.

Experiential Diversity: Geographic Origin, Education, Occupation, Religion, Interests, etc.

True diversity includes the richness of experiences found in society. In other words, where people are from, what they do and what they know. American society is comprised of people representing the spectrum of religions, occupations, and education levels in addition to geographic origin.

Regardless of race, gender, or ethnicity, people living in a small town in the midwestern United States have a much different perspective from those living in a big city on the eastern seaboard. Individuals who are the first in their families to attend college have a different perspective than those who descend from families who have all attended institutions of higher education. People who work as artists, engineers or laborers bring varied knowledge, skills, and abilities. Those from different socioeconomic backgrounds contribute unique thoughts and ideas reflecting their social experiences. A rich variety of experiences and backgrounds, regardless of race, gender, or ethnicity, is a premier element of diversity.

Race, gender, or ethnicity can sometimes add diversity if people's experiences enrich their perspective. For instance, a young Black teenager who lived on a farm during the civil war in Sudan will have a much different set of experiences than a young, Black teenager who grew up at the same time in a rural area in the United States. Likewise, a White person raised in a small town in East Germany under Soviet rule before the Berlin Wall came down will have a much different set of experiences than a White person born and raised at the same time in a small town in the United States. As a matter of fact, the African American and Caucasian born and raised as neighbors, attending the same school in the same town in the United States, are likely to share more in common with each other than they would with the member of their race raised in a completely different culture and country.

At the middle to senior leader level in my career, I had the opportunity, and with it the significant responsibility, of running the Coast Guard's officer selection boards and panels. Those deliberative bodies select Coast Guard officers and enlisted members for promotion, postgraduate education and special assignments that significantly impact their careers and lives.

In building diverse board and panel memberships, the staff worked diligently to ensure fair representation for everyone under consideration. Although each board and panel membership included race, gender, and ethnic diversity, those were but a few of many relevant perspectives needed.

The diversity of a board or panel member's occupational specialty brought tangible value to the selection process. Therefore, the staff selected members representing the spectrum of Coast Guard communities including aviation, surface operations, shore operations, engineering, information technology, finance and supply, training and education, and legal.

A diversified board and panel membership also included, among myriad experiences and perspectives, officers who had served both domestically and/or internationally, in special assignments with other departments or agencies, and in various geographic operating areas. Including a diversity of experience and background brought valuable perspectives to the board room table to interpret the officer evaluation reports elemental to selection decisions.

Running Coast Guard selection boards and panels confirmed my beliefs about diversity. What people have done and what they know (e.g., diversity of experience) is far more impactful to achieving a fair and optimal outcome than is diversity based solely on outward appearance.

Cognitive Diversity: Perspective and Personality

Perhaps the least understood, and most meaningful, type of diversity is cognitive diversity, which relates to the mind and brain. Cognitive diversity represents how people think, particularly as pertains to new, uncertain, and complex situations. It covers mental reasoning, intellectual curiosity, and personality traits.

Cognitive diversity isn't directly associated with race, gender, or ethnicity. A Military Leadership Diversity Commission issue paper examined several studies on the relationship between gender and personality versus race/ethnicity and personality. Results indicated the differences in personality *between* members of different races, genders, and ethnicities are minor, whereas differences in personalities are greater *within* those demographic groups.[24]

In other words, the differences between men and women and between the different racial and ethnic cohorts aren't as large as the spectrum of personalities present within any given cohort. For instance, a man and a woman who both have the same personality type may be more similar in many respects than two women with completely different personality types. It follows from the study results that increasing demographic diversity won't necessarily increase cognitive diversity. To increase cognitive diversity, an organization or a team must actively recruit or assign people with different personalities.

Those findings resonated with me. Throughout my career, people asked me for advice based on the presumption that all women thought the same. Nothing could be further from the truth! I've served with groups of women who looked like me but whose personalities and perspectives set them as far apart as the walls of the Grand Canyon. Likewise, I've participated in outwardly diverse-looking but effectively homogenous teams comprised of people with perspectives so similar they all fit together as uniformly as brown and white eggs nestled in a carton. I can attest from experience that better results come from the teams rich in cognitive diversity.

Since it recruits people from all over the United States and its territories, the Coast Guard is replete with cognitive diversity. When I commanded the cutter *Reliance*, the crew of seventy-five was predominately male and Caucasian. There were only a couple of women and a few minorities. Although seemingly homogenous, the crew was only non-diverse in terms of outward appearances. The strength that comes from different personalities and ways of thinking made it possible for *Reliance* to execute its missions in the aftermath of the terrorist attacks of 9-11.

In the months following that fateful day, *Reliance* patrolled for weeks on end offshore from New York City. The mission was to keep America safe and secure by inspecting large merchant vessels determined to be of high interest coming into New York harbor. Those vessels required more scrutiny to ensure they didn't pose a threat upon entering port.

Having been diverted from our normal law enforcement and search and rescue duties, the crew wasn't adequately trained for the new mission. They didn't have the expertise to conduct thorough inspections of merchant vessels. The crew had to adapt, and we drew upon their different mental frameworks and ideas to solve the many complex problems we faced.

One such instance was the case of the *Palermo Senator*, a freighter that had entered New York harbor from overseas to offload cargo. Post 9-11, the security situation in the nation's ports had been significantly heightened, triggering increased vessel inspections. The Coast Guard inspection of *Palermo Senator* revealed low levels of radiation which, it was feared, could have been emanating from some sort of nuclear device. Given the potential threat, the vessel was ordered back out to sea and directed to wait in a specific area several miles offshore while the cargo was analyzed.

Reliance was ordered to enforce a security zone, or perimeter, around the *Palermo Senator*. Authorities didn't want to alarm the public, so concern about the source of radiation remained closely held. Yet the situation had the president of the United States' full attention. I later learned President George W. Bush had spoken personally with the Coast Guard commander in charge of operations in the port of New York during the incident.

On the ship, we called together senior leaders and developed a plan to address the situation. We had no template, or what we in the Coast Guard call a "drill card," for this evolution. We didn't know how long we would be on patrol enforcing the security zone, but we knew we needed to refresh ourselves on the procedures to prepare for and respond to a potential nuclear incident.

The team engaged in robust discussion and debate about what to do and what not to do. For instance, we considered the appropriate level of precaution to take in safeguarding the crew. We had seen what happened with the Coast Guard cutter assigned to share security zone duties with us. Given the potential threat of a nuclear detonation, that ship decided to keep its crew locked down inside the ship, day and night. We got word the crew was stir-crazy and stressed with the constant worry of pending disaster. We decided we didn't want to create a similar environment on board *Reliance* and resisted the temptation to follow their lead.

Since everyone felt comfortable expressing different ideas, we considered a wide range of options and decided upon a sensible, balanced approach. We reasoned, "Let's face it, if there is a nuclear device on board the *Palermo Senator*, and it goes off with us patrolling inside the security zone, we're going to be zapped no matter what." Why create stress and anxiety when we had no control over what might happen?

To keep the crew mentally, emotionally, and physically prepared for a contingency, we chose a course of action that maintained business as usual, carrying out the normal underway routine of the day. We drilled the crew on the procedures necessary to prepare for a worst-case scenario. We conducted business with professionalism and accomplished the mission.

In the end, the *Palermo Senator* case was anticlimactic. After comprehensive inspections, including one by the Navy SEALs, the radiation detected on board the *Palermo Senator* was found to come from harmless clay tiles. Everyone breathed a collective sigh of relief. The *Palermo Senator* incident enriched my appreciation of the value of stepping back to consider all perspectives, thereby avoiding the groupthink trap, before making important decisions.

Although the value of cognitive diversity seems obvious to me, the long-standing association of diversity with outward appearances runs deep in our society and must be addressed. Alison Reynolds and David Lewis published interesting research on cognitive diversity in the *Harvard Business Review*. Their findings matched my observations of teams over the years: teams diverse in factors of outward appearance alone (i.e. race, gender, ethnicity) didn't improve group performance. Instead, they found the higher-performing teams were rich in cognitive diversity. I was intrigued by their conclusion that, while cognitive diversity is plentiful in society, it's seldom recognized or valued. Too often, homogenous organizational cultures stifle individualism and reward conformity.[25]

Unfortunately, evidence of this problem abounds throughout society today. People in the group convinced they're on the right side of an issue—or worse yet, on the right side of justice—seek to suppress, rather than understand, those on the other side. In seeking a deeper understanding of what we hold to be true, we all have a responsibility to reach out our hand to meet people on the other side of an issue where they are. The goal must be to bridge the differences by better *understanding* others' beliefs, not by *undermining* those beliefs.

American society desperately needs more leaders with the moral courage to promote civil discourse that will unite and strengthen, not divide and weaken. Those leaders of character must encourage different—yes, even dissenting—points of view. Conversations and discussions in a diverse workplace must be approached with openness, curiosity, and most importantly, humility. If such conversations are grounded in respect, the full benefits of diversity may be realized.

Of the three diversity categories discussed, I believe cognitive diversity is the most impactful yet is the least understood or valued. Cognitive diversity transcends the segregation sometimes associated with demographic and experiential diversity. People who learn to understand and respect each other's perspectives and beliefs can leverage their differences to create innovative, productive outcomes in the workplace.

Although cognitive diversity is integral, each of the three categories of diversity has its unique place in adding value. My duties leading people locally and an organization globally required me to continually solicit a wide variety of thoughts, ideas, and perspectives. I learned to achieve the best results, a leader must bring the right people to the table and actively solicit input from each of them. The best ideas often come from individuals who sit quietly until called upon, not those who can't wait to speak. Leaders of character who respect their people and who learn how to tap their workforce to harness the power of the full spectrum of diversity will meet with success.

Getting Diversity Right

Starting with how it accesses new members, the Coast Guard has done a lot to get diversity right. When young people arrive at the Academy or the Recruit Training Center, they're immediately assigned to a company. All members of the company participate in the boot camp–style basic training experience together as a team. Trainees don't get to choose their companies and pick people who are like them. Rather, they're assigned to their teams randomly, regardless of race, gender, ethnicity, or any other diversity factors. They must work through their differences together, which can be hard for young people whose perspectives may not yet have been challenged.

After much effort and many failures, the new cadets and recruits eventually bond with the shared purpose of overcoming adversity by solving problems together. As a result, they come to value each member of the team and appreciate others' unique contributions.

The most poignant experience of self-discovery I've ever witnessed is when young cadets or recruits emerge at the end of their basic training experience. At that moment, they proudly realize they have discovered what they're capable of, both as individuals and as part of a team. Now, that's real power. By the time those young officers and enlisted personnel report into their first Coast Guard units, they have already learned the value of diversity. Most importantly, they understand it to be far greater than race, gender, or ethnicity.

On the other side of the coin, I witnessed initiatives that stifled diversity during an official benchmarking visit to a college in the California state university system. It astonished me to hear that, unlike my educational experiences, students reporting in to start their first year got to select their team. Many of them felt pressured to immediately join an affinity group based solely on their race, gender, or ethnicity, ostensibly to create a feeling of belonging in unfamiliar surroundings.

A student of Japanese origin told me he loved drums, but to associate with others who shared the same interest, he had to join the African American affinity group. It bewildered me that the college didn't have affinity groups for those with shared interests, like playing drums. Such groups would truly enhance an inclusive culture by bringing members of demographically diverse cohorts together. How powerful it would be for students from varied backgrounds to participate in a drum club and learn how people from countries all over the world use drums in their cultures.

Although the university's student population was eighty-five percent diverse in terms of race and ethnicity, I came away feeling like the Coast Guard Academy, despite being only about twenty-five percent diverse, displayed far more functional diversity. Unfortunately, an institution of higher education can become a barrier to achieving the benefits of diversity if it encourages affinity narrowly based on outwardly visible characteristics like race, gender, and ethnicity instead of broadly through shared interests.

Back when I was a student at graduate school in the early 1990s, I received an invitation to join the newly established Women in Management affinity group. Feeling a little rebellious at being singled out, yet again, based on my gender, I told them I would join a Leaders in Management group open to all but not a group segregated by gender.

I'd worked hard all my life to be included and wasn't interested in joining a group that was, by definition, exclusive. It seemed regressive to me. I succeeded throughout my career by looking forward and choosing the progressive option to integrate and unite, not to segregate and divide.

Since then, my perspective has broadened as I've matured and come to better understand human nature. People associate with others who look like themselves for numerous reasons and tend to build relationships within their demographic group. In addition to gender-neutral groups, I've joined some women's affinity groups and find value in them.

I also enjoy spending time in person with groups of women who share common interests, like swimming. Some of the women in my local community have been swimming together for years, forming lasting friendships. We've watched children grow up, attended weddings, and supported each other during times of need. I also participated for many years in a stimulating classic book club whose members were very well-read women of about the same age. Our similarities were balanced by our differences, resulting from our varied backgrounds and how we thought. In another testament to the benefits of cognitive diversity, we could all read the same book and come away with completely different interpretations and reactions. We enjoyed learning and growing from each other's diverse experiences and perspectives.

Although associating with people who look like yourself is comfortable, a balanced perspective is necessary. I firmly believe people should deliberately venture outside of their comfort zone to associate across racial, gender, and ethnic groups. Choosing to associate solely based on outward appearances has drawbacks. For one, it forgoes all the richness to be gained from association with others who may look different but with whom you have shared interests. Even worse, it retards integration by presuming people must be of the same race, gender, or ethnicity to have anything in common.

Integration doesn't mean giving up your identity or lessening the value of the unique perspective you bring. Undeniably, I added value to the Coast Guard throughout my career due to my status as a female in a mostly male environment. *But never did I let my gender define me or allow someone else to define me by my gender.*

What matters most in the Coast Guard is proficiency and performance. In all my time serving, I never encountered anyone being rescued who cared whether their rescuer was a man or a woman, Black or White, Christian or Jew, enlisted or officer. The value someone contributes through performance, accomplishment, and achievement is what matters.

While serving as an ensign aboard the cutter *Glacier* in 1982, I led a small, operational workgroup called the Combat Information Center. The group composition was nearly fifty percent African American with the leader, me, being a woman. We formed a cohesive, fully integrated team of truly diverse people who respected each other based on our knowledge, skills, and abilities. The leading petty officer Radarman Second Class Bob Washington, an African American, taught me and showed me the ropes. An extremely patient professional, he helped me learn how to lead as a new division officer.

For five months during the Operation Deep Freeze '83 Antarctic support mission, we served together as a close-knit team. We trusted each other with our lives and with the safety of the ship and crew. We were the ones who, while on watch, scanned the radars for approaching ships or other hazards. We vectored the assigned helicopters away from the ship on their missions and safely back again.

It was irrelevant that we were a team of mixed races and genders. Job qualifications and performance were what mattered. We succeeded as a team in large part because the Coast Guard trained and prepared us to perform our duties. We had all earned our places through strong performance both on advancement exams and in the workplace, which fostered a positive work environment supportive of mutual respect and trust.

Bringing people who look, act, and think differently together in a workplace is hard, but the benefits are evident when the differences are leveraged to unite and strengthen, not to divide and weaken. The model, Succeeding in an Organization, reflects the importance of a healthy system of interdependence between society, organizations, and individuals. The entire system benefits when organizations commit to reflect and respect the full diversity of the population they serve and when individuals commit to achieve excellence.

WHAT IS INCLUSION?

As organizations progressed in implementing cultural change, it became apparent that diversity alone couldn't achieve the desired effect. Although diversity can help produce a strong team of people with different perspectives, more is needed for the team to achieve its full potential. The concept of inclusion was added to enrich the context of what it means to create a workplace climate in which every individual is valued, respected, and encouraged to grow, learn, and succeed.

Diversity, as a concept, might be construed as *passive*, whereas inclusion is *active*. Diversity is the state of being of a team; it reflects who they are and how they contribute in terms of their demographic, experiential, and cognitive diversity. Inclusion is how the organization harnesses the full value of its members and the teams they form. Inclusion means reaching out a hand to meet people where they are and welcoming them into the workplace and onto the team.

To succeed in uniting a diverse workforce, organizations must create programs to integrate and include individuals from a variety of cultures, with different experiences and cognitive frameworks. Otherwise, the differences can divide. People of assorted races, ethnicities, and beliefs have gone to war over their differences since the beginning of time. It takes strong leadership and deliberate effort to create unity and push aside division.

To unify a diverse team, all members must understand the shared purpose and feel like their contributions matter. When Jeh Johnson was installed as secretary of Homeland Security in 2013, he recognized an immediate need and started a unity of effort initiative to bring together a divided department.

The Department of Homeland Security had been established in 2002 as one of many actions following the terrorist attacks of 9-11. The department was formed by bringing together twenty-two disparate agencies, each with its own character, culture, and values. Some, like the Coast Guard, transferred intact. Others, like the Customs Service, were broken up and integrated into newly formed agencies, called components. The components had little in common aside from some connection to homeland security.

At first, it seemed like the diversity of the new Department caused nothing but division. None of the agencies being brought in wanted to change or compromise in any fashion. They fought to maintain their structure and identity. The atmosphere was rife with competition for scarce resources and status in the new organization. Conditions improved as the years passed, but from my perspective, the Department of Homeland Security never truly unified.

In about 2008, the Department embarked upon its first-ever Quadrennial Homeland Security Review, a requirement of the

Homeland Security Act of 2002. I was fortunate to participate as a member of the team that generated the inaugural strategy document that the Department delivered to Congress in 2010.

It was rough-and-tumble during the meetings, as the components jockeyed to develop and support departmental missions into which their component missions would neatly fit. Imagine the challenge of trying to fit the Coast Guard's statutorily mandated pollution response, icebreaking, and buoy-tending missions into a discrete homeland security mission.

Although contentious, the process provided the components a much deeper understanding and appreciation of the value each brought to the Department. Fleshing out a set of departmental missions with associated goals and objectives proved a productive first step toward unity and purpose. But more was needed.

Secretary Johnson brought a truly inclusive perspective to the Department. He honestly cared about the morale and well-being of the people on the front lines who executed and supported the missions. Morale was low, and the secretary realized something was missing. By the time he arrived, the Department had implemented an organizational construct and a process to develop strategy. Yet no one had taken the next step to unify by aligning the components with shared values and a shared purpose.

Recognizing the Department would be stronger—and America safer—with a united front, Secretary Johnson decided to promulgate a mission statement. It had been fourteen years since the Department had been established. The time was right.

The secretary could have gathered his trusted senior staff, put them in a room for a few days, and come up with a satisfactory product. Instead, he chose the inclusive route. He reached out to the entire workforce, imploring everyone in the Department to contribute thoughts and ideas.

Secretary Johnson made and posted a video, targeting employees at all levels and in every component. He also conducted personal outreach. One day as I sat in my office going through e-mails, a note from Secretary Johnson popped onto the screen. I blinked to be sure I wasn't mistaken. Yes, it was the secretary, not a surrogate, who had sent me a personal note. In it, he asked for ideas regarding the fundamental elements of a mission statement and recommendations on the specific wording. I sat down the same day and put together a proposed mission statement and my supporting thoughts, enthused with the opportunity to contribute.

Not long afterward, Secretary Johnson called a meeting for all senior leaders in the Department. We gathered in anticipation to hear him speak. Following his remarks, he proudly presented the new Department of Homeland Security Mission Statement, accompanied by an inspirational video showing every component conducting its missions.

The mission statement is elegant in its simplicity. It captures the essence of an incredibly complex mission in fifteen impactful words. Grounded in shared values, it's a clarion call for unity. Most importantly, everyone in the Department felt ownership. That day, I witnessed in Secretary Johnson a powerful example of what it means to lead with character.

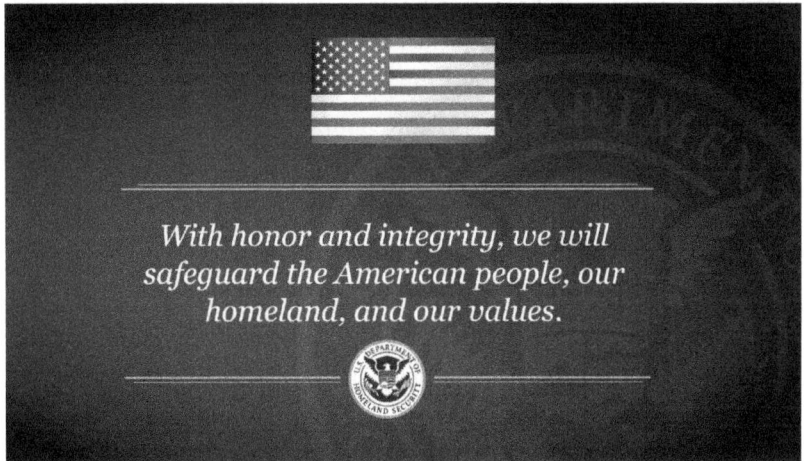

Department of Homeland Security Mission Statement

Getting Inclusion Right

Creating an inclusive workplace requires active engagement by participants at all levels. Culture won't change, regardless of how strongly inclusion is supported at the top, unless all people do their part. Individuals must reach out and invite others to participate—in a teamwork effort, an office outing, or a simple conversation. Equally as important, people must extend their hand and ask to be included instead of waiting passively for an invitation. Getting inclusion right also requires people to demonstrate the moral courage to intervene to correct anti-inclusive behaviors.

A healthy workplace climate relies on effective communication. Members of the workforce should listen and learn from their coworkers, thereby opening their minds to different ideas and perspectives. In America's ever-more-divided society, creating a workplace climate of inclusion means members must guard against the temptation to associate only with others who think and believe like they do.

Limiting interactions to like-minded people excludes other viewpoints and can lead to confirmation bias. Such bias results in a tendency for people to engage in selective retention and interpretation. It causes people to look for, prefer, and remember information in a way that supports their preexisting beliefs or hypotheses, even if evidence proves the beliefs to be false. That behavior will only serve to divide and weaken a workplace, not unite and strengthen it.

To create a culture of inclusion, people must first recognize and then set aside their own confirmation bias. Next, they must actively engage with others and seek to understand a range of viewpoints. I listened to a great TED Talk by Celeste Headlee, who spoke on how to have constructive conversations. She advised people to listen intently during conversations and "be prepared to be amazed" by the other person.[26] Reaching out a hand to welcome and include someone means truly valuing and respecting that fellow human being by listening, learning, and preparing to be amazed by what is heard. The world would be a much better place if everyone subscribed to that philosophy.

Throughout my career, I was often the first, the only, or one of the few women in the workplace. Women were seldom, if ever, listened to with amazement. The Coast Guard did the right thing and opened doors for women early on, but that didn't mean the mission was fully accomplished. From the beginning, women were often ignored and sometimes isolated, even by our peers. We didn't feel valued or appreciated.

From cadet to admiral, there were times when I was the only woman in a group and had to work hard to be included. Starting with my early years at the Coast Guard Academy, I ended up being the only woman in my company of approximately thirty cadets. Two cadets normally shared a barracks room, but as the only woman, I was assigned my own room.

Having a room all to myself might sound like a good thing, but trust me, it was not. Cadets survived in that exacting environment by working together to share information and overcome adversity. Living alone and isolated as the only woman, I had to work extra hard to be sure I didn't miss anything. At times, I didn't receive notice of a mandatory event, resulting in punishment leading to further isolation.

As a senior officer, I often participated as the lone woman in a room filled with my peers. Even at that level, I had to make a concerted effort to insert my views and often felt like people unintentionally talked around me. Even when my gender would have lent perspective, such as when discussing issues pertaining to women, the men rarely thought to ask my opinion.

Despite often feeling less included as the only woman, I came to realize it was my responsibility to step up and make my voice heard. I learned not to blame others or the organization. During my early years at sea on ships, I heard the guys making plans to go out after work or in a foreign port call. I wasn't asked to join them. At first, I chose to feel left out. The situation was particularly vexing because the ship's policy required crew members who left the ship during a port call in a foreign country to go out on liberty in groups of at least two or more for safety's sake. Out of necessity, I mustered up the courage to ask the guys if I could join them. Invariably, the guys gladly included me. Since I resided in a separate berthing area, they had simply not thought to ask me.

I learned to work my way into conversations and seize the initiative to invite myself to the table. If I had waited for someone in a male-dominated discussion group to ask my opinion, I would have been sitting silent forever. Although initially uncomfortable with this tactic, I realized most of the men already used it and finally stepped up and adapted my style.

Looking back, I believe my success came from taking personal responsibility for examining my role in each situation and asking myself what I could have done differently. An organization and its leadership can only do so much to create an inclusive climate. Employees are obligated to actively engage to achieve favorable outcomes.

WHAT IS EQUITY?

To me, equity means members of a society or an organization should all have access to the tools or opportunities they need to succeed. Pursuing equity requires recognizing that not everyone starts in the same place, and there may be barriers impacting some people more than others. As a result, changes to programs, policies, and processes may be necessary to help everyone participate and have the chance to succeed.

When I commanded the Coast Guard's Recruit Training Center, we had few women among the instructor staff. In the seamanship division, one woman served among the many men. A top performer, she had earned her coworkers' respect. After giving birth and taking maternity leave, she eagerly anticipated returning to the spartan workplace to resume her role training recruits. But there would be a barrier: the facility had no private place to express breast milk.

The male instructors rallied around their shipmate and took the initiative to set aside an adequate space so she would be comfortable.

It was heart-warming to witness their enthusiasm to provide their female coworker an accommodation she needed to be at her best. The Coast Guard has since put policy in place requiring units to provide space for new mothers. I marvel at how far our humanitarian service has progressed since I joined so many years ago.

Getting Equity Right

Compared with diversity and inclusion, equity is the toughest to address and the hardest to get right. In life, the playing field will never be level, nor will the outcomes ever be equal. Life is frustratingly unfair.

Effective equity programs don't pit people against each other; they strengthen and unite people and organizations. They strive to help everyone succeed by enabling equal opportunity. The second paragraph of the Declaration of Independence asserts, "We hold these truths to be self-evident, that all Men are created equal, that they are endowed by their Creator with certain unalienable Rights, that among these are Life, Liberty, and the Pursuit of Happiness."

Nowhere in that founding document is there a guarantee that all individuals, although created equal, will achieve equal outcomes. Leaders of character, however, will do everything they can to help people chart their course, overcome obstacles, and succeed in achieving their goals. When I was serving as a junior officer onboard the icebreaker *Polar Star*, Betty reported aboard to serve as a deck watch officer on the ship's bridge. Her duties required her to look out the window to see what was going on in the water and on the decks below. But Betty was short and couldn't see out the windows. She worried about how she was going to stand her watch. The next day, a handmade stand appeared on the bridge beneath a window. Crewmembers had noticed her challenge and had taken the initiative to provide a solution. Not long after, stands were installed beneath all the windows, making it easier for everyone to perform their duty.

Equity should never be misinterpreted to mean lowering standards, creating a double standard, or removing requirements. Organizations are responsible for providing programs to help every person succeed, and individuals are responsible for pursuing their goals and objectives through hard work and perseverance. When the organization and the individual both do their part, success is more likely to follow.

This concept hit home for me while attending the Coast Guard Academy. In high school, I graduated in the top five percent of a large class of nearly 400 students. The Academy was an entirely different story. Despite working incredibly hard, I struggled academically and graduated in the lower half of my class. It was tough, and very humbling, to accept the fact that in a more competitive environment, I was very average among exceptional peers. Quite frankly, I wasn't as academically gifted as other students and had never had higher-level academic preparatory classes like calculus in high school. Without adequate academic preparation, all my hard work wasn't enough.

Thankfully, the Coast Guard Academy offered programs to help level the playing field for academically deficient students like me. I took advantage of those programs, seeking help from instructors and classmates after hours. In turn, I succeeded in passing the academic portion of my Academy requirements.

Unfortunately, organizations desiring to diversify sometimes design programs enabling people to succeed without meeting the standards, or they change the standards so less qualified people can meet them. My experience has been that efforts to manufacture equal outcomes are apt to do more harm than good. They can divide the workforce, create resentment and unrealistic expectations, and lower performance.

As American society continues to diversify, Pew research shows the nation is more divided now than ever.[27] Therefore, it is incumbent upon organizations to implement equity measures positively to unite and strengthen individuals, teams, and organizations, rather than further dividing and weakening them.

The Coast Guard and the other armed forces are superior examples of excellent organizations in which diverse cohorts, regardless of societal inequities, can thrive. Newly accessed members from all walks of life enter at the lowest level in their service. Benefits, including housing, healthcare, parental leave, childcare, clothing, and food allowances supplement modest salaries and level the playing field. Throughout their career, service members receive the training and education needed to advance their knowledge, skills, and abilities and move up to lead and succeed at the next level. In turn, the armed forces demand individual accountability and responsibility. Each service member accepts the terms by signing a contract, then solemnly taking the oath of office, swearing to support and defend the Constitution of the United States of America.

The Coast Guard, and each of the other Armed Forces, gives members the chance to succeed, regardless of opportunities presented or challenges faced earlier in life. Of course, the work is never finished, and requires commitment from leaders at all levels. Organizations must strive for continuous improvement in creating respectful, inclusive workplaces where everyone can succeed. This calls for cultural change.

IMPLEMENTING CULTURAL CHANGE

Cultural change is never easy. People resist any kind of change, even if it will undeniably result in better outcomes. To be effective, change must be implemented deliberately, with targeted communication across the entire organization.

Cultivating and sustaining a positive climate and culture is akin to a marriage; it requires continual effort and commitment from everyone in the workplace. Most importantly, organizations must "do the right thing right." Getting cultural change wrong can sow the seeds of division and block necessary change from taking effect. To implement cultural change, you should take the following steps:

Implementing Cultural Change
- Treat everyone fairly and with respect
- Create programs and policies leveraging differences to unite and strengthen versus divide and weaken

- Avoid labeling or stereotyping individuals or groups
- Create a welcoming, inclusive workplace where people know they're valued as both individuals and members of the team
- Provide qualified individuals an equal chance for promotions and other opportunities
- Ensure members understand and feel ownership of the organization's mission, vision, and goals
- Help members overcome obstacles or barriers that may hold them back
- Make performance expectations clear and provide timely, relevant feedback
- Hold everyone accountable for their behavior and performance
- Reward outstanding performance by clearly distinguishing between levels of achievement

Getting Cultural Change Right

The Coast Guard has served as an exemplar, embracing diversity and implementing positive cultural change. From the time the Service started integrating women in the 1970s, it committed to ensuring women had parity with men. Although accommodations such as berthing were not widely available in the beginning, women were offered access to every occupational specialty. That included serving aboard the Coast Guard's version of warships, which were 378-foot cutters equipped with weapons systems.

I was assigned to one of those ships in the summer of 1979 on a five-week cadet cruise. I stood watch in the Combat Information Center and participated in live-fire exercises. At the time, the Coast Guard was the only armed service that didn't exclude women from any career field or occupational specialty. Unfortunately, my female counterparts at the US Naval Academy, where I once desired to study, weren't presented an equivalent option to train on board Navy warships. That made it far more difficult for them to be accepted as equals by the men.

Had I attended the Naval Academy instead of the Coast Guard Academy, I would have been denied, by combat exclusion laws and policies, from pursuing a career as a line officer at sea. I'm thankful the Coast Guard provided me equal access and parity from the start, enabling me to achieve my interpretation of success. Allowing women to serve side-by-side with men on the front line of operations created a presumption of equality. That, in turn, helped shape a culture that gradually embraced acceptance of women in the Service.

Despite good intentions, an organization can misstep by singling out members from less-represented cohorts for opportunities outside of the normal process. I witnessed this time and again and personally experienced it throughout my career. Advancing people ahead of their equally or better-qualified peers based solely on race, gender, or ethnicity can undermine diversity, inclusion, and equity efforts.

While serving aboard the cutter *Confidence* as a mid-grade officer, I found myself in the awkward position of turning down an exceptional opportunity that would have accelerated me ahead of my peers. It was an invitation to participate in the Coast Guard's prestigious senior service school program. Senior service schools include the armed forces war colleges, executive programs at top-tier universities, and high-profile fellowships. The program is only available to senior officers.

One day while moored in homeport, my assignment officer called. Such calls were rare and always elicited both excitement and anxiety. I was up for transfer and eagerly anticipated what fate had in store for me. To my surprise, he offered me a once-in-a-career opportunity to attend a year-long, senior-level National Security Fellowship at Harvard University.

Stunned, I blurted out, "How can that be? I'm only a lieutenant commander, and I'm not eligible for a few more years. I know the senior service school program is only available to senior commanders and captains who are in the eligibility zone."

My assignment officer replied, "Don't worry, the Coast Guard has decided to reach down and select women and minorities early, ahead of their peers." He explained how the Service desired to accelerate the representation of women and minorities at the senior level of the organization, so it made an exception to the rules. On hearing that, I summarily refused the Harvard National Security Fellowship. The Coast Guard didn't publicly advertise its decision to "deep select"[xiii] women and minorities ahead of their peers for senior service school. The program was personally offered to certain individuals. I turned down the Harvard fellowship because I didn't want that kind of opportunity. *I wanted a fair chance to compete on a level playing field but not an unfair advantage.* I felt patronized for having been offered a double standard, based on my gender.

I wondered what my peers would have thought if they had seen my name on the selection list when it hadn't appeared in the previously published eligibility zone. I think it would have diminished their trust in the organization and led them to resent me. Such an outcome would retard, not advance, cultural change.

A few years later, I was serving in officer personnel management and my job included responsibility for the same senior service school program. I fielded a question from the higher-ups as to why so few women existed in the pipeline for senior service school. Restraining myself, I politely reminded them of the earlier, informal policy to deep select women ahead of their peers. The unintended consequence of that preferential treatment program was a several-year gap of top candidates. Unfortunately, the Coast Guard appeared to be holding women back when, in fact, the opposite was true. In turning down the Harvard fellowship, I clung to my values, preserving both trust in the system and my self-respect.

Organizations must accept that it takes time to grow eligible candidates. This is particularly true in the armed forces, where people advance up the ranks based in a large part on years of experience. A sustainable strategy recruits, trains and retains top talent at all levels,

---

xiii   The term "deep select" means the organization reaches down below the established zone of eligible individuals to select those who have not yet met the standard eligibility criteria, which often includes time in grade.

covering the spectrum of diversity. Then, it provides equal opportunity for all and equity programs as needed so everyone can achieve their full potential. Although it can take time and patience, such a strategy will result in a more inclusive culture and higher performing organization.

Cultural change is hard, and getting it right is even harder. Individuals must be evaluated on their performance and behavior, not classified by cohort. People should be respected for what they do, not judged for who they are or what they look like. Leading with character means creating a culture of respect that values every person, encourages active participation, and gives everyone a fair chance to succeed but not an unfair advantage.

Creating a Culture of Respect

Respect is a small but very powerful word. It breaks down barriers in a way nothing else can. Only by creating a culture of respect can an organization succeed in implementing diversity, inclusion, and equity programs that unite and strengthen, not divide and weaken. Creating a culture of respect requires people to actively engage in a shared commitment to building trust and earning respect. That applies to relationships between peers, between supervisors and subordinates, and with an organization's customers and stakeholders. All members of the workforce, from the lowest-paid person to the top executive, deserve to be treated with respect and decency for who they are and what they contribute to the mission.

It's no coincidence that respect is central to the Coast Guard's core values of honor, respect, and devotion to duty. The Service's founding father, Secretary of the Treasury Alexander Hamilton, made sure of that. He established the Coast Guard's predecessor, the Revenue Cutter Service in 1790 to enforce the fledgling nation's laws on the high seas.

Alexander Hamilton instilled in the Revenue Cutter Service a culture of respect that has endured over the past 230 years to the modern-day Coast Guard. Since the United States had recently fought a war to escape tyranny and earn independence, Alexander Hamilton foresaw challenges the officers of the Revenue Cutter Service would face in enforcing laws on fellow citizens. He knew success depended upon building trust and creating a culture of mutual respect between citizens and their government.

Sagely, he instructed his officers to comport themselves with prudence, moderation, and good temper, charging them as follows:

> *They will always keep in mind that their countrymen are freemen, and, as such, are impatient of everything that bears the least mark of a domineering spirit. They will, therefore, refrain, with the most guarded circumspection, from whatever has the semblance of haughtiness, rudeness, or insult.*[28]

With those wise words, Alexander Hamilton instilled a culture of respect that enabled the Revenue Cutter Service to adapt and thrive over the centuries.

Creating and sustaining a culture of respect in an organization is no easy task and requires engaged leadership at every level. Unfortunately, people tend to take respect for granted and fail to realize that respect must be earned in the workplace every single day. This requirement applies even to the most senior executives, who should never presume respect derives from position power alone. Seeking to earn the respect of their subordinates will help executives maintain their humility, a central tenant of servant leadership.

Giving and earning respect can be as simple as acknowledging someone's achievement with a compliment or perhaps a handwritten note. I'll always remember the handwritten note I received from Secretary of Homeland Security Jeh Johnson, congratulating me on my new assignment. My respect for him increased, and I reflected, "If he makes time to write personal notes, I'm going to pay his example forward and write more notes myself."

There are countless ways to demonstrate civility and respect in the workplace, and leaders of character will discover and employ them. Those who respect others will earn respect themselves, creating a virtuous cycle leading to a positive workplace.

The Power of Effective Communication

Effective communication, like Alexander Hamilton's letter to the officers of the Revenue Cutter Service, builds and maintains trust, which is essential to creating a culture of respect. This was reinforced to me while serving as executive assistant to the commandant, Admiral Allen. I managed execution of the commandant's vision by communicating with other senior leaders answering questions, directing efforts, and resolving conflicts.

I was pleased with the progress the team was making as we steadily built trust in and support for the commandant's vision across the organization. One day, I could sense Admiral Allen was frustrated with me, but I didn't know why.

He looked at me and uttered with agitation, "Radar return, Sandy, radar return!"

Since we had both served on ships at sea, he chose a nautical reference to the shipboard radar scope to help me understand what he was looking for. Watchstanders on the bridge of a ship use radar to obtain a picture of the operating environment so they can navigate and avoid threats. Performing well on watch isn't enough; the officer of the deck must keep the commanding officer advised so he or she has the situational awareness needed to make command decisions.

In my attempt to shield Admiral Allen from the daily grind, I'd inadvertently denied him the information he needed to follow our progress. Taking the cue, I started providing Admiral Allen a weekly status report with the "radar return," detailing key issues and accomplishments. My report gave him the high-level information he needed and offered us an opportunity to align on expectations.

I learned to appreciate anew the power of effective communication in building trust and earning respect.

Organizational change is never easy, and cultural change is the hardest. Most organizational changes pertain to certain concrete aspects of the organization, be it structure, processes and procedures, service delivery or the like. Cultural change focuses on the individual, making it uniquely personal. Leading with character requires creating a strong culture of respect that supports diversity, inclusion, and equity initiatives that value every member of the workforce.

Stage Three: Resilience (Personal) / Courage and Confidence

> *The question isn't who is going to let me;*
> *it's who is going to stop me.*
>
> —Ayn Rand

At the pinnacle of the Succeeding in an Organization model is the individual component. It features resilience in the form of courage and confidence. That part of the pyramid is where you have the power to control outcomes. To succeed, you should spend most of your time working hard and persevering to achieve your goals, rather than being distracted by societal and organizational issues mostly beyond your control.

Although hard work and perseverance are necessary elements of success, they will only get you so far. You must also harness the inner resilience needed to overcome obstacles as you lead in uncharted waters. The characteristics of courage and confidence are personal qualities that strengthen your resilience and keep you on track.

Once again, Aristotle's golden mean adds a valuable perspective. Courage, in this interpretation, is a precise balance of having the right amount of both fear and confidence. Fear and confidence are not opposite concepts on a line, the balance of which is courage.

Rather, they are two distinct continua, the intersection of which is where courage is found. Finding that intersection requires you to search to discover the right amount of fear and the right amount of confidence to fit a given situation. Throughout my career, I often struggled to find the ideal balance between fear and confidence.

While serving as a mid-grade officer in a staff position, I received orders back to sea as executive officer aboard the cutter *Confidence* (aptly named given my situation). Although quite experienced with eight years of sea duty, this would be my first time serving as a senior leader on board one of the Coast Guard's major cutters.

I was excited and ready to go back to sea in a leadership position and expected to report aboard during the normal summer transfer season. There remained four busy months in my high visibility position as a program reviewer at Coast Guard Headquarters. Suddenly, phone calls from the ship started coming. The incumbent informed me I had to report aboard as soon as possible to oversee preparations for an important readiness evaluation. I expressed my concerns and explained the need for balance. Prominent programming and budgeting issues demanded resolution in my current job, which required an on-site relief. Undeterred, the incumbent demonstrated relentless persistence, insisting that passing the readiness evaluation depended on my presence.

Having served at sea for many years, I was very familiar with those standard, fleet-wide readiness evaluations. They consisted of team evolutions led by senior enlisted and junior officer leaders. The executive officer plays a central role in preparing the ship and crew to achieve the necessary readiness, but the preparations would be finished, and the crew ready, by the time I reported aboard. Nonetheless, the persistent pressure caused me to experience the tension between fear and confidence. Was there something I was missing? I knew I was ready for the job but couldn't help feeling a little apprehensive.

Searching inward, I managed to balance the relatively unfounded fear with my substantiated confidence, and I stood by my convictions.

I concluded the incumbent and I were simply two very different leaders. That didn't mean either of us was right or wrong. It meant I needed to believe in myself and my leadership abilities and accept I couldn't control what he thought. I held to my intended reporting date. I decided to arrive prior to the ship getting underway to transit from homeport to the readiness evaluation location. I knew that would allow enough time to familiarize and prepare.

Upon reporting aboard, I detected a climate characterized by stress and, in some cases, fear imposed by a perfectionist who micromanaged people. The junior officers, in particular, had fought to find the courage to persevere along that continuum representing the tension between confidence and fear. They had been, in some cases, afraid to approach the executive officer.

During the relief process, which included meeting with senior leaders in the crew, I became encouraged. The department head responsible for most of the pending readiness evaluation evolutions assured me, "Don't worry, ma'am. We've got this."

His reassurance was exactly what I needed to validate my confidence.

I found the ship well prepared and the crew eager to demonstrate their skill. They made me proud by performing admirably during the readiness evaluation. I set to work restoring leadership responsibility to the crew, striving to build a positive environment in which people could flourish and succeed. I learned the importance of trusting my instincts and persevering with confidence to stand up for what I knew was right.

The Succeeding in an Organization model demonstrates the value of an integrated approach. There must be laws and policies enabling access and opportunity for all to participate. Then, cultural change is necessary to ensure people can strive to reach their potential and, in so doing, help optimize organizational performance.

Perhaps most pertinent of all, individuals must understand and accept that the playing field will never be level. They must work hard and persevere toward their goals and exhibit the courage and confidence to adapt and thrive. Despite the laws and policies providing me access to opportunities and the Coast Guard's positive culture of respect, it wasn't until I found courage and confidence that I started to realize success.

PART THREE

Leading the Organization

★ ★ ★

The key to successful leadership today is influence,
not authority.

—Ken Blanchard

REACHING THE EXECUTIVE LEVEL of any organization requires an extended journey of professional and leadership development. Serving in the US Coast Guard, the journey to flag officer rank, or admiral, took me twenty-eight years. The armed forces promotion process is an "up or out" system, with little opportunity to accelerate beyond your peer group. A certain degree of proficiency and leadership development is presumed based on experience gained at each level. At each promotion point, officers in a peer group are evaluated, with those who are found best qualified selected to move up to the next level.

In the Coast Guard, only about one percent of officers make it from ensign to admiral. The few who rise to the top are obligated to lead with character, placing the needs of the Service and their people first. In any organization, executives assume the role and obligation to set the mission, vision, and values that drive a positive culture, enabling people to succeed.

Executives must master the art of decision-making, which often requires demonstrating the moral courage to accept a reasonable level of risk. They should develop and publish a leadership philosophy, crafted with the hindsight of looking back on years of experience leading at every level. Perhaps most meaningful of all, executives must take personal responsibility for succession management, "returning to port" to groom and bring aboard the next generation of leaders of character who are motivated and ready to step up to replace them one day.

CHAPTER TWELVE

RETURNING TO PORT

*Memories of our lives, of our works and
our deeds will continue in others.*

—Rosa Parks

HIGH ABOVE THE ANTARCTIC Ocean, the helicopter beat its way along the ice edge, following it down the coast to our destination, Shackleton's hut at Cape Royd's, Antarctica. It was January 2018, and I'd made the long trip down to Antarctica to familiarize myself with the logistics required to support the National Science Foundation mission. In my position as the vice admiral leading the Coast Guard's mission support organization, supporting the Antarctic operations fell under my purview.

The skilled National Science Foundation pilot set the helicopter carefully down on the ice near Shackleton's famous hut, and our small travel party scrambled out, tightening our parkas against the biting wind. The hut was preserved precisely as it had been left after serving as the base of operations for the 1907-1909 Nimrod Expedition. That was an early attempt in the race, led by the famous British explorer Ernest Shackleton, to the geographic South Pole. Cans of meat, seal skins, clothing, and bedding remained as they had been left, preserved indefinitely in the frigid, parched polar air.

After exploring the hut, we slipped and slid for a couple hundred yards, following our noses along the ice to a large penguin rookery, where about 1,800 nesting pairs were raising huge chicks, clumsy and downy. The dedicated parents tobogganed relentlessly back and forth from the rookery to the sea, catching fish to feed the insatiable, squabbling young. The constant communication between 1,800 pairs of penguins and their demanding chicks set up a cacophony reminiscent of what you would hear in a reception hall during a huge celebration where everyone was competing to talk over each other.

Weddell seals and a variety of whales made their homes near the rookery, adding to the commotion as they all took advantage of the abundant fishing and feeding supplied by the nutrient-rich Antarctic waters. The chaotic scene overwhelmed our senses with sights, sounds, and smells the like of which we had never experienced.

Earlier in the morning, the helicopter had ferried us from McMurdo Station, the main National Science Foundation station, along the coast to the tiny refueling depot at Marble Point. Manned only during the Antarctic summer, Marble Point was operated by two people who refueled helicopters conducting scientific research in the Dry Valleys and beyond. One of the Coast Guard's missions was to break the ice surrounding Marble Point to provide a channel for ships to refuel the vital supply point.

After visiting Shackleton's hut and the penguin rookery, we loaded back into the helicopter and embarked on what would be, for me, the penultimate experience of the trip. Flying out over the sea, we caught sight of what looked like a small, red blob on the horizon, in stark relief on the gleaming white ice. As the helicopter thumped ever closer, the blob emerged as my very own *Polar Star*, the same ship I'd sailed aboard to Antarctica conducting Operation Deep Freeze '85. Now, a new generation of Coast Guard men and women were participating in Operation Deep Freeze '18, and my job was to support that effort.

What a testimony to the Coast Guard's mission support capability that the same icebreaker I served aboard during my first year in the Coast Guard as an ensign was still in service when I stepped aboard thirty-three years later in my last year as a vice admiral! As I posed for a picture with the ship's captain and crew on the ice in front of *Polar Star*, I thought back to those idyllic days breaking ice in Antarctica. I never dreamed of making it to admiral, but through hard work and perseverance and with the help of forces beyond my control, it happened, nonetheless.

The privilege of being asked to serve at the executive level inspired me to resolve to be worthy of the trust placed in me to lead at the top of the organization. I was proud to ultimately return to Antarctica, where I started my career as an ensign, to help ready the next generation of Coast Guard women and men who would relieve me one day.

CHAPTER THIRTEEN

THE POWER OF GIVING BACK

It is every man's obligation to put back into the world at least the equivalent of what he takes out of it.

—Albert Einstein

ON A BEAUTIFUL SUMMER evening, my husband and I were taking our customary Friday jaunt on the National Mall in the heart of our capitol. The year was 2010, and I served at Coast Guard Headquarters in Washington, DC, as Admiral Allen's executive assistant. At the end of an arduous week, Bob and I enjoyed exploring the sights, sounds, and tastes of the eclectic neighborhoods surrounding Capitol Hill.

I slowly decompressed, gradually allowing myself to relax. We could hear the electric beat of one of the armed forces bands playing a concert on the capitol steps. We admired the graceful elms reaching out their leafy arms to bathe us in cool shadows. We inhaled the tantalizing scent of the food trucks wafting on the breeze, triggering our hunger.

Suddenly, the serenity was shattered when my work phone rudely rang. It jolted me to remember I was on call twenty-four hours a day, seven days a week. Suspecting the worst, I mused, *Darn, right in the middle of a delightful evening out, here comes another work requirement.*

Given the demands of my job, I could seldom expect an undisturbed leisure activity or meal. The unwelcome call came from the commandant all right, but it wasn't what I expected. Instead of tasking, he informed me I'd been selected for flag rank, or admiral. Shocked, I stood rooted to the ground and looked at Bob. He and I both knew our world would soon be changing dramatically.

I felt incredibly honored to have been offered the privilege of serving at the executive level in the Coast Guard and fortunate to have been placed in jobs that prepared me for the responsibility, starting with leading as an ensign on the *Glacier* and *Polar Star*. Yet when the time finally came to step into the new role, it was hard getting used to it.

Even before I was officially promoted, people started treating me differently, and expectations changed. I was still the same person, but instead of offering alternatives and conferring with me to determine the best solution, people looked up to me for direction. Because no formal guide for new flag officers existed and there were few people to ask for advice, you had to learn along the way.

Upon promotion to rear admiral, I put on my first star[xiv] as director of the Coast Guard Reserve Force. On my initial overseas trip, I ventured to the Middle East to visit our reservists who provided security and logistics support services in the Persian Gulf region. Aside from myself, my team was comprised of all men. We drove a big, black sport utility vehicle to conduct unit visits.

One day, our travels took us to a US armed forces installation in Kuwait. Lacking full confidence in executive protocol, I mistakenly sat in the front passenger seat, instead of the appropriate seat in the back behind the front passenger seat. To keep a low profile for security reasons, we did not wear the blouses indicating our rank during transit. As a result, there was no way to determine the senior person in the vehicle, aside from the seating protocol.

When we arrived at the imposing gate to clear security, the guard, keenly aware of the protocol, spoke into his handheld radio informing

---

xiv   A star is the insignia denoting a rear admiral, lower half. It is worn on the collar or hat. A rear admiral, upper half rates two stars, a vice admiral rates three and an admiral rates four.

others on the installation, "The football has arrived." He smartly saluted one of my male subordinates sitting in the back seat where I belonged.

For those not familiar with military-speak, the "football" is the senior executive, who's supposed to be in the right rear seat. At first, I thought the guard may have overlooked me because of my gender, perhaps presuming "the football" was a man. I soon realized that our protocol error was to blame. We proceeded through the checkpoint and broke out in laughter at the mistaken identity error. We joked among ourselves that we had increased my security through our protocol snafu.

The football incident taught me a valuable lesson in what it takes to transition to the executive level. From the moment leaders assume an executive role, they're under a microscope. Every little detail matters—down to where they sit. What worked at the lower levels isn't enough to succeed at the executive level. New executives must prepare to meet the expectations and requirements of their highly visible position. I used my first assignment as a flag officer to grasp expectations and start the mental transition from the tactical to the strategic level.

When halfway through my two-year assignment as director of the Reserve Force the Service issued executive leadership orders, I was told to plan on remaining in my current job and not expect reassignment for another year. Shortly thereafter, I received an unexpected phone call from the vice commandant. Again, I was offered an exciting new opportunity. Something must have changed, because the vice commandant told me I was being reassigned to the Coast Guard Academy, to serve as superintendent, which is equivalent to president of a small college.

The news stunned me. Superintendent of the Coast Guard Academy was the dream job I could never have even imagined. Since the superintendent position is a four-year tour of duty, the chances of the timing working out were slim. I realized my selection for the position was a quirk of fate—or as I would say, part of God's plan—and felt instantly humbled.

Although I had no experience leading in higher education, the Coast Guard had prepared me well for the next level of command. The Coast Guard Academy, like all the armed forces service academies, is a military institution first and foremost, with governance through a chain of command.[xv] Proven leadership ability is the primary qualification for the role of superintendent.

Presiding over an institution of higher education, with its myriad complexities, would require leadership at a new level. To complicate matters, I found myself once again summoned to face the media spotlight, as the first woman to lead an armed forces service academy. Although deeply honored to be recognized and congratulated by so many influential people, including members of Congress and the Administration, I knew the congratulations came with high expectations.

Yet again, all eyes would be on me to watch and see how the first woman would perform. I wouldn't have the luxury of reporting into the Academy and taking the typical ninety days to conduct an assessment on which to base my vision and strategic intent. I needed to arrive well-prepared if I were to succeed.

Hence, I put together a plan. Since each of the other service academies had an experienced superintendent at the helm, I decided to visit them and learn all I could. Within a couple of months, I benchmarked best practices at the Naval Academy, Military Academy, Air Force Academy, and Merchant Marine Academy. I had the unique opportunity to experience life at each of those exceptional institutions from both the cadet/midshipman perspective and the senior leader perspective. My fellow superintendents graciously welcomed me and offered valuable insights.

I was struck by how much the four diverse institutions had in common. The cadets and midshipmen at each academy came from

---

xv   Each branch of the military operates through a chain of command, with orders and task direction passed down from higher up to the lower levels. Likewise, service members at the lower levels make requests and pass reports up the chain of command to their superiors.

the same pool of high-quality young people. The mission at each academy was fundamentally the same: to develop leaders of character in service to the United States. Since each academy executed the mission differently, I learned a lot about what it took to succeed. I leveraged the best of all I saw to develop my vision for taking the Coast Guard Academy to the next level of excellence.

I had a head start in preparing for the new role as superintendent through my duties as a member of the Academy's Board of Trustees. In my role as a trustee, I learned about all the issues facing the Academy and understood the challenges and opportunities. Between the highly valuable benchmarking visits and my experience as a trustee, I developed the makings of a strategic intent before being installed as superintendent.

I knew the audience would be watching closely when I stepped up to give my remarks upon assuming command. To build trust in my ability to lead the organization, I set forth five focus areas that would serve as the foundation for my strategic intent: strengthen partnerships; leverage the Academy's unique value to benefit the Coast Guard, Department of Homeland Security, and beyond; shape and balance the cadet learning experience through the core curriculum review; examine staffing and organizational alignment in a modernized Coast Guard; and build a more diverse officer corps.

Over the ensuing weeks, as I thought about the overarching message implied by those five focus areas, my vision for the Academy emerged. As an institution of higher education, we had a lot to offer the Coast Guard, the Department of Homeland Security, and beyond, but we needed to actively market our value.

One morning while out walking, it struck me. We would strive to become "locally relevant and nationally prominent." Upon arriving at my office, I wrote down the slogan on a piece of paper and simply posted it on the door. I wanted to gauge people's reactions. As it turns out, the vision caught on and was quickly adopted throughout the Academy community.

The slogan served as a positive inspiration to unite the Academy in a shared purpose. Cadet athletes representing the Academy by competing at the national level elevated the institution's prestige, which helped recruiting efforts. Cadets who served in leadership roles building a local Habitat for Humanity house brought the Academy recognition and respect from the local community. Standing up the Center for Arctic Study and Policy showcased the Academy's academic research value to both the Coast Guard and the international community.

In those first weeks, while developing my vision and implementing strategic intent, people asked me, "What does it mean to you to be the first female superintendent?"

I told them, "I'm honored to serve as a role model but do not view being the first female superintendent as a milestone. Rather, it's a natural progression in the Coast Guard's efforts to create a climate of inclusion and a culture of respect that provides each individual an equal opportunity to advance her or his career and contribute to vital Coast Guard missions."

At the executive level, leading with character means continually seeking ways to give back, including shifting focus away from yourself to the organization and its people.

Despite my best efforts to downplay being the first female superintendent, some people couldn't see past my gender. Those with the most deeply entrenched mindsets were the older alumni, some of whom questioned whether a woman was qualified to lead "their academy."

My first homecoming football game as the newly installed superintendent was off to an exciting start. It was a picture-perfect day and, best of all, our Coast Guard Academy Bears were winning! Everyone was having a good time, catching up with friends and family, and enjoying the camaraderie. While standing in the bleachers speaking with some cadets and their families, our team scored a touchdown.

I went down on the bleachers with the cadets to pump out our traditional, celebratory push-ups in the spirit of the touchdown. Rising with a big smile, I looked right into the dour face of an alumnus from the fifty-year class. To put it in perspective, he graduated from the Academy in 1961, when I was one year old.

The gentleman stared at me disdainfully. Defiant, he interrogated me right there in front of all the spectators, saying, "That's a big job you've got. Are you sure you're up for it?"

Shocked, I said, "Yes, it is a big job. I'm honored to have it, and I intend to do my best." I shrugged it off and went about my business.

A few hours later, we gathered for a reception in honor of the fifty-year class in our Alumni Center. The atmosphere was celebratory, as our football team had won by a longshot. Making my way through the crowded room, I spied a respected member of the class whom I knew well. I embraced him and kissed him on the cheek.

Then a voice behind me spoke out, "I want a kiss, too."

Turning around, I was thunderstruck to see the same man who had questioned my competence a few hours earlier. Seizing an opportunity, I embraced him and gave him a peck on the cheek. We exchanged pleasantries, with no mention of the previous incident. Watching his classmates interact with me must have led him to see me more personally, and that changed his perspective.

The incident with my supervisor on the *Katmai Bay* had taught me how to deal with those awkward circumstances of being judged. I chose to reach out my hand to meet people where they were, instead of judging them in turn. Trying to win over the non-believers by getting to know and understand them, rather than resorting to resentment and anger, is the better, more noble way to advance a civil society.

I found that once someone got to know me as a person, not as the nebulous "first female this or that," he or she looked at me differently and with more respect. Was it hard being on the defensive and having to earn respect as such a senior person? Surely it was. I also recognized that being a trailblazer, for better or worse, comes with the obligation to clear obstacles from the trail as you encounter them. Those experiences taught me the value of looking at every new encounter as an opportunity to earn the respect of the people around me. As a result, I tried harder to understand and relate to people—to meet them where they are—and I'm a better leader for it.

During my four years leading the Coast Guard Academy, I learned the importance of developing a vision and setting forth a strategic intent to focus a diverse workforce. Without a vision of a shared purpose, different people and groups will naturally develop different—often competing—priorities and goals. At the Academy, constant tension existed between the three main departments: athletics, academics, and professional development. With so many requirements for cadets to meet, there was never enough time in a day. It took dedication for the senior leadership team to balance those requirements constructively. They needed to pull together and focus on the core mission, vision, and strategic imperatives to which we all subscribed.

This meant paying attention to the bigger picture, including initiatives not falling within the purview of any one division or department. Physical security, although a vital function, didn't reside within the purview of the three primary domains. Hence, it had no senior champion below the superintendent's level.

During my visits to other colleges, universities, and service academies, I noticed the dorms or barracks all had external door locks, mostly in the form of key card access. In comparison, the Academy's aging cadet barracks, housing approximately 1,000 students, were wide open day and night. With about fifty entrances, it would be daunting and expensive to outfit the old building with modern locks. But it had to be done.

My desire to implement physical security measures was met with skepticism by division leaders whose resources were already heavily strained. I strived to help people look past the temporary difficulties to envision the future benefits. Unequivocally, my top priority was the safety and security of the cadets for whom I was absolutely responsible. An executive does not delegate that responsibility; it comes with the privilege of command.

When welcoming a new class of incoming cadets and their parents, I would tell the parents, although I had no children of my own, I considered myself the mother of 1,000 young students entrusted to my care. Instantly, the parents relaxed and felt more trustful based on my demonstrated, personal commitment to their sons and daughters. Afterward, I always felt as if there was a covenant between the parents and me, and I meant to honor it.

Regarding the cadet barracks, it was incumbent on me to present my vision to senior leadership and demonstrate the importance of cadet safety and security to our mission. We forged ahead, forming a cross-functional team to lead the effort. It was disruptive and took a couple of years to implement, but we completed the project.

Today, it's hard to imagine a campus lacking basic physical security measures to protect students in their dorms or cadets in their barracks. Senior executives must look across the entire enterprise, as only they can, to determine the top institutional priorities. Those priorities must then be tied to strategic intent and implemented by making the tough, but necessary, trade-off decisions on where to best invest scarce resources.

At the tactical level, every single day of my tenure as superintendent involved extreme preparation for the daily spotlight. From shining shoes and pressing shirts to preparing appropriate remarks for my many engagements, being ready in all the seemingly small ways was essential. The small things are what most people at the Academy saw day after day, and how I presented myself defined my reputation internally.

Moving to the strategic level, my job also required preparation for significant external events with greater overall reach and impact beyond the Academy. Such activities included major keynotes, media interviews, and representing the institution and the Coast Guard at local and international venues. Those external engagements reflected on the Academy and often the entire Coast Guard, requiring my full attention to adequately prepare.

An executive must master the art of prioritizing where to invest that most precious resource—time. As I prepared for my role at the Coast Guard Academy, Vice Admiral Mike Miller at the Naval Academy shared some valuable insights on time management. He sagely advised me, "Do only what only the superintendent can do."

I lived by those wise words, making every effort to delegate certain recognition ceremonies and local speaking engagements down to the appropriate levels. Further empowering my senior leaders not only eased my burden, it gave them more ownership of and satisfaction in leading their departments and divisions.

One evening, when I was in the final year of my four-year tour as superintendent, Bob and I were hosting a small reception at our quarters. We had the rare privilege of hosting the commandant Admiral Zukunft, who had traveled up to visit the Academy. There came a time when the commandant and I found ourselves alone in the library. In the middle of a conversation about books and cadets, he abruptly asked me a question that again changed my life. "Would you like to come to Coast Guard Headquarters to serve as my deputy commandant for mission support?"[xvi]

As with the previous phone calls from the commandant and vice commandant offering me exceptional executive leadership opportunities, I was temporarily caught off guard. The position was a step up from rear admiral to vice admiral. It offered the chance to continue giving back, helping move the organization forward. I was surprised, because normally, the next step for an academy superintendent is retirement.

---

xvi The deputy commandant for mission support is the vice admiral who leads the approximately one-half of the Coast Guard dedicated to supporting the Service's missions and people. Functions include personnel and pay, medical, training and education, force readiness, engineering and logistics, information technology, acquisition and procurement, contracting, and security.

It had been thirty years since a superintendent was retained on active duty, so I wasn't expecting to be asked to continue in service at the next level. I stared at the commandant in disbelief before finding words to stammer an answer in the affirmative.

In the following years, we both laughed recollecting that encounter. I'd unintentionally given him the impression of hesitating about taking a new job, with the accompanying promotion. I was, in fact, thrilled with the opportunity to apply my leadership at the next level, supporting Coast Guard missions and people.

CHAPTER FOURTEEN

DEVELOPING A VISION AND STRATEGIC INTENT

Strategy without tactics is the slowest route to victory.
Tactics without strategy is the noise before defeat.

—Sun Tzu

AT THE EXECUTIVE LEVEL, A leader's most immediate priority should be developing a vision and implementing a strategic intent to guide the workforce and move the organization forward. Here are the steps to set forth and achieve your goals and objectives:

Achieving Executive Goals and Objectives
- Promulgate a vision
- Manage change
- Create an innovation culture

Promulgate a Vision

Engaged leaders of character spend years preparing to lead at the executive level, intentionally looking beyond the tactical to the longer view. Upon assuming duties as commandant of the Coast Guard, Admiral Thad Allen set forth a powerful vision for the Service. Throughout his career, Admiral Allen had commanded many operational units, both afloat and ashore, and exuded command presence. At his best when confronting a crisis, he recognized and seized an opportunity in the face of every challenge.

A naturally insightful leader, Admiral Allen had looked to the future to assess prospective threats and opportunities for decades as he rose through the ranks of Coast Guard leadership. He was passionate about mentoring junior people who would replace him someday and encouraged them to look with a discerning eye for areas that needed improvement. He recounted how he had spent years "packing his seabag,[xvii*]" filling it with things to fix as he moved up to the next levels in the Coast Guard. As commandant, he set about unpacking that seabag to improve the Service.

Admiral Allen immediately stood up a strategic transformation team led by a flag officer. He published ten commandant intent action orders directing implementation of his vision for sweeping change. The effort was named Coast Guard Modernization.[xviii] It would entail the largest organizational change in modern Coast Guard history.

Leaving tactical matters to others, Admiral Allen focused his attention on the bigger picture, championing the Coast Guard's early long-range strategic planning efforts. In the late 1990s, he spearheaded the Coast Guard's Project Long View, which morphed into Project Evergreen in the early 2000s. Long View was an over-the-horizon, strategic planning initiative designed to create and sustain strategic intent in the Coast Guard.[29]

Long View projected a range of potential scenarios designed to anticipate the Coast Guard's future operating environment. From

---

xvii   In the sea services—the Coast Guard, Marines, and Navy—a seabag is a canvas bag, like a nautical suitcase, that members use to pack their belongings when traveling to and from a ship. It has an elongated shape designed to fit down a ship's scuttle, which is a round, watertight fitting separating the decks on a ship.
xviii*   Admiral Allen's organizational change effort was named "modernization." Unlike modernization in the Department of Defense, which means recapitalization of ships and aircraft, Coast Guard modernization transformed the entire Service. Modernization delivered an entirely new organizational construct that was designed to improve both mission support and mission execution. It was the biggest organizational change in modern Coast Guard history.

there, the exercise engaged diverse teams to analyze each scenario. The teams were directed to imagine new ways of doing business, new products, or new mission areas to best position the Coast Guard to address future challenges and take advantage of opportunities.

While assigned to the cutter *Confidence*, I received an invitation to travel to Washington, DC, to serve as a member of the inaugural Long View strategic team. I was surprised, honored, and eager to see what the project involved. As one of the more junior participants, I distinctly remember how much my perspective differed from the majority of the members who were older, predominantly white, male executives.

Only two women, both of us relatively junior, participated in the entire group of what must have been between thirty-five and forty people. At the end of a session, the other woman showed the courage to stand up and speak out, but one of the flag officers brushed her off. He seemed to dismiss her ideas as naïve and too far out of the mainstream. I thought she was spot-on and was disappointed to learn some of the senior executives were so set in their world views. Serving on the Long View team helped me understand the value of diverse perspectives and shaped the more strategic outlook I would need as a flag officer.

Long View and the subsequent Evergreen process proved to be a valuable framework for a service whose motto is *Semper Paratus*. Given its legacy response culture, the Coast Guard needed Long View to force it to embrace the strategic perspective necessary to develop relevant programs. For instance, Long View is responsible for the Coast Guard's implementation of crucial maritime domain awareness initiatives, which help keep our nation safe and secure against all threats and hazards.

Long View's strategic scenario development also added value by highlighting the emerging relevance of the polar regions. Drawing on that analysis, the Service developed an enterprise-level Arctic strategy, established a Center for Arctic Study and Policy at the Coast Guard Academy, and initiated a major acquisition program to build new polar security cutters.

Despite the enduring value of the Evergreen process, the Coast Guard didn't have a repeatable method to fully institutionalize it as an essential part of the overarching strategic planning, programming, and budgeting process. To remedy the shortcoming, Admiral Allen directed me to establish a new office of Enterprise Strategic Management. The new office, reporting directly to the vice commandant, elevated Evergreen to the enterprise level.

Although the new organizational construct added value from inception, it did not, unfortunately, survive the next leadership transition. Nonetheless, Evergreen remained a valuable link in the planning, programming, and budgeting chain. Connecting long-term strategic planning back to the immediate programming and budgeting process should be an objective for every organization. Executives are responsible for scanning the horizon for threats and opportunities, adjusting course as necessary, and developing a strategic intent to best position the organization.

In developing his strategic intent for the organization, Admiral Allen not only looked to the future, he learned from the past. Throughout his career, he recognized several significant inflection points, each of which drove the need for organizational change. Among them were the Magnuson-Stevens Fisheries Conservation and Management Act of 1976 (implemented to manage declining US fish stocks) and the Oil Pollution Act of 1990 (implemented as a result of the Exxon Valdez oil spill in 1989), both of which significantly increased the Coast Guard's regulatory functions.

A steep rise in migrant and contraband smuggling during the 1990s intensified and expanded the Coast Guard's law enforcement functions. Inclusion of the Coast Guard as a member of the national intelligence community in 2001 required a new organizational construct.

The events of 9-11, with the Coast Guard's subsequent transition from the Department of Transportation to the Department of Homeland Security, required integration with an entirely new set of interagency partners. Hurricane Katrina in 2005 highlighted the need for unity of effort and influential on-scene command.

Deployment of Coast Guard forces to the Middle East in support of Department of Defense missions elevated the Service's national defense mission. Emergence of the Arctic as an operational domain required adapting operations and support to a more hostile operating environment. Most recently, threats in cyberspace spurred the Coast Guard to stand up a cyber command and to establish a cyber workforce.

All those inflection points called for more Coast Guard. They required the Service to deliver more interagency engagement; more interoperability; expanded local, national, and global presence; more capable ships, planes, and boats; and modernized mission support systems and processes, including Information Technology infrastructure. Most of all, they required better-trained, specialized people to support the new requirements and meet new expectations.

Emerging demands triggered the Coast Guard to rapidly mature and transform from a small, coastal maritime service to a much larger, more capable organization with global reach. There came a tipping point when the Service couldn't continue doing business the same way if it were to remain relevant and fully capable of executing its many statutory missions.

Unfortunately, very few people recognized the tipping point. Most leaders, even top executives, failed to embrace the need for change. Admiral Allen not only recognized the tipping point but understood the urgency of taking prompt action so the Coast Guard could address the issues on its own terms to achieve a better outcome. He warned, if the Service dragged its feet, "someone else outside the organization will dictate terms to us."

To the benefit of the Coast Guard and the nation, Admiral Allen boldly seized the initiative and developed a comprehensive plan to modernize the organization to meet the needs of a new era. But even as Service chief, he met with significant resistance. His sweeping modernization effort required significant change that would initially result in disruption and uncertainty. That change needed to be properly managed from the start.

Manage Change

Making the transition from the tactical to the strategic means being prepared to imagine necessary changes, as did Admiral Allen. Developing a vision is the first step and the easier part. The hard part comes in the next steps of seeking buy-in from the senior leadership team, preparing the organization for the change, then implementing the change and seeing it through until fully institutionalized.

Admiral Allen believed in me and offered me the opportunity to serve as his executive assistant to help drive organizational change during the modernization effort. Trust me, it was harder than hard. Even when change is indisputably for the better, naysayers abound. Some will try, either actively or passively, to undermine the change effort. From my experience, the leader who demonstrates the moral courage to propose needed change had better "stand by for heavy rolls" of resistance, as we would say in the maritime services.

Many factors contribute to an organizational culture of resistance. Most notable are the institutional mindsets of those who desire to maintain the status quo. They may question, "If everything is working fine, why change?"

I call this the stewardship mentality. Leading with character means embracing change and stepping out boldly to help move the organization forward.

Another contributing factor is the "silo mentality" that characterizes many organizations. If an organization's functional areas aren't connected but operate as independent silos, people within each functional area will likely see only the value they deliver. They may be unable or unwilling to accept their functional area as but one part, and perhaps not the most important part, of the bigger organizational construct. As a result, change to their functional area may be perceived as a threat to their place, power, or scope of responsibility within the organization.

Creating an organizational construct requiring cross-functional interaction can alleviate some of the friction and advance change. Such a construct was at the heart of Admiral Allen's modernization effort. Before that, the organization's functions (operations, engineering, acquisition, marine safety, etc.) resided within competitive silos, each led by a rear admiral. Those senior executives each operated in the interest of their organization, bringing problems and conflicts up to the chief of staff,[xix] a vice admiral, for resolution. There was great incentive to *compete*, but little incentive to *collaborate* or *compromise*.

Modernization created four interactive peer entities, known as the "big four." Each was led by a vice admiral, all reporting up to the vice commandant. The deputy commandant for mission support, deputy commandant for operations, Atlantic area commander, and Pacific area commander were supported by a governance structure requiring integration at every level across their organizations. The "big four" worked through issues, resolved conflicts, and tabled solutions up to the vice commandant and, as necessary, to the commandant. In the modernized Coast Guard, collaboration and cooperation were baked into the organizational construct, resulting in more transparency and ownership of decisions.

Despite the promise of a better system, Admiral Allen's modernization effort met with considerable resistance. The only sure way to overcome resistance to change is through trust. Building trust in the change is hard on the front end when evidence does not yet exist to validate the new organizational constructs and processes. The workforce must have trust in both the leader implementing the change and in the change itself.

At the same time the Coast Guard was rolling out its modernization plan, Amazon launched a major modernization effort. Both organizations would have to change and manage the associated risks. There are notable differences in the change management process for a government organization compared to a private sector company. These differences illustrate the challenges the Coast Guard faced.

---

xix   The chief of staff was a vice admiral and the third-senior officer in Coast Guard Headquarters. The position fell below the commandant and vice commandant and coordinated efforts between functional areas.

Speculation swirled when Amazon expanded almost overnight from selling books to offering merchandise online in competition with traditional retail stores. At first, many people couldn't imagine ordering an item online from home when they could be participating in that great American past time—an outing to the shopping mall.

Amazon knew it had to build customer trust quickly by demonstrating the advantages of shopping online. The company invested in technology and focused on customer service, vastly improving consumer access and the overall shopping experience for many people. People soon started to trust the new way of shopping.

Like Amazon, the Coast Guard had to build trust in its modernization effort upfront. Unlike Amazon, the Service lacked the resources to build trust quickly. Without the necessary information technology systems and personnel, the process would be slower and require much effort before the benefits could be realized.

Therefore, Admiral Allen had to rely on the trust he had built over the years through his personal and professional power. In managing the response to crisis incidents such as the terrorist attacks of 9-11 and Hurricane Katrina, Admiral Allen led with character to unify local, state, and federal responders in service to devastated communities. He built trust both outside the Coast Guard and with the Coast Guard workforce. The modernization effort moved forward, in large part, because people trusted Admiral Allen.

Since his term as commandant was limited to four years, Admiral Allen had to move forward as quickly as possible. He needed the full support of the workforce. He and Master Chief Petty Officer of the Coast Guard Skip Bowen traveled around the Coast Guard, conducting outreach sessions to explain modernization and the need for change. Junior personnel were generally receptive and understood the necessity to adapt systems and processes to a changing world.

Senior leadership was the most influential cohort and the toughest to persuade. If they didn't support modernization, their subordinates were unlikely to do so. Unfortunately, it was the senior leaders who presented the most significant impediments to success. Although many outwardly supported modernization, some saw the change as a threat or simply didn't see the need for change. Some were skeptical, questioning what could be wrong with a system in which they had risen to the top.

The naysayers couldn't see past the tactical to the strategic imperative to change. Using a ship's radar plot as an analogy, they were "stuck in relative plot." Radar is the equipment used to detect other ships or aircraft. It can be operated in either relative or true plot. In relative plot, a ship is positioned at the center, with other vessels or aircraft in a relative display around it. In other words, everything revolves around the ship at the center. This is a useful perspective for determining how other ships or aircraft in the area are moving in comparison. For instance, relative plot is used to evaluate the risk of collision or a ship's place in a formation.

In true plot, a ship is positioned in actual relation to the other vessels or aircraft within the scope of the radar's antenna. In other words, a ship appears as one of many moving on their respective courses. The plot shows the bigger picture of what's happening and how the ship fits as part of that picture.

Senior leaders entrenched in a tactical mindset, or stuck in relative plot, posed a threat to the Coast Guard's modernization effort. They couldn't see beyond themselves at center with the world rotating around them and had grown overly comfortable remaining in place. Leading with character means demonstrating the self-awareness to switch over to true plot, putting the organization and its people at the center.

Executives must look past performance alone to put the right person in the right job at the right time. They should select trusted change agents who can pull together productive teams to lead the implementation. Such people need to be among the organization's very best—strong leaders who are fully empowered to lean forward and make the tough decisions needed to effect the change. Experiential and cognitive diversity factors should be considered to optimize the teams. There may be some team leads who need to have a high emotional intelligence quotient, while others need to be more assertive and directive.

One of the most controversial decisions Admiral Allen made in the early days of his modernization effort was installing a senior Coast Guard aviator to lead the Surface Forces Logistics Center in Baltimore, Maryland. That was anathema to the afloat community! The Surface Forces Logistics Center supported cutters and boats, not aircraft. The precursor organization had always been led by a senior member of the afloat community.

An aviator, Rear Admiral (then-Captain) Mark Butt was selected to lead modernization at the Surface Forces Logistics Center. Years earlier, the aviation community had successfully modernized its logistics service delivery at the Aviation Logistics Center in Elizabeth City, North Carolina. Aviators understood the business model. Rear Admiral Butt had been instrumental in implementing aviation logistics management programs and processes.

He was the right leader at the right time and place, presenting himself in a professional, no-nonsense manner, with zero tolerance for excuses or shoddy analysis. Rear Admiral Butt had a brilliant mind, and it was in his blood to challenge assumptions. He framed problems differently than most people, leading to broader, informed discussions and better decisions. He operated in true plot, keenly visualizing how every piece fit together in the bigger picture and possessing a unique ability to anticipate the long-term benefits beyond the short-term limitations.

The afloat community was up in arms at the decision to assign an aviator, but Admiral Allen remained resolute. He recognized the right leader for the job wasn't someone who knew cutters and boats; it had to be someone who knew the business processes necessary to modernize service delivery, be it to support aircraft, or cutters and boats. Looking back, the decision was ingenious.

Rear Admiral Butt took bold, necessary actions an insider in the afloat community wouldn't likely have embraced. Thousands of parts that had been carried in each cutter's hold were removed and transferred to a warehouse at the Surface Forces Logistics Center, where they could be issued as the need arose. Thus, the Surface Forces Logistics Center effectively, and far more efficiently, supported an entire fleet from a centralized inventory control point. At first, many cutter commanding officers railed against losing control of those parts, believing the change threatened their command authority and ability to execute their missions.

Although it took time to build trust, the new system reduced costs and improved service delivery. This experience demonstrated to me that senior executives will fail or succeed based on the people they select to lead in the foremost positions driving organizational change.

Create an Innovation Culture

It takes moral courage to lead at the executive level, to set a bold vision and then take the risks associated with implementing the vision. Understanding change management is necessary, as is cultivating a culture receptive to change. Such a culture starts with a workplace that encourages and rewards innovation and ideas originating from the lowest levels of the organization.

When Admiral Allen's modernization effort got started, the Coast Guard didn't have the benefit of a change-centric, progressive innovation culture. To address the shortcoming, he reinvigorated the Service's innovation program. Having been formally established in 2000, the program needed an injection of positive energy and momentum. Hence, a small innovation office was identified, resourced, and provided strategic guidance and advocacy through an Innovation Council comprised of mid- and senior-level leaders.

The innovation program, still in place today, contains both top-down and bottom-up avenues to ensure a robust exchange of ideas. At the heart of the program are the Captain Niels P. Thomsen innovation awards, designed to encourage innovation and recognize those who presented ideas for Service-wide improvements.

The awards are named after the Coast Guard innovator who invented the buoy chain stopper, a device that dramatically improved the safety of buoy-tending operations. Each year, awards in several categories are presented in front of the Coast Guard senior executive corps. The Coast Guard's innovation program continues to mature, most prominently with a crowdsourcing tool enabling prospective innovators to share and discuss ideas online.

Even if leadership makes innovation a priority, infusing it throughout an organization's culture is hard. No matter how well-designed or advocated for at the top of an organization, unless it's supported by mid-level leaders, an innovation program is unlikely to succeed.

Often, mid-level leaders don't take the time to entertain and evaluate subordinates' new ideas. They're focused on and consumed by the work at hand and have limited resources to apply beyond that. There can also be a cultural misperception that newer or more junior people have less knowledge and experience and, therefore, don't have ideas worth considering.

To achieve their strategic intent in a more competitive and complex world, executives must be able to harness the value of every member of the workforce, from the entry-level to the senior leaders. Given the right encouragement and incentives, people should have the opportunity to make their organization better.

When I was in command of the cutter *Reliance*, I learned a lot about my crew by sitting down with each new report, from the senior-most to the junior-most, for a "welcome aboard" interview. The knowledge, skills, and abilities brought by the Coast Guard's newest recruits always impressed me. Some had served as community firemen before enlisting and already understood more about damage control than most of the ship's engineers. Others had taught and arrived with a sage understanding of how to train and develop a workforce. Remarkably, some had earned bachelor's or even master's degrees. Those newest members could contribute substantially to improving the ship—if only their supervisors would let them.

Creating an innovation culture takes persistent effort and dedicated support at the executive level. To succeed, organizations must break down barriers to harness the full value and power of their diverse workforce, particularly the most junior members. They must encourage and incentivize innovation by members through both formal and informal recognition programs. Perhaps most important of all, they must be willing to accept reasonable risks associated with developing and implementing new solutions.

Making the transition to the executive suite is challenging. Executives must will themselves to move beyond the tactical performance within their functional area that worked well for them at the lower levels. To succeed at the executive level, a leader must imagine a better future for the organization and its people, implement strategic intent to drive toward that vision, build and inspire the teams that will lead the necessary change, and remove obstacles. Even with all that effort, success is elusive. The executive must encourage and reward innovation, as did Admiral Allen, energizing the organization to improve, advance, and grow.

CHAPTER FIFTEEN

THE ART OF DECISION-MAKING

*In any moment of decision, the best thing you can do is the
right thing, the next best thing you can do is the wrong thing,
and the worst thing you can do is nothing.*

—Theodore Roosevelt

ADAPTIVE, FLEXIBLE ORGANIZATIONS CREATE cultures
that empower their members and encourage decision-making at
the appropriate levels. They prepare and train their people to act
when needed without having to wait for permission—to seize an
opportunity or manage a crisis.

Senior executives should motivate subordinates to take calculated
risks and reward them when they do so. Likewise, leaders should seize
the initiative to make timely decisions. In the Coast Guard, decisions
are pushed down to the lowest, most reasonable level. People are
empowered, for example, to take immediate action to save lives,
enforce laws, or solve a problem.

Respect for autonomy has been part of the Coast Guard's long-
standing culture from the time of its inception as the Revenue
Cutter Service in 1790. Then, as now, cutter commanding officers
were empowered to represent and serve the fledgling United States
government by conducting independent enforcement operations at
sea. In 1915, the present-day Coast Guard was formed by consolidating
maritime agencies, including the Revenue Cutter Service, the Life

Saving Service, and the Lighthouse Service. The result was a diverse set of authorities reflecting the bias for immediate response action that characterized the founding agencies.

The Coast Guard's motto, *Semper Paratus*, couldn't be more fitting. Today, the Coast Guard is one of the only federal agencies with the authority to immediately respond to an incident or disaster in any one of the United States or its territories. Those authorities allowed the Coast Guard to begin rescuing thousands of stranded people during two significant domestic natural disasters: Hurricane Katrina in 2005 and Hurricane Harvey in 2017. Local Coast Guard leaders didn't have to wait to request permission from up the chain of command or for an invitation from a governor. They were authorized to act immediately using what's called "on-scene initiative."

The pages of Coast Guard history books are replete with amazing feats performed by junior personnel empowered to make consequential life and death decisions. One of the most remarkable is the heroic rescue memorialized in the 2016 Disney film *The Finest Hours*. The film recounts the rescue of thirty-two crew members from the SS *Pendleton*, a merchant ship that broke up off the coast of Massachusetts on February 18th, 1952, during a devastating nor'easter.

Boatswain's Mate Petty Officer First Class Bernie Webber, a true Coast Guard hero, was the boat coxswain on watch that fateful night at Coast Guard Station Chatham. Upon receiving the distress call, he didn't hesitate. He made the monumental decision to strike out into the teeth of the storm, crossing the deadly bar[xx] to face the raging sea. Battling fifty-foot waves in his thirty-six-foot motor lifeboat, he and his crew of three defied the odds of capsizing and safely navigated to the distressed vessel.

Although the *Pendleton* had broken in two, Petty Officer Webber managed to maneuver close enough in the heavy seas to rescue

---

xx A bar is a sandy shoal at the entrance to a harbor. It is normally located between two jetties that make up a narrow entry point that causes incoming waves to build up to dangerous heights, particularly when the seas are already storm-driven.

thirty-two crewmen off the stern section of the sinking ship. As the men scrambled down the Jacob's ladder[xxi] of the ship, Petty Officer Webber had to reposition his boat to safely embark them in the heaving seas. With the exhausted men on board, Petty Officer Webber turned through the seas and miraculously made it safely back to Chatham Harbor.

A Coast Guard cutter offers another superb example of empowerment. Cutter commanding officers must empower their crews while at the same time managing risk. To do so, they issue clear guidance in the form of standing orders and navigation standards, and they promulgate a command philosophy. Commanding officers supplement those enduring directives with daily and/or nightly orders, which govern expectations while the officers aren't immediately available. In the Coast Guard, we have a saying, "In an emergency, you act as you have trained." Disciplined training prepares a crew to react instinctively during situations requiring immediate action, even in the absence of their commanding officer.

The cutter *Reliance* had returned to homeport at the Portsmouth Naval Shipyard in Kittery, Maine, following a six-week patrol. Another ship was in our normal berth, and we had been assigned a different one further down along the granite quay wall. It lacked the robust fender system that normally cushioned us. We put over the ship's fenders and mooring lines, securing *Reliance* to the quay wall; all appeared to be well.

When the work was finished, most of the crew eagerly headed home to their families, including the senior leadership. A small duty section of watchstanders remained on board. Not long after everyone had departed, the watchstanders noticed something highly unusual. The ship had started to list, or lean, over to one side. A strong ebb current flowed out of the deep river where *Reliance* was moored. The water rushed past, rapidly lowering the water level of the river, which has a substantial tidal range of about ten feet.

---

xxi A Jacob's ladder is a convenient rope ladder hung over the side of a ship so people can climb aboard from or disembark to a small boat.

The receding water left the ship hanging precariously by its stabilizing fin on a previously unknown underwater ledge jutting out from the rugged granite-block quay wall. Such a situation had never happened at the previous berth, and the watchstanders were concerned that *Reliance*, displacing well over 1,000 tons, could fall off the granite ledge and snap back, slamming the quay wall. The resultant impact could cause underwater damage and possibly lead to the ship's sinking in thirty feet of water.

By then, I'd already left the ship and was unavailable to consult. The watchstanders unhesitatingly took decisive action to protect the ship; they lit off the engine plant, secured the ship's hatches and scuttles, and notified the appropriate authorities.

The watchstanders contacted me soon after and briefed me on the situation. I drove back to the ship and commended them for taking immediate action and making decisions as trained. Fortunately, the situation resolved on its own when the incoming tide refloated *Reliance* without mishap. The shipyard, having learned their lesson on the danger of an inadequate fender system the hard way, took immediate action to remedy the problem. The lesson I learned that night was the value of training, then trusting, the crew to perform well in my absence during an unforeseen emergency.

Impediments to Decision-Making

Decision-making is at the heart of leadership and comes with a huge level of responsibility. Along with the privilege of command comes the burden of command—making what can be life and death decisions. Framing command in this manner—a balance between privilege and burden—can help you maintain the humility required to lead with character.

In a well-led organization, easy decisions are made by empowered subordinates below the executive level. Only high-consequence decisions requiring tough, trade-off determinations should make it to the executive's desk. Executives must take decisive action to manage risk, often without all the information they would like to have.

Decision-assistance tools are readily available, but there is no panacea. Although they can provide information and insight to help inform executive decisions, no technical application or generic management tool can adequately substitute for thoughtful, executive decision-making. Executives must step up to master the art of decision-making, or their people and their organization will suffer. I have observed executives fall into the following decision-making traps that demoralize their people and weaken their organization:

Impediments to Decision-Making
- Paralysis by analysis syndrome
- Consensus conundrum
- Being nice illusion

Paralysis by Analysis Syndrome

Every subordinate yearns to follow a leader who acts decisively when circumstances dictate. Instead, leaders often disappoint by hesitating to make a decision, stalling in the hope of one more piece of information. They fall victim to the "paralysis by analysis" syndrome, setting aside the tough decisions. Their indecision often leads to deterioration of trust, missed opportunities for the organization, and frustration for its members.

Leaders should expect the best, most relevant information their staff can provide. They must also realize and accept there will be times when the available information might not seem like enough. That's particularly true in complex situations or crises. Sometimes, the most urgent decisions must be made with the scantiest information.

I recall speaking with a colleague who had been deployed to the Gulf Coast to assist with messaging on the federal response to a damaging hurricane. His responsibilities included preparing a Coast

Guard flag officer in a significant leadership position to brief officials and the media on the status of the collective response efforts. People wanted and needed a status report, answers, and assurance.

My colleague described, with much frustration, his failed attempt to persuade the flag officer to make confident, decisive statements. With the situation constantly evolving, the flag officer deferred, waiting for one more piece of information he hoped would come at any minute. Meanwhile, people on the scene were losing patience with, and confidence in, the Coast Guard.

Always quick with a story or anecdote, my colleague attributed the flag officer's hesitation to make a command decision to his background in maritime pollution response. Often, the immediate response to an oil spill is to contain it with a long, floating barrier called a boom. After a spill is boomed off and thereby contained, responders have time to deliberate the best cleanup method. My colleague likened the flag officer's indecision to figuratively "putting a boom around it" to contain the problem until a more complete picture emerged. Unfortunately, the flag officer's indecision jeopardized trust in both the Coast Guard and the entire interagency response effort.

Early in my career, I came across a quote by George Patton. "A good plan violently executed today is better than a perfect plan executed next week." Those wise words forever served as my decision-making guide. Leading with character means analyzing the risks and taking responsibility to make the tough decisions, even if doing so means facing criticism. Leaders must believe in themselves and their people and trust their instincts. While there are seldom any perfect decisions, there are many necessary decisions, and the sound decision made today is always superior to one that's deferred until it's too late.

Consensus Conundrum

Some executives defer decisions to avoid conflict when stakeholders disagree. That can result in the "consensus conundrum." To avert this pitfall, executives should subscribe to what I call "the rule of three Cs." Be wise with *cooperation* and *collaboration* but be wary of *consensus*. Savvy leaders understand the value of leveraging cooperation and collaboration to facilitate problem-solving and decision-making. They also understand—and avoid—the risk of trying to achieve consensus.

Tough decisions pushed up to the executive level seldom enjoy consensus. If people all agreed, the decision would have been made at a lower level. Instead, a truly diverse team advising a senior executive should display a healthy difference in perspectives. Not everyone will agree, which should be considered a strength, not a weakness. A robust selection of ideas and options will better inform the decision-maker.

Coast Guard executive leadership has evolved from a competitive to a more cooperative and collaborative culture. Going back to Aristotle's golden mean, there must be a healthy balance between the extremes of competition and consensus. In a resource-constrained environment, programs should be collaboratively evaluated and funding adjusted according to the organization's needs.

During my years as an executive leading the Coast Guard's mission support organization, I witnessed the adverse effects of the consensus conundrum. The Service was experiencing annual budget reductions as the administration and Congress advanced their top priorities. Each year, the Coast Guard addressed the problem by cutting every program equally, regardless of its significance or status.

The Evergreen strategic planning framework would have served a useful purpose to adjudicate between programs, but the Coast Guard never fully institutionalized it. Instead, program managers competed for the limited resources, and who could blame them? The Coast Guard's performance evaluation system rewards those who obtain more funding for their programs, not those who collaborate and make the hard decisions to cut, even if it means their program gets reduced. The recurring, across-the-board cuts weakened many crucial programs, causing organizational stress and performance degradation across the entire organization.

Decision-makers seeking consensus failed to make the tough, trade-off decisions needed to evaluate competing programs. Some, like cutter, boat, and aircraft operations, can be cut by reducing deployment hours, then resuming operations if funding is restored. If, on the other hand, training funding is cut, the center continues to operate but at a reduced level inadequate to support required training for ongoing operations and maintenance. Since every program was cut, with support programs taking the biggest cuts, the consensus conundrum resulted in decreased readiness directly impacting mission execution.

Over the years, the Coast Guard resigned itself to "doing more with less" in the face of persistent funding shortfalls. In keeping with its response culture, devoted Coast Guard professionals would not let mission performance suffer. Instead, they worked themselves to exhaustion. The Service's former commandant Admiral Paul Zukunft stepped up to address the problem head-on during his four-year tenure from 2014-2018.

Admiral Zukunft made it a top priority to change the self-defeating "doing more with less" mentality to an inspirational "doing more with more" outlook. He made the bold decision to discriminate between programs by prioritizing them based on Service need. He then took his arguments for increased funding for the Service's top priorities up to Coast Guard overseers in the administration and Congress. Under Admiral Zukunft's leadership, support for Coast Guard programs and funding increased, as did the morale of the workforce.

Leading with character means finding and accepting the golden mean between competition and consensus. It means making the right decisions for the organization and its people and managing expectations of those who might feel offended. I recall a memorable talk offering a lasting lesson in this regard from Mrs. Grace Nelson, wife of Senator Bill Nelson. The Coast Guard had invited her to address a semi-annual senior executive conference I attended. Her heartfelt talk centered on the individual's responsibility to improve civil discourse in our democratic process. Her message resonated in an agenda filled with briefings on tough and divisive topics like the budget and politics.

Inevitably, there will be times when people don't agree with what someone else says or does, but they can choose how to react. Too often, people take offense at the slightest provocation instead of trying to understand the other person or the bigger picture. Mrs. Nelson sagely advised the audience to "choose to live unoffended." I found her words simply elegant and relevant to the complication of dealing with people whose programs suffered cuts following the making of tough decisions. I posted her quote near my desk to serve as a daily reminder to lead with character by choosing to react with dignity in the face of adversity.

Being Nice Illusion

Some executives mistakenly equate leading to cheerleading, especially if that style worked for them as they moved up in an organization. They believe if they're nice and well-liked, people will perform and behave well for them. But the opposite is often true. Leaders must anticipate there will be somebody, somewhere in the organization, ready to take advantage of the situation if they create a vacuum by not actively engaging. I have walked into new jobs where my first task was to improve a workplace climate that had degenerated because a supervisor failed to hold employees accountable for bad behavior or substandard performance.

In certain situations, cheerleading can be constructive. An executive position requiring daily collaboration with interagency partners might benefit from a leader whose role is to encourage and support cross-functional efforts. On the other hand, an executive position comprised of diverse cohorts with competing interests and motivations might need a decisive, firm hand at the helm to actively manage distractions and keep the organization focused on its mission. High-performing organizations recognize that different positions require leaders with different personalities and perspectives, and they assign the person with the right acumen for the job at hand.

As leaders explore ways to connect with their workforce, they may see being nice as a virtue. Nowhere in a leader's job description is there a requirement to be nice. Leaders who prioritize being nice may end up achieving their goal of being liked, but they may not be respected or effective. The demands of executive-level decision-making don't allow a leader to be universally nice. Leaders are expected to be respectful, fair, and decisive. They are expected to take care of their people and, equally as important, to hold them accountable. They must achieve good outcomes and meet the organization's mission. When executives make tough trade-offs between programs and people, those decisions can create conflict.

Intuitive leaders of character know how to engage with all employees, from the junior-most to those more senior. They use personal and professional power, not position power, whenever possible. They discern when to be nice, when to be exacting, and when to get down to the business of deciding. They demonstrate the moral courage to make tough decisions with the available information and to manage the consequences as best they can.

Decision-Making Steps

From the entry-level to the executive suite—from ensign to admiral—I've observed the harmful effects, on both individuals and organizations, of leaders who could not or would not make decisions. To make sound, timely decisions, follow these steps:

Decision-Making Steps
- Define the problem and desired end state
- Build the team and specify roles
- Manage risk and maintain decision momentum
- Determine how much information is enough—the 85% solution
- Make the decision!

DEFINE THE PROBLEM AND DESIRED END STATE

When I reported in as the vice admiral leading the Coast Guard's mission support enterprise in the summer of 2015, one of my top priorities was to support the commandant's newly promulgated Coast Guard cyber strategy. I immediately noticed significant problems with the mission support organization's service delivery. The Coast Guard's command, control, communications, computers, and information technology (C4IT) enterprise, for which I was responsible, wasn't properly positioned to support the new cyber strategy. The C4IT infrastructure, organizational construct, governance, business processes, and resourcing were inadequate. Therefore, the organization was unable to keep pace with rapid advancements and increasing threats in the C4IT domain.

Shortly after starting in my new role, the Coast Guard met a significant cybersecurity challenge. Malicious actors tried to attack the Coast Guard data network, which is the critical infrastructure supporting computers and information systems across the Service. In response, we worked with US Cyber Command to stand up a crisis action team. The effort was part of a unified response to mitigate known vulnerabilities in information technology infrastructure throughout the Coast Guard organization.

Although the crisis action team provided an immediate, effective response to the cyber attack, it was obvious the Coast Guard needed to be much better prepared to address emerging threats. The attempted intrusion demonstrated the need for a more secure, efficient, effective C4IT platform and a better staffed, trained, equipped, and resourced cyber program.

The first step in addressing the problem was reaching out to my counterpart and primary stakeholder, the deputy commandant for operations. As the vice admiral in charge of Coast Guard operations policy, he was responsible for the Service's newly established cyber program. We agreed the problems surrounding the inadequate C4IT business line should be addressed at the enterprise level to ensure full support, including adequate resourcing. We decided a task force would be the appropriate vehicle to address the problems. Thus, we prepared a Cyber-CIO-C4IT task force charter for the vice commandant, which he quickly signed.

BUILD THE TEAM AND SPECIFY ROLES

Next, we set out to build the Cyber-CIO-C4IT task force team. The top priority was identifying the right leader to chair it. We wanted a senior executive who not only knew the business but who could provide the necessary leadership. We found the right individual from within the mission support enterprise. Mr. Al Curry, a civilian senior executive with C4IT experience, served as the Coast Guard's deputy chief engineer. Mr. Curry had completed an entire career in the US Navy, giving him a broad operational and support perspective. A well-respected leader of character whom people trusted, he brought much-needed professional and personal power to the effort.

After assigning the Cyber-CIO-C4IT task force chair, we turned our attention to staffing the task force. We looked for motivated individuals with the right attitude and proper skills. Equally as important, we needed cognitive diversity to develop an optimal set of alternatives—differences in thinking, personality, and perspectives. Although differences can lead to disagreement, such friction produces collaboration and cooperation, generating a deeper analysis of the issues. Cognitive diversity shields a decision-making process from confirmation bias, which causes individuals with similar viewpoints to align to the point of excluding or not even considering ideas outside their comfort zones.

We also needed diversity of experience and background reflecting the needs and perspectives of all stakeholders. Looking across the Coast Guard, we drew not only from headquarters staff but reached out to tap vested personnel from the field and fleet. It was imperative to include both mission support professionals and operational customers working and operating within the current C4IT construct. We also brought in personnel responsible for programming and budgeting, communications, acquisitions, and other stakeholders.

After building the team, we began structuring the task force. As a result of its reach and complexity, we needed to identify discrete lines of effort. We then created integrated product teams to lead those lines of effort. Identifying the right senior leaders to preside over the integrated product teams was vital. They had to be hands-on leaders who fully supported the Cyber-CIO-C4IT transformation and who could lead diverse teams in a complex environment.

With the Cyber-CIO-C4IT task force staffed and organized, we aligned the team by setting expectations. The team developed a plan of action and milestones to manage and track the task force deliverables. As with every significant organizational change effort, we needed a tested project management plan and associated tools. During every Cyber-CIO-C4IT task force briefing, the team presented us, the senior executives, the key decision points. Although we always wished we had more information and seldom achieved consensus, we diligently kept the effort moving forward.

MANAGE RISK AND MAINTAIN
DECISION MOMENTUM

From the start, the enterprise-level Cyber-CIO-C4IT transformation involved considerable risk in gaining organizational buy-in, particularly from some older, civilian employees with deeply entrenched mindsets. Being nice wouldn't work with individuals who resisted the needed change; it required intrusive, decisive leadership to either bring them on board or hold them accountable.

Among other risks was obtaining adequate resources from overseers in the administration and Congress, some of whom didn't understand what modernizing the C4IT organization and standing up a cyber program meant and why it needed to be done. Gaining support necessitated building trust in the Cyber-CIO-C4IT transformation effort.

Although we managed a plethora of risks, one eclipsed all others. I worried most about the possibility of the effort losing momentum with the arrival of new senior executive leaders who might have different priorities. Success would require gaining and maintaining what I call organizational "decision momentum." This is the energy that surges through an entire organization or a single staff element when developing alternatives, recommendations, or courses of action to inform an executive decision.

To maintain positive momentum with the Cyber-CIO-C4IT transformation, we relied on the plan of action and milestones. It powered the effort by presenting specified key decision points supported with the available information, which was never enough given the complexity of the effort. Nonetheless, we made important decisions with the best information we had.

DETERMINE HOW MUCH INFORMATION IS ENOUGH—THE 85% SOLUTION

Over the years, I discovered tools to help me make decisions without all the desired information. When I attended the Kellogg Graduate School of Management, we learned the concept of marginal analysis. At some point in a production process, a cost point presents at which all the affordable quality or reliability has been achieved. Any additional quality or reliability will cost exponentially more, for little additional value.

Translating that economic concept to decision-making is a natural fit. At a certain effort point, all the information reasonably needed to support a decision is available. Substantial time, effort, and other costs will be required to achieve a marginal amount of additional information to aid the decision-maker. In other words, leaders must be willing and able to make many decisions when they have enough information for what I call "an 85% solution." Leaders who calculate risk understand they must maintain decision momentum by prioritizing requirements, analyzing risk, evaluating alternatives, and making decisions with the best information they have.

I looked at the Cyber-CIO-C4IT transformation effort as a picture to be painted, one stroke at a time. In the beginning, the blank canvas made it harder to decide where to start. After each decision, another brush stroke was added, further fleshing out the picture. As the picture began to take shape, the decisions fell into place a little easier, providing more insight to inform subsequent decisions. Thus, as the Cyber-CIO-C4IT transformation effort progressed, the picture became clearer, resulting in greater trust, stronger support, and excitement as stakeholders started to visualize the outcome.

The Cyber-CIO-C4IT transformation was a multi-year effort that endured through senior executive leadership transitions because it achieved and maintained decision momentum early in the process. At its core, leadership is all about decision-making, which is an *art*, not a *science*. High-performing organizations need leaders, particularly at the executive level, who have mastered the art of decision-making. Leaders who cannot or will not make timely decisions fail in their duty to their people and the organization. Leading with character requires managing risk and making the tough, trade-off decisions necessary—and expected—at the executive level.

★ CHAPTER SIXTEEN ★

CREATING A
LEADERSHIP PHILOSOPHY

*A great leader's courage to fulfill his vision comes
from passion, not position.*

—John Maxwell

NOT UNTIL STEPPING UP as superintendent at the Coast Guard Academy did I fully realize the importance of being able to clearly articulate a leadership philosophy. A leadership philosophy is your perspective on what you believe makes a leader of character. Far more than a list of desirable leadership attributes, a leadership philosophy helps subordinates better understand their executive.

In short, a leadership philosophy is directed to the workforce and tells people *who the executive is* while a strategic intent is directed to the organization and tells people *what the executive wants.* Insightful executives can use a well-crafted leadership philosophy as a tool to implement and advance their strategic intent. Most importantly, a leadership philosophy should set expectations for leading with character.

It took me many years to fully mature my thoughts on leadership. Crafting a leadership philosophy is an iterative process. It starts at the entry-level when students or new workers are developing as leaders. As superintendent of the Coast Guard Academy, I enjoyed listening to cadets present their nascent leadership philosophies in class. Some sounded off bold and sure, while others wavered with some uncertainty. They all shared the same excitement about the prospect of putting their leadership philosophy into practice. As they grow and develop as leaders of character, the cadets' leadership philosophies evolve to reflect the maturity and wisdom derived from their rich leadership development experiences.

My leadership philosophy is grounded in the principle of engaged leadership. Engaged leadership means connecting with your people by getting out and about to meet them where they are in their workplaces. Engaged leadership means serving your people, ensuring they're fully capable and motivated to perform their duties. It means understanding your people to help them realize their full potential. I exercised engaged leadership by mentoring subordinates to further their development as leaders of character. To serve as a good mentor to younger people, like cadets, I needed to understand what mattered to them.

One day at the Academy while out and about, I met a mother who was visiting. Renee had a child at the Naval Academy preparatory school in Newport, Rhode Island, but was curious about the Coast Guard Academy. We had a lot in common in addition to our shared passion to develop young people. Renee was also a pioneer, a professional woman of color who had worked for years in the information technology sector. I was immediately drawn to her energy, enthusiasm, and confidence. I asked for her thoughts on how the Coast Guard Academy could reach out and attract prospective cadets from a broader segment of society. She sagely advised me, "Sandy, the secret to inspiring young people is to meet them where they are."

Using situational awareness to discover what young people are interested in, then finding a way to translate their interest to the missions of the Coast Guard, is what it means to meet them where they are. For instance, most young people are constantly connected with their mobile devices and view the world through the lens of that technology. They may be excited to learn about the cockpit of a Coast Guard aircraft, the bridge of a Coast Guard ship or a Coast Guard command center, which are equipped with the most advanced technology. They may be interested to learn that Coast Guard missions are executed in a collaborative environment by cohesive teams.

Showing young people how the Coast Guard offers them a chance to use technology, like their smartphone, in serving a purpose greater than themselves is powerful. They may imagine working as part of a capable team to save lives, clean up the environment, enforce laws, and protect critical infrastructure. Helping them visualize the possibilities could motivate them to enlist in the Coast Guard or apply to the Coast Guard Academy.

My new understanding of situational awareness in meeting people where they are served me well in learning to understand and mentor entry-level workers. I knew I couldn't expect the same behavior and decision-making from a student or entry-level worker as I expected of myself. Rather than expressing disappointment when young people inevitably made mistakes and poor decisions, I reminded myself to reach out and try to understand them better. In so doing, I could guide them in advancing to the next level of their potential.

Engaged leadership—meeting people where they are—consists of these three enduring principles applicable at all levels in an organization:

Engaged Leadership
- Build trust and earn respect
- Believe in yourself and others
- Demonstrate moral courage

Build Trust and Earn Respect

Few things help an individual more than to place responsibility upon him, and to let him know that you trust him.

—Booker T. Washington

Perhaps the most important requirement for a leader of character is to build trust and earn respect. Build and earn are active verbs demanding continual engagement. The two words fit together and complement each other. I tend to view the building trust element as pertaining more to the organization, while the earning respect element has more to do with the people. By building trust, a leader can create happiness and boost productivity in the workplace.[30] A happy and productive workplace is likely one with a strong culture of respect, enabling individuals to thrive and the organization to succeed.

Building trust and earning respect is hard, partly because many people don't comprehend the subtle context of the words *build* and *earn*. Picture the word *build*. Civil engineers build bridges, children build sandcastles, birds build nests. Now picture the word *earn*. Workers earn money, scouts earn merit badges, athletes earn fame. In the workplace, people don't think about trust as something that has to be built one piece at a time. Nor do they think about respect as something that must be earned, one step at a time. Trust and respect don't necessarily exist in the workplace until they're actively built and earned. And that requires time and effort. Engaged leaders of character create the conditions to nurture growth of these crucial core values.

To set the foundation for building trust, executives must ensure processes and policies that personally and/or professionally impact the workforce are standard, repeatable, and reliable. Members may not always understand or like the outcome of a process, but if they know they're being fairly treated, they're more likely to trust the organization and show loyalty to it.

A happy and productive workplace also depends upon trust among members of the workforce. Interpersonal trust requires mutual respect. Each person in the workplace, from the senior executive to the most junior, entry-level employee, should continually strive to earn the respect of others. Although I admit to not always meeting my expectations, as a senior executive, I endeavored to set the example by starting each day with a renewed effort to build trust and earn the respect of those around me.

Upon reporting to my new position as deputy commandant for mission support, I stepped up to lead a large organization consisting of about one-half of the Coast Guard's workforce. The mission support organization, newly established as part of Admiral Allen's modernization effort, had a long way to go to reach full operating capability. Much work remained to develop policy and institutionalize structures and processes that would build trust in the new organization.

Regrettably, the position I filled had been vacant, due to unforeseen circumstances, for over a year. Several initiatives, both short- and longer-term, simple and complex, awaited executive action and decisions. Meanwhile, the organization was losing hard-earned momentum, people were losing motivation, and operational customers weren't gaining the improved support services they expected. I needed to act quickly.

It was my duty to support every Coast Guard mission and every Coast Guard person. To succeed, we needed to gain the trust of the fellow Coast Guard men and women we served. It was imperative to cultivate a customer-focused culture, and I found out how hard that would be. I'd pulled together a small, informal team to develop themes for my strategic vision, called a commander's intent.[xxii] During our initial meeting, I let the team know my vision needed to address improved customer service.

---

xxii   In the Armed Forces, the commander's intent is the clear, concise direction a leader provides the force to achieve a desired outcome. The commander's intent framework has been adopted by some in the business world.

To my surprise, the team members responded in unison with the same concern. "Admiral, we can't call them customers. They'll get the wrong impression and think they have a choice in the service we provide. Our job is to provide standard support services. We give them what they *need*, not what they *want*."

I was appalled to learn that this traditional, institutional mindset persisted several years after the Coast Guard's modernization effort had begun.

My years at Kellogg Business School had taught me a lot about customer service, and I knew a high-performing organization was fully capable of delivering standard service with reasonable choices. Take McDonald's, for instance. As a fast-food chain, the restaurant provides a host of standard choices and a menu to choose from. Customers can select a hamburger, chicken, or fish sandwich; they can add fries or upsize a drink. There was nothing, except institutional mindsets, to stop Coast Guard mission support from providing similarly tailored customer service.

To advance my strategic vision, I leaned on the exceptional mission support staff. Within the first week, we promulgated my commander's intent, which can be found in appendix two. In it, I announced three priorities to steer the mission support organization to set the Coast Guard on a course to make it more relevant, more respected, and better prepared to meet the challenges ahead.

Regarding the first priority, engaged leadership, I advanced the need for leaders to collaborate with customers to improve support service delivery. Second, with efficiency through innovation, I emphasized the value of a culture of stewardship to deliver excellent, yet cost-effective, mission support. Third, I set forth the need to provide transparency in delivering standard support services based on valid requirements.

Unlike on a Coast Guard cutter, I couldn't muster the crew to communicate. To achieve maximum impact, I relied upon e-mail and other communication vehicles to roll out each of my three priorities sequentially over a period of a couple of weeks. That way, I clearly communicated to a large audience, one priority at a time.

Promulgating my commander's intent rapidly to senior leaders in the mission support organization empowered them to personalize the message to their subordinates. Making my priorities their own gave them the ideal opportunity to focus their organization, motivate their people . . . and build trust.

One of the first concerns my senior staff brought to my attention was the many action items awaiting decision and implementation. Simultaneous with my commander's intent, I asked the team to put together a one hundred–day plan of quick-hitter items we could act on to create energy and enthusiasm. Each of the action items in the one hundred–day plan was assigned to a designated champion in an office charged with leading the implementation effort. The planning staff managed the progress of each action item and reported the implementation status for all to see.

As an example, with our new focus on customer service, we addressed the issue of spare parts delivery to remote locations, like Guam. At the time, we had one standard inventory control point for cutter and boat support in Baltimore, Maryland. Although this structure offered peak efficiency in terms of processing parts from a central location, it didn't adequately meet operational readiness needs in Guam. Since there is no express mail service to Guam, shipping parts the standard way didn't meet that customer's needs for timely repair to meet operational requirements. To resolve the problem, we developed a "push parts" program to proactively send the most commonly needed parts to Guam, where they were locally stored and available for immediate use in the event of an equipment or machinery casualty.

To build trust, it was imperative to include the operators, or customers, in support service delivery conversations. We had to understand their needs and address their concerns, as with the case of proactive delivery of spare parts to Guam. In the past, mission support had implemented new services that yielded enterprise-level efficiencies but caused unanticipated problems for the customer in the fleet or field. We needed to focus foremost on the customer.

I set out to visit the most remote outposts of Coast Guard operations, such as Guam and Alaska.

I told my team, "We're going to visit Guam in the summer and Alaska in the winter."

They looked at me like I was crazy, since most senior executives schedule their familiarization visits to coincide with the most favorable environmental conditions. To build trust and earn respect, I wanted to meet my customers where they were when the conditions were at their very worst. Thus, in small-town Alaska, we waited for hours in airports as flights were cancelled due to the weather, trudged around industrial facilities while freezing in the cold winter rain, heard stories about families dealing with seasonal affective disorder, and noticed the dearth of recreation and dining opportunities. In Guam, the mugginess enveloped and choked us. We suffered the relentless humidity in the living and dining quarters and felt the oppressive heat permeate our heavy standard uniform. We saw how long it took for parts and packages to arrive—instead of next day delivery, the best-case scenario was next week delivery.

Those trips were crucial to building trust and earning respect. Yet leaders don't always make those seemingly small investments, perhaps because there are no short-term rewards for doing so. The boss isn't likely to notice. But the customers and other stakeholders notice. Building trust and earning respect is like investing money, one dollar at a time. Eventually, the interest on those investments compounds and a person earns a reputation as an engaged leader of character who people want to follow.

The first few months in a new executive position are pivotal, filled with opportunities to recognize and seize. By bringing people together in teams to achieve some early victories and quick wins, a leader can build trust and unite the organization. Leading with character means sincerely humbling yourself to actively earn others' respect through personal and professional power. Doing so, while eschewing position power when possible, will motivate and inspire others to support your vision and strategic intent.

Believe in Yourself and Others

To be yourself in a world that is constantly trying to make you something else is the greatest accomplishment.

—Ralph Waldo Emerson

The Coast Guard excels at leadership development by providing motivated members boundless chances to test themselves. Those who are willing to work hard and persevere can excel, both as individuals and as team members. Despite working hard and persevering, some talented people still fall short. They fail, in part, because they don't have the confidence to believe in themselves. Lack of self-confidence is an impediment to leadership in many ways. People who cannot believe in themselves are also unlikely to have the ability to believe in and lead subordinates.

I came across an insightful article in *The Atlantic* entitled "The Confidence Gap," which helped inform my thoughts on the importance of believing in yourself. The authors, both women, set out to demonstrate the existence of a gap in the level of confidence between women and men. This gap in confidence doesn't correlate with competence. Yet, the authors report, "evidence shows that women are less self-assured than men—and that to succeed, confidence matters as much as competence."[31]

The findings don't mean every woman is less confident than every man. Plenty of men lack confidence. The findings should compel executives to understand the dynamic that could be at work in a mixed-gender group and to reach out to those who hold back. Engaged leaders employ techniques to ensure everyone in the workplace feels included and valued.

One day, while serving as superintendent at the Academy, I was invited to observe an engineering class. The class was made up mostly of men with a few women. Beforehand, the male instructor asked me to watch for the difference in class participation between the men and the women. During class, I saw how the men raised their hands unhesitatingly but often gave partial answers. Then the instructor specifically called on one of the women, who hadn't raised her hand. She delivered the perfectly correct answer. After class, the instructor informed me she was one of his smartest students. To ensure the women participated, he sometimes had to call on them individually as opposed to relying on the voluntary show of hands.

"The Confidence Gap" article resonated with me because I was that young woman who lacked self-confidence. I seldom raised my hand, despite being as competent as the next person. There were times when I wanted to contribute but couldn't break into the lively, male-dominated discussions.

The men never asked, "Sandy, what do you think?"

Rather, I had to compete with a room full of seemingly confident men.

There came a savored moment during my service as military aide to Secretary Skinner when I turned a corner regarding confidence. I'd done my best to earn his trust, and he believed in me. On matters of national significance, he would turn to me and ask, "Sandy, what do you think?"

The first time the secretary asked my opinion, I was taken aback. In those days, it was very unusual for a Coast Guard senior leader to ask a junior subordinate for her opinion. Secretary Skinner understood the value of a wide range of perspectives. My opinion was one of many he routinely solicited from a variety of people, both junior and senior. By asking for my thoughts, Secretary Skinner conveyed to me a sense of value that boosted my confidence.

Having broken the ice, so to speak, from thenceforward, I felt more empowered to work my way into discussions. With my new confidence came the realization that not having a voice at the table was mostly my fault. The problem couldn't be blamed on the more assertive men; rather, it was my failure to believe in myself. I needed to adapt my personality so I could stand up for myself and be a better leader. I realized I owed that duty not only to myself but to the people I would lead. Thus, I endeavored to pay forward Secretary Skinner's belief in me.

While serving as deputy commandant for mission support, I traveled around the Coast Guard to visit both mission support and operational units. During those visits, I reached out to meet people where they were to better understand their problems and concerns. I quickly recognized a significant problem that was eroding the confidence of some in the mission support organization.

Before the Coast Guard's modernization effort, operational commanders controlled both operations and, to a large extent, all the maintenance and support of their ships, boats, aircraft, equipment, and facilities. Modernization divided maintenance and support into two parts. First was the operational level or day-to-day maintenance, which would remain under the purview of the operational commander. Second was the depot level or longer-term maintenance, which would move to the mission support organization.

The transition wasn't an easy one for either mission support or operations. Many operational commanders resisted giving up control over part of their maintenance and support to a new organization they didn't know and did not yet trust. To make matters worse, the mission support organization struggled to get certain aspects of service delivery and support right for the customer.

Although support improved and costs decreased dramatically in most areas, that wasn't what the customers noticed. They noticed only the problems. As human nature would have it, with another organization responsible for support and service delivery, the principle of moral hazard set in. It became easy for some in operations to pay less attention to their support duties, allowing routine operational maintenance to back up. The result was unplanned depot-level support requirements for the mission support organization.

At times, the mission support workforce felt like they were being blamed for things beyond their control. Under the new system, it was hard for junior leaders to defend their service delivery to more senior operational commanders. During my early unit visits, I noticed the morale of some units was down as a result of a steady drumbeat of complaints and criticism.

As I discussed this problem with my staff, a great idea emerged—to tell the story of mission support successes. We knew we needed to keep our workforce confident and motivated to maintain our momentum to build out the organization, as we still had much work to do. My superb planning staff put its talented people to work finding a way to show progress. Using volumes of performance data, they developed a storyboard displaying the remarkable outcomes the organization was achieving across the Coast Guard.

Creating transparency through a visible display of achievement boosted morale in the mission support workforce. It also provided members a tool with the information necessary to stand up to and counteract criticism. For months after creating the storyboard and explaining it during unit visits, we received positive feedback. Mission support personnel from around the Service could visualize their contributions and were happy to see the positive impact of their hard work. By actively and visibly demonstrating belief in the mission support workforce, we built confidence and boosted organizational performance.

Demonstrate Moral Courage

It is curious that physical courage should be
so common in the world and moral courage so rare.

—Mark Twain

Leading with character requires moral courage, a core value that is difficult to clearly define. It's often said that moral courage is doing the right thing when no one is looking. I don't agree with that definition. I believe a leader of character should be *expected* to do the right thing when no one is looking—that takes honesty, not courage. Honesty is doing the right thing when you're behind closed doors when no one is looking. Moral courage is doing the right thing when you're in the spotlight and everyone is looking and judging. It's much harder to stand up and boldly do the right thing in public when you must make a weighty decision that others may question.

The responsibility to demonstrate moral courage is a key principle of my leadership philosophy because the toughest decisions leaders must make are the very visible, controversial ones. These are decisions that involve enforcing standards that have been allowed to lapse, holding someone accountable for previously unaddressed poor performance or misbehavior, or standing up for someone or something in which you believe. Absent moral courage, leaders avoid such decisions, losing trust and sowing discontent in the workplace.

Mark Twain's musing that physical courage is so common, while moral courage is so rare, applies to this day. Physical courage is universally lauded and rewarded. History books are filled with exploits of heroes who demonstrated praiseworthy physical courage. The stories of moral courage are much harder to find. Moral courage isn't always lauded or rewarded. It's sometimes even condemned.

Those who demonstrate physical courage often do so in a moment of crisis, responding to external stimuli. They react by risking bodily harm to help another or to serve the greater good. Moral courage, on the other hand, results from a more deliberate response to internal stimuli. Demonstrating moral courage requires examining your core values, then standing up to do the right thing, always, even in the face of criticism or judgment.

My outlook on moral courage has been shaped most profoundly by observing those who failed to do the right thing when they had the chance. I witnessed the resultant deleterious effects on the workforce and even the organization. Serving as a leader in various personnel management positions required me to enforce standards and offered me unique insights into human behavior.

In one such position, I was a senior leader running the Coast Guard's officer promotion board process. My duties involved taking calls from officers with questions about the outcome of a given promotion board. Generally, those calls came from distressed officers who hadn't been selected for promotion. Sometimes the calls came from supervisors who wanted to find out all they could about why their high-performing subordinate hadn't been selected. Although I couldn't discuss the confidential deliberations of the promotion board, I would review officers' service records and counsel them as best I could.

After publishing the results of a promotion board, I received an unusual call from a very senior officer serving as chief of staff, an executive level position, at a large Coast Guard unit. The chief of staff was senior to me, and he demanded to know why a certain officer under his command, who wasn't a top performer, had been selected for promotion to the next level. I pulled the officer's service record that had been put before the promotion board. To my consternation, the senior officer on the phone was the person who had given the officer a positive promotion recommendation on his most recent evaluation report.

When I tactfully brought this fact to the chief of staff's attention, he said to me, with considerable irritation, "Well, I thought the board would see through that!"

In other words, he had hoped to avoid having to confront the officer with a negative performance evaluation and believed his endorsement would be weak enough that the board would "read between the lines" and not select the officer for advancement. In failing to accurately document the officer's performance, the chief of staff demonstrated to others under his command that he couldn't be trusted to do the right thing.

Contrary to the chief of staff's presumption, the Coast Guard promotion board process doesn't work that way. Promotion boards rely on the assumption that evaluation reports accurately reflect an individual's performance. As a result of the chief of staff's failure to demonstrate moral courage, an officer was selected for promotion who perhaps shouldn't have been. Unfortunately, that officer took the place of another officer who wasn't selected but who may have been more deserving.

On the other hand, I witnessed prime examples of leaders who, despite the risks, stood up to do the right thing. During his tenure as secretary of Transportation, Secretary Skinner earned the moniker "Master of Disaster" as a result of stepping up to lead the federal responses to the Exxon Valdez oil spill, Hurricane Hugo and the San Francisco earthquake. Remarkably, those disasters rocked the United States in quick succession during the year 1989.

At the time, the Federal Emergency Management Agency was still a small, independent organization unequipped to lead major disaster response efforts. The Stafford Disaster Relief and Emergency Assistance Act had been enacted in 1988, a few months before the disasters that struck in 1989. Although it set forth requirements for federal government support to local and state authorities, it hadn't yet been tried and tested.

Without a proven playbook, and not officially designated as the cabinet member responsible for disaster response, Secretary Skinner demonstrated the courage to step up to face the challenge. While others stood by waiting for more information when disaster struck, Secretary Skinner boldly harnessed the power of his transportation resources, notably the US Coast Guard, to rapidly respond on behalf of President Bush. My tour of duty with Secretary Skinner became a huge lesson in crisis leadership through the lens of moral courage.

The first news reports of the oil tanker Exxon Valdez's running aground in Prince William Sound outside of Valdez, Alaska, came in as those of us on the secretary's staff arrived at work the morning of

March 24, 1989. We knew it was bad, but no one knew the magnitude
of the spill. As reports came in, we learned 11 million gallons of crude
oil had leaked into the pristine waterway, making it the largest oil
spill in US history. Coating 1,300 miles of coastline, the oil threatened
wildlife populations and livelihoods, causing an environmental and
political crisis.

Secretary Skinner and his leadership team sprang into action. He
immediately reached out to invite Mr. Lee Raymond, the president of
Exxon, to meet with him in Washington, DC, to discuss the response
effort. The requirements outlined in the Oil Pollution Act of 1990
were not yet in effect (OPA 90 resulted from the Exxon Valdez
disaster). Technically, no one government or private sector entity
bore responsibility for the cleanup.

Secretary Skinner knew he needed to provide a strong federal
response but faced significant limitations. For instance, the cleanup crew deployed to work in the muck on cold beaches in Valdez,
Alaska, would need thousands of pairs of socks and other gear. As
he sat with Mr. Raymond in his office, he lamented the logistical
hurdles of government contracting, which made rapid procurement
of critical supplies impossible.

Mr. Raymond interjected, "I can have ten thousand pairs of socks
on the scene in Alaska practically overnight."

Thus, we began a productive partnership between government
and industry to address a natural disaster too big and complex for
either one to solve alone.

Shortly after the spill, Secretary Skinner flew to Valdez to
personally meet with disaffected stakeholders. This was a task his
staff would rather have seen him delegate to a surrogate. We knew
he would be in the spotlight, bearing the brunt of the criticism. Many
locals, particularly fishermen, had come to the shocking realization
their livelihoods and way of life were threatened as a result of the
pollution. They were angry, distressed, frustrated, fearful for their
futures, and ready to vent. They wanted the federal government to fix
the problem, now.

Secretary Skinner didn't have all the answers in the early days of the disaster, but he had the situational awareness to realize how important it was to show the people President Bush cared about them. He did his best to explain what the federal government was doing and to respond to people's concerns. By demonstrating the moral courage to personally appear on the scene in front of hostile audiences, Secretary Skinner earned the respect of local leaders.

Shortly after the Exxon Valdez disaster, on September 10, 1989, Hurricane Hugo hit the Caribbean and the southeast United States as a Category 4 storm. It was the strongest hurricane to strike the East Coast north of Florida since the Georgia hurricane of 1898. Hugo left devastation and shock in its wake. The storm caused dozens of deaths, left one hundred thousand homeless, and caused over $9 billion in damage. People needed help.

The secretary immediately mobilized the Federal Aviation Administration jet to personally observe the damage. We first stopped in St. Thomas, a hard-hit island where the United States has a Department of Transportation presence. Since our plane was the first to land on the devastated island in the wake of the storm, the Federal Aviation Administration personnel had to clear the debris off the runway. They were thrilled to see the secretary! His presence assured them he cared and was taking immediate action to address the significant damage and severe operational impacts.

When we landed in Charleston, South Carolina, which had sustained the worst of the damage, large swaths of the waterfront were ravaged and deserted. I'd never witnessed such destruction and couldn't imagine the area ever recovering. Secretary Skinner was met with angst and concern regarding relief efforts. Once more, he demonstrated the moral courage to serve as the face of the federal government in a devastating situation.

Less than a month later, on October 17, 1989, the San Francisco Bay area was rocked by the 6.9 magnitude Loma Prieta earthquake. The massive quake, triggered by the San Andreas Fault, was the strongest to strike the area since 1906. It claimed sixty-three lives and resulted in nearly 3,800 injuries and $6 billion dollars in damage. The Bay Area transportation system suffered the worst damage, paralyzing the city and surrounding area.

By early the following morning, Secretary Skinner arrived on the scene with Vice President Quayle, assessing damage even as many people remained trapped, with fires and gas leaks raging. Secretary Skinner engaged with devastated communities and reassured distraught local leaders of the federal government's commitment. He quickly determined the level of damage to the expansive Bay Area infrastructure and prioritized how best to provide federal aid, from first responders, to grants, to repairing bridges and highways.

Through his disaster response efforts, Secretary Skinner taught me moral courage through crisis leadership. I witnessed the value of leading by example in immediately responding to affected, distressed populations, even without having all the information. I learned the importance of trust in building partnerships to solve overwhelming problems. Most importantly, I came to understand that leading with character means demonstrating the moral courage to step up to face public and media scrutiny and do the right thing, no matter how hard it may be.

The principles that comprise my leadership philosophy, *build trust and earn respect, believe in yourself and others*, and *demonstrate moral courage*, have served me well in setting expectations and achieving results. Every executive should prepare a leadership philosophy built upon his or her personal core values and that reflects the organization's core values. The leadership philosophy should both inspire and guide, serving as a beacon to motivate aspiring leaders of character.

★ CHAPTER SEVENTEEN ★

SUCCESSION MANAGEMENT

*At the end of the day it's not about what you have or even
what you've accomplished . . . it's about who you've lifted up,
who you've made better. It's about what you've given back.*

—Denzel Washington

LEADING AT THE EXECUTIVE level is, in some ways, like
commanding a ship. Executives must look forward, over the horizon,
to set the course for the organization. Equally as important, executives
must look astern to identify and develop the leaders of character who
will move up the ranks to replace them one day. Grooming competent,
capable subordinates to step up to lead at the next level is a wise, and
necessary, investment. The question is, "How do you motivate the
best members of the workforce to remain with the organization and
desire to advance?"

Motivation is a powerful force that drives people to continue even
when they feel like quitting. It transcends the virtues of hard work
and perseverance, which come from within. Motivation depends
upon external factors over which an employee has no control, like
an inspirational leader or a positive workplace environment. To
motivate subordinates and instill in them a desire to lead in the
organization, you should follow these steps:

How to Motivate Subordinates

- Set the example
- Raise expectations
- Empower subordinates
- Provide resources
- Reward excellence

Set the Example

The Coast Guard shines as a model of motivational leadership. Retention of members of the workforce is remarkably high compared to the other armed forces. When asked why, the Service's former commandant, Admiral Paul Zukunft explained, "It really begins with good leadership. Our leaders really, truly do look out for their people and not for themselves."[32]

Admiral Zukunft personified the selfless, servant leader whom people choose to follow. As commandant, he set the example every day, modeling selfless service to the Coast Guard and its people.

Admiral Zukunft's leadership style makes me think back to when, as a senior executive, I assumed responsibility for developing the theme, itinerary, and speakers for the Coast Guard's semi-annual senior executive leadership conference. We reached out to the famous author and speaker Simon Sinek, inviting him to share his thoughts on leadership from his book *Leaders Eat Last*.[33] With a reputation for delivering a captivating talk, he was in high demand. We were thrilled when he agreed!

Mr. Sinek talked about leadership, sharing his experiences working with the US Marines. He had approached the Marines asking about the secret to their success leading on the battlefield under arduous conditions. He wanted to understand why Marines would lay down their lives for others whom they may not even know. He learned that the Marine Corps culture supports taking care of the junior enlisted personnel. Those Marines can then get on with the business of taking care of each other and the mission. Hence, at mealtime, junior Marines eat first, and their leaders eat last.

Mr. Sinek spoke before lunch, so he could remain afterward to dine with his audience, the senior executives. Mr. Sinek delivered an incredibly inspiring presentation, causing us all to contemplate our leadership styles. When the talk ended, everyone headed out to enjoy a prepared lunch in the adjoining conference room.

I almost laughed out loud at what I saw. People milled around talking, but no one dared to step up to the loaded buffet table! What senior executive would venture to be first in line after a motivational leadership talk extolling the virtues of leaders eating last? Thankfully, the senior executive spouses also attended the talk and saved us all by starting through the buffet line first.

Admiral Zukunft was the senior-most leader in attendance for Mr. Sinek's talk. He already had the lesson "leaders eat last" down pat. I'd seen him hosting events at his quarters during which he not only ate last but personally cooked for his guests! Most famous were the big July Fourth gatherings, which involved well over one hundred attendees, including service members and their families. During those festive occasions, our commandant could be seen at the grill, toiling in the heat in his Hawaiian shirt, happily serving up burgers and hotdogs.

Hearkening back to the importance of emotional intelligence, executives must possess situational awareness to understand how their work habits and personal actions impact their people. Leading by example means creating a workplace climate that inspires subordinates to want to move up to take more responsible, demanding jobs. Supervisors who spend most of their time in the office and don't have a healthy work-life balance are probably not people who subordinates want to emulate. They may look up at their boss and think, "Wow, I don't want her job if that's what's expected."

While working for former vice commandant of the Coast Guard Admiral Dave Pekoske, I was impressed to watch him routinely dedicate time out of the office for exercise. Despite the pressing demands, he directed the staff to block his calendar, and he went out for a run every day. He did so not only for his own health and well-being but to set the example for his subordinates.

In an office environment characterized by high expectations and even higher stress, that white space on the boss's calendar was a welcome sight. It allowed his subordinates to breathe a sigh of relief and tacitly permitted us to take an hour of personal time. Following Vice Admiral Pekoske's example, when I reached the executive level, I made it a point to block my calendar for an hour at lunchtime.

In their own ways, leaders like Admiral Zukunft and Vice Admiral Pekoske cultivated a workplace culture that inspired and motivated Coast Guard men and women. People enjoy being part of an organization with strong core values and leaders they trust and respect. When Coast Guard members retire, they often remark, "I joined the Coast Guard for the missions and opportunity to serve but stayed because of the people."

Leading with character means inspiring people to choose to stay with the organization they are so proud to be a part of.

Raise Expectations

Most people want to work for an organization that sets high performance, behavior, conduct, and ethical standards that apply equally across the workforce. Motivational leaders raise expectations for adherence to standards, creating a fair and respectful workplace that allows everyone to thrive and achieve top performance.

In the armed forces, compliance with established standards is necessary to preserve the good order and discipline that sets the conditions for individual and unit success. A model example of an executive who raised expectations for workplace conduct is Australian Army General David Morrison.

A few years ago, the Australian Army faced a misconduct problem involving the inappropriate treatment of female soldiers. General Morrison took immediate action, delivering a passionate, forceful address reinforcing the standard of conduct expected of everyone in the Australian Army. He finished his speech with a resounding admonition, "The standard you walk past is the standard you accept."[34]

General Morrison's powerful speech is available online, and I encourage every leader to invest a few minutes to watch it. His speech resonated from Australia across the Pacific Ocean to the US Armed Forces, where people commended it as a prime example of motivational leadership. At the time, I was serving as superintendent at the Coast Guard Academy. General Morrison's compelling message inspired Academy leaders, including cadet leaders, to raise expectations for adherence to established standards. General Morrison made it clear that leaders of character have an obligation—one could even say a moral obligation—to appropriately address failure to adhere to established standards.

Raising expectations and compelling compliance is difficult. It requires emotionally intelligent leaders to purposefully draw upon their self-awareness and situational awareness. To succeed, they must address the awkward matter of appropriately confronting and questioning people regarding their actions or behavior. The approach will necessarily differ depending on the status of the person or people failing to meet a standard. It's one thing to hold accountable the relatively powerless, junior enlisted personnel in the Australian Army or cadets at the Coast Guard Academy. An entirely different method of engagement is required to address the shortcomings or misbehavior of senior, experienced members of the workforce.

Be it a minor infraction or something more significant, such as an ethical lapse by a junior or a senior person, any failure to adhere to standards must be addressed. Yet leaders, even those who adhere to the standards themselves, walk past infractions. They rationalize that it's someone else's job to hold the person accountable, or it's too much trouble to hold the person accountable.

In his book *The Power of Noticing*, Max H. Bazerman offers compelling insights into what motivates leaders to tacitly accept failure to adhere to standards. He discusses the concept of "motivated blindness," which he defines as "the systemic failure to notice others' unethical behavior when it's not in our best interest to do so."

He argues that when people have a vested self-interest in a situation, they have a hard time seeing past their bias to notice misconduct, making it difficult to properly assess the problem.[35] A companion to motivated blindness is confirmation bias, which can result when people believe a well-liked person couldn't possibly do anything wrong.

It takes moral courage to raise expectations and hold people accountable, particularly when standards have been ignored over time and non-adherence has become accepted. Motivated blindness and confirmation bias make it easier for leaders to walk past problems rather than to address them head-on. This conundrum can even be found in cases involving senior, influential members of the federal government workforce. Take, for instance, a senior civilian who has built a positive reputation over years of employment and achievement. The person has supporters who steadfastly refuse to believe the accomplished person they know and respect could have done anything wrong.

A leader who steps up to hold such a person accountable for not adhering to standards runs the risk of being called out and judged. Since law and policy limit the information leaders can disclose about personnel actions and investigations into misconduct, there are very few options for communicating and explaining the situation.

Complicating matters, the employee subject to the proceedings tells the story he or she wants people to hear and files grievances against leaders who took action to hold him or her accountable. Doing the right thing by holding someone accountable then becomes a long, drawn-out process that erodes trust and diverts leadership from focusing on the mission. In the extreme version of these cases, executives who hold people accountable become the target of criticism themselves, even if they have done everything right in accordance with the personnel management and legal proceedings requirements.

During my tenure as superintendent at the Coast Guard Academy, a matter arose that posed a moral dilemma. A senior, influential employee was found to be behaving in a manner that harmed students and threatened the institution's standing. Upon learning of the behavior, I carefully considered the situation and took measured actions to hold the person accountable and remedy the situation.

Although my actions supported good order and discipline in the workplace, people outside the organization who knew the member refused to believe he could be involved in any wrongdoing. They expressed concern about my addressing the violations. The tension continued even after an investigation clearly demonstrated the misconduct. That didn't satisfy the naysayers, who were too blinded by confirmation bias to accept the truth. As a result of interference by those misguided outside influencers, my actions were questioned by my supervisor, and I—not the person who had committed the misconduct—ended up having to explain myself.

Nonetheless, I doggedly followed the appropriate processes to move the case forward. Based on the evidence, we notified the senior employee that he would be fired. The civilian personnel management rules allowed him the option to retire instead of being fired, and he chose retirement. Since we treated the member with respect and carefully protected his privacy during the proceedings, people not aware of the details of the case thought he retired by choice.

The situation posed significant and unforeseen challenges, as can be the case when you raise expectations for compliance with standards. Nonetheless, we achieved our goals of ensuring the well-being of the students, preserving the integrity of the Coast Guard Academy, and restoring the workforce's trust in the system.

It requires courage to hold accountable senior members of the workforce who engage in misconduct, particularly if it involves junior people with little power or influence. The senior person is often the one who long-time supporters want to believe. Making matters worse, junior personnel are often hesitant or afraid to say anything about a senior person's misconduct. That's particularly true in a training environment where the senior person has authority over those who are junior.

The most junior, vulnerable individuals in an organization deserve a workplace that supports their personal and professional development. They are, after all, the ones who are in line to move up and lead at the executive level one day. Leaders who set low expectations and walk past standards that aren't being met leave behind disappointment and poor morale. Leaders who raise expectations and ensure adherence to standards will create a climate of trust and respect that values members and motivates them to remain with the organization to lead at the next level.

Empower Subordinates

Most people aspire to grow and develop in the workplace. Some actively seek more responsibility, but others can become comfortable with their current position and apprehensive about reaching higher. Executives must motivate their people to reach for more responsibility by encouraging and empowering them to take calculated risks and learn from their failures. As the saying goes, "There's no growth in the comfort zone and no comfort in the growth zone."

Inspirational leaders seek out subordinates who are thirsting for more responsibility, then place trust in them to stretch further without intrusive meddling. That can unleash a cascade of innovation as the empowered members reach high to make improvements and advance the organization. At every level of the Coast Guard, I was fortunate to have supervisors who believed in me and gave me autonomy to develop innovative solutions and make impactful decisions.

While serving in my first year as superintendent of the Coast Guard Academy, my administrative assistant informed me Rear Admiral Jonathan Bailey, director of the National Oceanic and Atmospheric Administration (NOAA) Commissioned Officer Corps, desired to meet with me. I'd recently read the US Merchant Marine Academy in

Kings Point, New York, had announced it would no longer host NOAA's Basic Officer Training Course. The NOAA Corps is a uniformed, but not armed, federal service and has a collaborative relationship with the Coast Guard. I presumed Rear Admiral Bailey might be looking for a new partner to host his officer accession training.

In addition to its four-year cadet education mission, the Coast Guard Academy also performs the Service's four-month officer candidate training mission, which is akin to the NOAA Basic Officer Training Course. I became intrigued by the possibilities and eagerly anticipated my pending meeting with Rear Admiral Bailey. Experience had taught me that organizations succeed in becoming more relevant when they recognize and seize opportunities to meet emerging demands.

When we met, Rear Admiral Bailey and I connected immediately. He impressed me from the start. He'd served for many years at sea, as I had. We both shared a passion, as senior leaders, for ensuring the continued prosperity of our organizations and our people. We understood the critical importance of developing the next generation of leaders who would replace us one day.

Rear Admiral Bailey shared with me his vision to integrate NOAA's Basic Officer Training Course with the Coast Guard's Officer Candidate School. He offered it would strengthen both our services. From accession, Coast Guard and NOAA officers would train and serve alongside each other in the maritime domain. Both Rear Admiral Bailey and I were excited with the possibility that integrating our accession training could lead to a closer relationship for both services in mission execution and mission support. Already, the Coast Guard and NOAA worked together in conducting some missions, particularly those that support the environment. Each service operated a fleet of cutters and ships, with some sharing home ports.

I quickly recognized the opportunity and immediately agreed to evaluate our ability to accommodate his program. I asked my staff to work the issue. The prospect of welcoming NOAA to the Coast

Guard Academy met with widespread, although cautious, enthusiasm. Integrating the two officer accession training programs had much promise but wouldn't be easy.

Foremost, the Coast Guard Academy is space-constrained, situated on a compact 103 acres. Locating adequate classroom capacity would require creative solutions, as would integrating the NOAA officer candidates into the dining, physical training, medical, and other facilities. Another hurdle would be blending the two programs, which differed in duration and content. Accommodating NOAA would require dedication and innovation on the part of both staffs.

Enthusiastically, I presented the proposal to my supervisor Vice Admiral John Currier, who was then serving in a newly created position, deputy commandant for mission support. Understandably, he expressed some concerns. I couldn't answer all his questions, as some unknowns needed to be worked out as the process moved forward. Yes, the Coast Guard would be accepting some risk, but I assured him I firmly believed the benefits to the Service would be well worth it. I was thrilled when he allowed me to proceed, giving me full autonomy to implement the new program.

The Coast Guard Academy and NOAA teams enthusiastically collaborated, developing innovative solutions to reach a mutually beneficial outcome. We drew up provisions for an interagency agreement. NOAA agreed to pay its share of the program costs and provide instructors. NOAA also decided to switch to the Coast Guard training uniform and to maximize joint classroom training, among other accommodations. The Coast Guard Academy agreed to provide logistics support, including classroom space and access to facilities, to assimilate the NOAA officer candidates into the Coast Guard Officer Candidate School program.

Since NOAA had been abruptly deprived of its accessions training location with a new class in the pipeline, we had to work fast to establish the new program at the Coast Guard Academy. Within a relatively short period of time, we welcomed the inaugural NOAA

Basic Officer Training Course students in August 2012. We then formalized the arrangement with an interagency agreement.

I proudly watched the program prosper beyond our expectations. The students and training staffs looked beyond the inconveniences that accompany a new start. They embraced the significant benefits accruing to both services. What a thrill it was to join the combined NOAA and Coast Guard officer candidates during their training cruise on board the *Eagle* a few months later. Watching them pull together on a line to set a sail, just as I'd done decades earlier, gave me deep satisfaction. The future of both services was bright, and I envisioned one of the Coast Guard officer candidates possibly replacing me one day.

In May 2014, the combined Coast Guard Officer Candidate School and NOAA Basic Officer Training Course graduating classes presented the director of the NOAA Corps and me with a brass geodetic survey marker. The marker proudly commemorated the Academy's status as a joint service training center. The NOAA administrator Doctor Kathryn Sullivan and I placed the survey marker in a memorial park at the Academy as a testament to the enduring relationship between our two services.

With the Coast Guard Academy serving as the sole geographic accession source for all Coast Guard and NOAA officers, the connection between the two services soon deepened. In October 2014, the Coast Guard and NOAA signed a fleet plan and officer exchange memorandum of understanding. Areas of collaboration included repairing NOAA ships at the Coast Guard shipyard in Baltimore, Maryland, and advancing the United States' Arctic preparedness.

The venture succeeded because Vice Admiral Currier believed in me and empowered me to implement a significant organizational change. On the foundation of his confidence, key stakeholders in both organizations, from the student to the executive level, built and advanced the change effort. As a result, both the Coast Guard and NOAA became stronger and better connected by jointly investing in strengthening their accession programs and, ultimately, their succession management programs.

Managing an organizational change at the Coast Guard Academy provided valuable experience that prepared and motivated me for the next level of leadership in the Coast Guard. As a tribute to Vice Admiral Currier, I moved up to serve in the position he had held, deputy commandant for mission support. In that position, I drew upon all my change management experience to meet the challenges of maturing the newly established mission support enterprise.

Provide Necessary Resources

Perhaps the most fundamental requirement of a productive workplace is access to the resources people need to do their jobs. The appropriate tools, equipment, and clothing are crucial, particularly for those on the front lines of mission execution and mission support. Likewise, modern facilities, assets, and information technology systems are indispensable. Too often, these basic support requirements are unsatisfactorily met as scarce funding is directed to meet operational needs.

Despite their important role in driving performance and job satisfaction, failure to pay attention to resources can blindside a leader. As a work environment slowly degrades, people can grow accustomed to and accepting of the lower standard as it gradually becomes the norm.

When I was a young officer commanding the cutter *Katmai Bay*, my chief engineer, Chief Warrant Officer Mike Smith, taught me a lifelong lesson in leadership. Mike was a taciturn engineer but devoted to his duty and the people who worked for him. One day he brought me a procurement request for tools his engineers needed to perform maintenance and repairs. I noticed the brand was top quality, like Snap-On or Dewalt, and therefore expensive. Believing an attribute of good leadership was to exercise discretion and frugality with the budget, I questioned him as to why we weren't procuring the tools from a less expensive supplier. I asked why they wouldn't be good enough.

Chief Warrant Officer Smith looked me in the eye with barely concealed exasperation and explained, "These men leave their families and come in every day to work long hours maintaining and fixing machinery to keep the ship running in all kinds of adverse conditions. The tools reflect their pride in their work. It's all we can do for them. We can't pay them more, but we can buy them good tools to show them how much we value what they do."

I felt ignorant and naive after that lecture from my chief engineer. From then on, I made every effort to understand my people and provide them with what they needed to motivate them to perform.

While serving as deputy commandant for mission support, I was constantly frustrated by the inability to obtain adequate resources to keep up with accelerating information technology systems and equipment demands. One of my biggest disappointments was the inability to deliver needed technology to the people conducting Coast Guard operations.

With consternation, I observed the adverse impact this failure had on a workforce accustomed to the benefits of private sector technology. At home, people could purchase from Amazon with a couple of clicks. The next day, they would report to work in the Coast Guard to encounter a very different scenario. Many jobs required members to spend hours trying to navigate ancient or complex purchasing, logistics, and other systems.

I know first-hand of Coast Guard members who, despite loving the Coast Guard, its missions, and its people, left the Service out of frustration with the archaic equipment and technology. Once, while visiting Facebook's headquarters to learn more about their human resource practices, I met a member of the company's security force. He proudly informed me he had been in the Coast Guard before joining Facebook and had loved his job serving our country. When I asked why he left, he told me he could no longer tolerate the obsolete information technology systems that posed a daily frustration. At Facebook, he was provided with top quality resources to do his job.

Modern buildings and workspaces are equally as important in motivating the workforce. Achieving excellence is elusive when the organization fails to provide basic necessities. During my tenure as superintendent, the Coast Guard Academy's vital healthcare clinic operated out of an antiquated building suffering from inadequate ventilation and electrical systems. Office spaces were crammed with window unit air conditioners, fans, air purifiers, and refrigerators that loaded up the electrical circuits. The budget was never enough to cover all the maintenance at the Academy, which had been constructed in the 1930s.

The clinic's maintenance problem caused repeated power failures that inconvenienced everyone and adversely impacted the healthcare service delivery mission. I can speak from personal experience on this matter. One day I was sitting in the dental chair and had been numbed up for a procedure. No sooner had the needle entered my gum than the power went out.

The dentist, mortified to have the superintendent in such an uncomfortable position, was helpless to rectify the situation. I made light of the matter and tried to relieve the dentist of any feeling of responsibility for something beyond her control. The incident served as a stark example of the adverse impact on morale and motivation when people don't have the facilities and workspaces they need to achieve the excellence they proudly pursue.

The Coast Guard never receives enough funding to support both the full range of operations and the infrastructure, systems, and equipment necessary to support those operations. Senior executives must lead with character to guard against a culture that fails to invest in the infrastructure required to support the mission. Otherwise, the mission will suffer, and so will the people who may lose motivation as they come to believe the organization doesn't care about them or what they do.

Executives must demonstrate the moral courage to make the tough trade-off decisions on where to best apply scarce resources. Their reward will be both mission success and retention of the highly valued workforce.

Reward Excellence

Organizations that pursue excellence must reward exceptional performance and recognize the accomplishments of individuals and teams. Doing so instills pride and motivates members to perform at their very best. Organizations need targeted recognition programs that include opportunities for every category of employee in the workforce. Above all else, recognition must be timely. Programs should include both formal and informal components and should distinguish top performers.

An organization must give deliberate thought to what motivates its members and devise impactful recognition programs. In the Coast Guard, a culture of selfless service inspires members to place a premium on team results that serve the greater good. Many appreciate being recognized as part of a successful team. That culture also supports quietly competent individuals who derive deep satisfaction from the work they do and who eschew formal recognition.

Leaders can demonstrate incredible personal power by publicly recognizing people, either formally or on the spot. Formal programs are easy to establish and thrive over time if they're properly institutionalized. Although formal recognition programs can be powerful and effective, I prefer the more spontaneous approach—to surprise someone unexpectedly in the workspace surrounded by his or her peers. A poignant method is to present someone with a small, but meaningful, token of recognition.

In the armed forces, command coins are widely used as a personal form of on-the-spot recognition. The prized coins are presented to individuals to recognize commendable performance in support of the commander and the mission. Long before the advent of coins, leaders of character found innovative ways to extemporaneously recognize their people.

I witnessed a great example of the power of recognition when serving as military aide to the secretary of transportation many years ago. Secretary Sam Skinner was advancing some high visibility policies and programs, most prominently the National Transportation Policy. He wanted a way to recognize everyday people who got the job done behind the scenes. After a discussion with the staff, the secretary came up with a Way to Go award in the form of a special and very coveted pin. He presented the pin to ordinary workers who had done something extraordinary. Because people didn't expect on-the-spot recognition from someone in a cabinet-level position, they were often in disbelief when notified.

While traveling on the government jet, Secretary Skinner—never one to sit idle for even a moment—asked me to place some Way to Go phone calls. He was in the habit of making the calls to people whose names and accomplishments had been passed up from the transportation modes or agencies.

Despite the technology limitations of communicating from the air in those days, I managed to place a call for a junior Coast Guard member at a small boat station in Eureka, California. Eureka is a small town in a very remote location. The person we were trying to reach was an enlisted member who served as a small boat coxswain. He had bravely executed an arduous search and rescue case in the dangerous waters of the Pacific Ocean.

The unit's administrative assistant answered (we called them secretaries back then). Competing with the static of a phone call from 30,000 feet, I tried to convey that the Secretary wanted to speak with the boatswain's mate; could she please put him on?

The administrative assistant (i.e. secretary) said, "Whose secretary?"

I said, "*The* Secretary."

She asked again, "Whose secretary?"

I don't think she ever understood who was calling but finally put the Coast Guard person on the line, probably telling him, "Somebody's secretary wants to talk with you, and they're calling from an airplane."

At first, the boatswain's mate didn't believe the caller was, in fact, the Coast Guard service secretary, the secretary of transportation. Secretary Skinner had a winning way with people, and the boatswain's mate finally caught on. Of course, he was shocked and thrilled to receive a personal Way to Go award call. I suspect he still tells that story to this day! The best executives model the way, leading with character to set the example for everyone in the organization.

There are many ways to recognize top-performing employees. Everybody is unique, and people have different preferences. Some people appreciate public recognition, while others may prefer a private venue. The desires of someone being recognized should be respected in an inclusive culture that understands and values differences.

There are times when recognition is about more than the member. Retirements, particularly of active-duty members who have served in uniform, are a case in point. Ideally, military members should be recognized with formal, public retirement ceremonies. Although there are many humble, high-performing people who would rather retire quietly, those dedicated individuals should be honored in front of their families, co-workers, and even the public, as appropriate.

Imagine the effect of a top Coast Guard employee walking out the door, having chosen to forgo a public retirement ceremony. The impression of the workforce might well be, "Wow, the Coast Guard didn't care much about her since there was no ceremony."

Retirement ceremonies provide a unique opportunity to focus on the bigger picture of a member's service to the nation. The honored traditions highlight the member's place in a long line of those who have, with their families, made personal sacrifices to serve a greater purpose.

When I was commanding the Coast Guard Cutter *Reliance*, a chief petty officer who had served for well over twenty years, many of them at sea, decided it was time to retire. He had spent much time away from his family, with six-week deployments being the norm for our ship.

When we assigned a project officer for his retirement ceremony, the chief petty officer came to speak with me, making his case for not wanting a public retirement in front of the crew. A quiet, humble leader with a serious, professional demeanor, the chief wasn't the type for fanfare. We had a respectful discussion during which I explained my view of the bigger picture and the importance of a formal ceremony on board the ship. In the end, he somewhat reluctantly agreed.

The day of the chief's retirement arrived. It dawned as a perfect, sunny day, which was unusual in the ship's homeport of Kittery, Maine. There's nothing quite like a military retirement ceremony, hosted on board the ship, and steeped in tradition. It comes with all the pomp and circumstance customary in honoring the Coast Guard's rich military, maritime heritage.

After a rendering of the National Anthem, I spoke about the chief's career, extolling his virtues and accomplishments. We then recognized him with a career service award. Next, I presented him with the letter of appreciation and official retirement certificate, both signed by President George W. Bush. We asked the chief's family to join us on the dais, where I presented his wife and children letters of appreciation from the Coast Guard commandant. The chief's family was moved to the core, with tears of pride and emotion in their eyes.

After the chief's retirement ceremony, his spouse approached to thank me. She recounted with deep emotion how much it meant for her and the children to learn about the remarkable things her husband had done. The chief had never been one to speak about his job at home. Knowing how much he had contributed made his wife understand and feel good about the sacrifices she and the children had made throughout his career.

Later, the chief himself sought me out and, in his quiet way, gave me heartfelt thanks for convincing him to go through with the formal ceremony. He saw what it meant to his family and his shipmates, and he felt the pride and satisfaction of the closure that accompanies capping off a distinguished career. The experience inspired me, too. I resolved to commit even more deeply to my duty to appropriately recognize deserving service members and their families.

The best recognition programs reward people who have performed above and beyond what is expected and who have distinguished themselves from their peers. In any given workplace, there will always be varying degrees of performance and achievement. People know who's going the extra mile to get the job done and who's taking shortcuts. They know which co-workers are serving others and which ones are serving themselves. People will be happy to see their hard-working, high-achieving colleagues singled out for recognition.

Some question the value of recognition programs that single out top performers, supposedly because such programs can lead to competition between employees. I've never found that to be true in a high-performing organization like the Coast Guard. Recognition doesn't have to lead to unhealthy competition; rather, it can raise performance and job satisfaction across the board.

An executive desiring to create a motivational work environment will find ways to encourage people to push themselves to excel while creating a collaborative environment rewarding both individuals and teams. Healthy competition can be a positive factor in an organization that has cultivated a culture of respect valuing everyone equally but rewarding excellence judiciously.

Survey data supports this premise. During my last position with the Coast Guard, I was responsible for administering the periodic Federal Employee Viewpoint Survey, a tool designed to evaluate the job satisfaction of civilian government personnel. Year after year, the single biggest source of dissatisfaction in the workplace was the failure of organizations to distinguish between top performers and those who are not.

For instance, the results of the 2018 survey indicated only a little more than one-third of federal employees believe promotions in their workplace are based on merit. Likewise, a little less than one-third believe their agencies take steps to deal with poor performers.[36]

One can infer from the survey results that people want their organization to deliberately distinguish between top and mediocre performers. Recognition programs lose their luster and credibility when multiple winners are selected for one award or when program standards are changed to include those not otherwise qualified.

Unfortunately, some leaders view it as more just and equitable to recognize everyone the same, regardless of performance or behavior. Subscribing to this approach denies top performers meaningful and deserved recognition, failing to distinguish them from their mediocre peers. Unfortunately, it validates the mediocre performers who have no incentive to do better. Consequently, the organization risks devolving to mediocrity as the top performers leave for more fulfilling, rewarding jobs with organizations that appreciate them.

Perhaps the best example of a truly merit-based award that has maintained its sanctity over the years is the Armed Forces Medal of Honor. In the entire history of the US Coast Guard, there has been only one recipient of that distinguished award. Signalman First Class Douglas Munro was awarded the Medal of Honor posthumously for heroism during World War II.

The Coast Guard participated across the Pacific and Atlantic theaters, from the shores of Guadalcanal to the beaches of Normandy, as part of the Navy during World War II. Petty Officer Munro oversaw a group of small, armed landing craft assigned to deliver and recover Marines to and from the beach in the battle of Guadalcanal.

On September 27, 1942, Petty Officer Munro was leading his group of landing craft with orders to recover Marines under the command of then–Lieutenant Colonel Chesty Puller. The Marines had met with an unexpectedly large Japanese invasion force that drove them to evacuate. While recovering the Marines, the landing craft came under heavy Japanese machinegun fire. Petty Officer Munro maneuvered his boat to place it between the other landing craft, the evacuating Marines, and the beach.

In saving the lives of countless Marines, Petty Officer Munro was killed by enemy gunfire. His last words were, "Did they get off?" As Alexander Hamilton so adroitly observed, "There is a certain enthusiasm in liberty that makes human nature rise above itself, in acts of bravery and heroism."

Petty Officer Munro rose above the fear and pandemonium that fateful day, demonstrating unusual courage that marked him a true hero. Scarcity is what gives everything worthwhile its value. Judicious awarding of the Medal of Honor has preserved its sanctity over time, ensuring inspirational heroes like Petty Officer Munro remain prominent. To be relevant, recognition programs must maintain their discipline, acknowledging the real heroes and top performers.

The Coast Guard's ranks are filled with young people like Petty Officer Munro. They come from small towns and big cities, with high school or college educations. Some are extroverts and others are introverts. They are officers, enlisted, and civilians. They are all different but share a common goal: to serve a purpose greater than themselves.

Leading with character, from the entry-level to the executive ranks, means living your core values, modeling the way, and motivating subordinates to want to move up in the organization. As a junior member of the Coast Guard, Petty Officer Munro set the example for leading with character. His courage and core values have motivated and inspired generations of Coast Guard men and women and Marines.

Young people like Petty Officer Munro place their trust in the Coast Guard and its leaders when they sign up and take the oath to serve. They deserve senior leaders who are engaged with their people and who cultivate a culture of respect in the workplace. Executives must lead selflessly, motivating people to remain with the organization and strive to move up to lead at the next level.

Motivational leaders set the example through their own conduct and behavior. They maintain good order and discipline in the workplace by raising expectations, empowering people to innovate and excel, providing necessary resources, and rewarding excellence. Forward-looking executives leave their organizations better, having groomed and inspired high-performing subordinates to step up to take their place one day.

CONCLUSION

It is not the critic who counts; not the man who points out how the strong man stumbles, or where the doer of deeds could have done them better. The credit belongs to the man who is actually in the arena, whose face is marred by dust and sweat and blood; who strives valiantly; who errs, who comes short again and again, because there is no effort without error and shortcoming; but who does actually strive to do the deeds; who knows great enthusiasms, the great devotions; who spends himself in a worthy cause; who at the best knows in the end the triumph of high achievement, and who at the worst, if he fails, at least fails while daring greatly, so that his place shall never be with those cold and timid souls who neither know victory nor defeat.

—Theodore Roosevelt

I WILL HAVE ACHIEVED my purpose if you have gained a greater understanding of leadership development and what it means to lead with character. With the right tools, leaders of character can succeed from the entry-level to the executive level of an organization. The leadership development journey starts in childhood with the development of personal values and continues at the entry-level in the workplace as individuals embark on their personal journey of self-discovery. During this formative time, people learn more about themselves, including the qualities (personality, abilities, and values) that make them who they are. From there, they begin to shape their passion and purpose.

Although hard work and perseverance are my watch words for success, there are other factors influencing people's ability to reach their full potential. Three equally important components must be satisfied and balanced, like a three-legged stool. First, it is imperative for government to implement the laws and policies offering all people equal access to opportunities to pursue their passion and purpose. Second, organizations must create a culture of respect that welcomes a diverse workforce by ensuring people feel included, are valued, and are given the opportunity to succeed. Finally, there is the individual component—the part that each person can control. Individuals must demonstrate the resilience, through the attributes of courage and confidence, to find their place in the organization and to demonstrate their value as contributing members of the team.

My own personal leadership journey is evidence that leaders of character can be made, even if they aren't natural-born leaders. Upon entering the US Coast Guard Academy as a cadet, I took the oath of office to support and defend the Constitution of the United States. From thence onward, the Coast Guard core values of honor, respect, and devotion to duty were ingrained in me. The Service offered me the chance to find my passion and purpose as part of something noble and much bigger than myself. It provided the challenges and opportunities necessary for me to mature from a shy, unconfident, young woman into a leader of character and to achieve my full potential at the top of the organization.

The Coast Guard believed in me, even when I didn't have the confidence to believe in myself as a developing leader of character. Thirty-three years after I entered the Coast Guard Academy as a cadet, I had the privilege to return as superintendent. There, I seized the awesome opportunity and responsibility to give back some of what the Coast Guard had given me by influencing the leadership development of approximately 1,000 cadets and officer candidates. The opportunity to give back by developing the leaders of character who would replace me one day was truly the highlight of my career.

I've shown that successful leaders of character share attributes relevant across time. The ancient philosophers, from Plato to Socrates to Aristotle, pondered and reflected upon the nature of man. What they observed back then regarding virtues, values, and ethics remains relevant. A prime example is President Abraham Lincoln, one of the strongest leaders of character our nation has ever known. When faced with the absolute toughest of choices, President Lincoln demonstrated exceptional moral courage to lead a young nation into civil war to fight for a just cause.

Although the world is a different place today than it was in the time of the ancient philosophers or President Lincoln, there is still no secret ingredient for success. Leaders of character are obligated to know themselves and their people well enough to develop leaders who are prepared to adapt and innovate to meet the demands of a changing world.

Today, more than ever, the world needs leaders of character dedicated to selfless service, leaders who set the example, who motivate their people to reach their full potential, and who adapt and innovate to lead their organization to excellence. These are leaders who see the glass as half full and filling up; they reach out their hand to bring subordinates up to where they need to be; they believe in implicit decency, not implicit bias; and they choose to live unoffended. These are the leaders who believe in themselves and their subordinates, who build trust and earn respect every day and who demonstrate moral courage, even when everyone is watching and judging them.

These are the leaders of character who, as Theodore Roosevelt so graphically described, were molded in the arena of life, covered in sweat, blood and dirt; when knocked down, they got back up again. They stepped up to overcome obstacles and sometimes failed. In the end, they emerged from the arena having experienced the highs and lows of life, having learned how to cope and having been humbled. They emerged as leaders of character—leaders people choose to follow—whose success will be measured not by their own accomplishments but by the achievements of their people and by whether they left the world a better place.

APPENDIX ONE: READING LIST

(Each of these volumes holds leadership
lessons waiting to be discovered)

Literature

And Quiet Flows the Don, Mikhail Sholokov

Atlas Shrugged, Ayn Rand

Billy Budd, Herman Melville

The Boys in the Boat, Daniel James Brown

The Bounty Trilogy, Charles Nordhoff and James Norman Hall

The Caine Mutiny, Herman Wouk

Candide, Voltaire

Captains Courageous, Rudyard Kipling

The Chosen, Chaim Potok

Crime and Punishment, Fyodor Dostoevsky

Decision in Philadelphia, Christopher Collier
and James Lincoln Collier

Don Quixote, Miguel de Cervantes

Dr. Zhivago, Boris Pasternak

Ghost Fleet: A Novel of the Next World War, P.W. Singer and August Cole

The Good Earth, Pearl S. Buck

Heart of Darkness, Joseph Conrad

Hard Times, Charles Dickens

Longitude, Dava Sobel

Lord Jim, Joseph Conrad

The Man who would be King, Rudyard Kipling

Man's Search for Meaning, Viktor Frankl

Mere Christianity, C.S. Lewis

The Old Man and the Sea, Ernest Hemmingway

The Red Badge of Courage, Stephen Crane

Rising Tide, John M. Barry

The Sea Wolf, Jack London

Siddhartha, Hermann Hesse

To Kill a Mockingbird, Harper Lee

Two Years Before the Mast, Richard Henry Dana

Typhoon, Joseph Conrad

Biographies/Memoirs

Alexander Hamilton, Ron Chernow

Chesty: The Story of Lieutenant General Lewis B. Puller, USMC, Jon T. Hoffman

Nimitz, E. B. Potter

Peter the Great, Robert K. Massie

South: The Story of Shackleton's Last Expedition 1914-17, Sir Ernest Shackleton

Steve Jobs, Walter Isaacson

Theodore Rex, Edmund Morris

West with the Night, Beryl Markham

Commander's Intent
Deputy Commandant for Mission Support

June 2015

Mission

The Deputy Commandant for Mission Support (DCMS) organization delivers the systems and people that enable the Coast Guard to efficiently and effectively perform its operational missions.

The Coast Guard exists to serve the people of the United States of America in the maritime domain. To successfully execute our missions, the Coast Guard must have a fully modernized and efficient DCMS organization. Mission support is the center of gravity for mission execution—people, cutters, aircraft, and systems require excellent support to meet the mission! DCMS must be affordable, accountable, and transparent, and we must be integrated, flexible, and responsive to Coast Guard operations.

Mission support has a rich and proud heritage of excellence and innovation. Although much has changed, and we have matured significantly since DCMS was established in April 2011, one thing that hasn't changed is our amazing people. They live our core values and are devoted to the duty of supporting Coast Guard operations. Our current environment is characterized by fiscal constraints and high expectations, including accountability, clean audits, and effective oversight. Our people will continue to meet these challenges head on!

DCMS Priorities

Engaged Leadership

In DCMS we lead at all levels, regardless of grade or position. We need leaders of character—with the integrity and courage to constructively challenge themselves, each other, and the system—who can

"We define success by reliable delivery of the required, affordable services our customer needs, not by how well we *think* we delivered the service."

Vice Admiral Sandra L. Stosz
Deputy Commandant for Mission Support

then lean in to make decisions that will effect positive change. We are servant leaders who put our **mission first,** and as leaders emphasize service delivery with a **customer focus.** We walk the deckplates; we actively engage with our customers to shape **positive outcomes.** We strive each day to build trust and to be the partner of choice. Equally as important, we must communicate internally to ensure every member of the DCMS organization understands their contribution to our mission and outcomes.

Efficiency through Innovation

We must emphasize a culture of efficiency while delivering excellent mission support. DCMS is the steward for about half of the Coast Guard's budget and workforce. We must be efficient and effective with every dollar and with every minute of our time. We must push authority down to the appropriate levels wherever possible.

Commander's Intent
Deputy Commandant for Mission Support

Logistics and Service Centers, Bases, Training Centers, and Asset Project Offices are particularly well-suited to lead the way to efficiency through innovation. They own the products and processes for service delivery, and are empowered to implement risk-informed and well thought-out changes with the required levels of service in full view. Working together with the responsible program manager, we will **find the hidden costs** and reprioritize to meet the greatest needs while achieving the highest returns. Specifically, we will:

- Partner with operations and align expectations in developing requirements to deliver services and systems that are affordable, sustainable, and, most importantly, capable of accomplishing the mission.

- Deliver a cost-effective support system that is tuned to the complexity of our extremely capable modern assets along with the need to pivot nimbly to address contingencies. Through business case reviews of our processes, and by developing and refining our product lines, we will maximize resources, optimize life cycle cost, find efficiencies, and deliver value.

Standard Service Delivery

Operations relies on standard service levels and understandable access points for all DCMS services. Our **Mission Support Business Model** brings a single point of accountability for a given asset or service, standardization and configuration control, centralized support, and resource prioritization into every aspect of the organization. These cornerstones meet today's demands and are underpinnings to initiatives, such as: Financial Management and Procurement Services and Human Capital Management.

The 418-foot National Security Cutter Hamilton cruises alongside the Fast Response Cutter William Flores off Miami Beach. The DCMS organization helped acquire these new assets and now supports their sustainment in the fleet.

The **value proposition of our business model is building trust, respect, and transparency** through accountability while ensuring controlled processes based on valid requirements. We will continue to fully develop the business model and deploy it where its strengths are the right approach for the Coast Guard.

Cause for Action

Serving the Nation is a privilege, and being part of the Coast Guard is an honor. More than any time in history, we have an opportunity within DCMS to shape the future of the Coast Guard in fundamental ways. Together, we will set our proud Service on a course that will make it more relevant, more respected, and better prepared to meet the challenges of the next century.

This is our Coast Guard.
We are Mission Support.

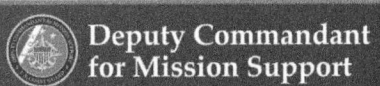

**Deputy Commandant
for Mission Support**

ACKNOWLEDGMENTS

I'M GRATEFUL TO ALL the leaders who influenced me throughout my career—the exceptional, the good, and even the not-so-good—for their part in my leadership development journey. Each one played an important role in helping me achieve my goals and fulfill my potential to become the best person and best leader of character I could be.

I owe a huge thanks to Shane Tews who inspired the title, *Breaking Ice and Breaking Glass* more than thirty years ago when the book was just a dream. I thank Secretary Sam Skinner and the entire Skinner team for their support over the years. Thanks to my sister-in-law Lynn Maize for helping me get the book started. The book was much improved by my dedicated readers including my mom, Joy Stosz, my brother, Mark Stowes, and my friends Camilla Bosanquet, Michelle Lauzon, Sandy Bushue, Tim and Lois Sheane, and Jeff Hathaway.

I'm thankful to those who provided input to my title and cover and who helped with the book launch. I'm honored by those accomplished leaders and authors who generously gave their time and effort to endorse my book. Thanks to the US Navy Institute Press, who peer-reviewed the book and provided valuable developmental editing. Thanks to my editor, Dawn Brotherton, who helped pull the book together. Thanks to my publisher, John Koehler, and his team at Koehler Books for bringing the book to market. Finally, thanks to all those who coached and mentored me during the writing and publishing processes.

ABOUT THE AUTHOR

VICE ADMIRAL SANDRA STOSZ served as a member of the US Coast Guard, a branch of the US Armed Forces, for thirty-six years. Graduating from the US Coast Guard Academy in 1982 with the third class to include women, she became the first female Academy graduate to attain the rank of rear admiral and, subsequently, vice admiral. From her first assignment as a junior officer on board the heavy icebreakers *Glacier* and *Polar Star*, where she broke the ice in both Arctic and the Antarctic waters, she has been breaking barriers as a pioneer for women in the Service ever since.

Vice Admiral Stosz served twelve years at sea, commanding two ships that performed law enforcement, search and rescue, homeland security, icebreaking, and other Coast Guard missions from the Great Lakes to the Caribbean Sea. Her ship and crew patrolled the waters off New York City in the wake of the terrorist attacks of September 11, 2001, keeping the nation safe and secure in the face of an emergent threat to the homeland.

Specializing in leadership development and change management, she modernized Coast Guard accession training and education programs as commander of the Coast Guard's recruit training center (enlisted boot camp) in Cape May, New Jersey, and as superintendent of the Coast Guard Academy (officer education and training) in New London, Connecticut. There, she became the first woman to lead one of the nation's armed forces service academies. She finished her career as the first woman to command the Coast Guard's 17,000-person mission support organization, responsible for engineering and logistics, information technology, acquisitions, human resources, training and education, and research and development.

Vice Admiral Stosz earned a Master of Business Administration from the Kellogg Graduate School of Management at Northwestern University and a Master of Arts in National Security Strategy from the National War College at the National Defense University.

Vice Admiral Stosz's military awards include two Coast Guard Distinguished Service Medals, three Legion of Merit Medals, and four Meritorious Service Medals. She is the recipient of the National Maritime Historical Society Distinguished Service Award; Soldiers, Sailors, Marines, Coast Guardsmen and Airmen's Club Distinguished Military Leadership Award; Girl Scouts of America Trail Blazer Award; Connecticut Women in Leadership Woman of the Year; and she was named in *Newsweek's The Daily Beast*, "150 Women who Shake the World."

NOTES

1   US Coast Guard, "Leadership Development Framework," *Comman-dant Instruction M5351.3*, Chapter 2 (May 9, 2006): 2-1. https://media. defense.gov/2017/Mar/16/2001717682/-1/-1/0/CIM_5351_3.PDF

2   Aristotle, *Poetics.*

3   Emanuele Castano, "Reading Literary Fiction Boosts Leadership Qualities," *Proceedings*, December 2020, 72-74.

4   Kenneth H. Blanchard, Ph.D. and Spencer Johnson, M.D., *The One Minute Manager* (New York: William Morrow and Co, Inc., 1982).

5   Donald T. Phillips and James M. Loy, *The Architecture of Leadership: Preparation Equals Performance* (Annapolis: US Naval Institute Press, 2008).

6   Daniel Golman, *Working with Emotional Intelligence* (New York: Bantam Books, 1998).

7   Russell Cropanzano, Deborah E. Rupp, Zinta S. Byrne, "The Relation-ship of Emotional Exhaustion to Work Attitudes, Job Performance, and Or-ganizational Citizenship Behaviors," *Journal of Applied Psychology* 88, no. 3 (2003): 160-169. https://web.archive.org/web/20100215224016/http:// www.ilir.uiuc.edu/rupp-papers/CropanzanoRuppByrneJAP2003.pdf

8   T.A. Wright and R. Cropanzano, "Emotional Exhaustion as a Pre-dictor of Job Performance and Voluntary Turnover," *Journal of Applied Psychology* 83, no. 1 (1998): 486-493. https://www.ncbi.nlm.nih.gov/pubmed/9648526

9   J. Van Cutsem, S. Marcora, K. De Pauw, et al, "The Effects of Mental Fatigue on Physical Performance: A Systematic Review," *Sports Med* 47 (2017): 1569. https://doi.org/10.1007/s40279-016-0672-0

10   Aristotle, *Nicomachean Ethics*, Book II.

11   Reinhold Niebuhr, from a sermon or prayer, circa early 1940s and included in, *A Book of Prayers and Services for the Armed Forces* (The Federal Council of Churches, 1944).

12   Thomas Paine, *The American Crisis*, 1776.

13   Jim Harter, "Employee Engagement on the Rise in the US," *Gallup News*, Aug 26, 2018. https://news.gallup.com/poll/241649/employee-engagement-rise.aspx?utm_source=link_wwwv9&utm_campaign=item_245786&utm_medium=copy

14   Susan Cain, *Quiet: The Power of Introverts in a World That Can't Stop Talking* (New York: Crown Publishers, 2012), 160-161.

15   Jon T. Hoffman, *Chesty: The Story of LGEN Lewis B. Puller, USMC* (New York: Random House, 2002), 14-15.

16   Ibid, 20-21.

17   Ibid, 43-57.

18   Bronnie Ware, *Top Five Regrets of the Dying: A Life Transformed by the Dearly Departing* (Hay House, Inc, 2012).

19   Coach Wooden, "Pyramid of Success," http://www.coachwooden. com/pyramid-of-success

20   "Remembering Frank Robinson," hosted by David Greene, Morning Edition, National Public Radio, February 8, 2019, https://www.npr. org/2019/02/08/692614165/remembering-frank-robinson

21   Verna Myers, https://learning.vernamyers.com/pages/about-vern-myers

22   Jason L. Riley, *Please Stop Helping Us: How Liberals Make It Harder for Blacks to Succeed* (New York: Encounter Books, 2014).

23   Office of Personnel Management: "Full-Time Permanent Age Distribution," September, 2017. https://www.opm.gov/policy-data-oversight/ data-analysis-documentation/federal-employment-reports/reports-pub-lications/full-time-permanent-age-distributions/

24   Military Leadership Diversity Commission, "Definition of Diversity," Issue Paper #4 http://mldc.whs.mil/

25   Alison Reynolds and David Lewis, "Teams Solve Problems Faster When They're More Cognitively Diverse," *Harvard Business Review*, March 30, 2017. https://hbr.org/2017/03/teams-solve-problems-faster-when-theyre-more-cognitively-diverse

26   Celeste Headlee, "Ten Ways to have a Better Conversation," recorded May, 2015 at *TEDxCreativeCoast*, video, 11:44, https://www.ted.com/ talks/celeste_headlee_10_ways_to_have_a_better_conversation.

27   Pew Research Center: US Politics and Policy, "Political Polarization: 1994-2017," October 20, 2017 https://www.people-press.org/interactives/ political-polarization-1994-2017/.

28   Alexander Hamilton, "Letter of Instruction to the Commanding Officers of the Revenue Cutters," June 4, 1791, https://media.defense.gov/2017/Jul/02/2001772367/-1/-1/0/HAMILTONLETTER.PDF

29   US Coast Guard, "Creating and Sustaining Strategic Intent in the US Coast Guard," July, 2008, https://www.uscg.mil/Portals/0/Strategy/EG2_Green_Book.pdf

30   Paul J. Zak, "The Neuroscience of Trust," *Harvard Business Review*, January-February 2017, 5, *https://hbr.org/2017/01/the-neuroscience-of-trust.*

31   Katty Kay and Claire Shipman, "The Confidence Gap," *The Atlantic*, April 14, 2014, 1. https://www.theatlantic.com/magazine/archive/2014/05/the-confidence-gap/359815/

32   Scott Maucione, "What's in the Coast Guard's Secret Sauce for High Retention?" *Federal News Network*, January 15, 2018, https://federalnewsnetwork.com/dod-personnel-notebook/2018/01/whats-in-the-coast-guards-secret-sauce-for-high-retention/

33   Simon Senik, *Leaders Eat Last* (New York: Portfolio, 2014).

34   David Morrison, Lieutenant General and Chief of the Australian Army, addressing the Australian Army on YouTube, June 13, 2013, https://speakola.com/ideas/david-morrison-adf-investigation-2013)

35   Max H. Bazerman, *The Power of Noticing: What the Best Leaders See* (New York: Simon & Schuster, 2014), 23-24.

36   US Office of Personnel Management, *Federal Employee Viewpoint Survey,* (Washington, DC: Office of Personnel Management, 2018), p. 5), https://www.opm.gov/fevs/reports/governmentwide-reports/governmentwide-management-report/governmentwide-report/2018/2018-governmentwide-management-report.pdf.

CPSIA information can be obtained
at www.ICGtesting.com
Printed in the USA
JSHW042101190921
18823JS00004B/13